CW00541338

Refugee Wales

Syrian Voices

Edited and selected by
Angham Abdullah, Beth Thomas and Chris Weedon

Refugee Wales: Syrian Voices is published with the support of:

Parthian, Cardigan SA43 1ED
www.parthianbooks.com
ISBN: 978-1-914595-30-1
Ebook ISBN 978-1-914595-31-8
First published in 2022 © Cardiff University & Amgueddfa Cymru-National Museum Wales
Edited and selected by Angham Abdullah, Beth Thomas and Chris Weedon
Cover image: "All at Sea 2" by Alison Lochhead. Photography: Luke Unsworth
Typeset by Elaine Sharples
Printed by Gomer Press, Llandysul, Wales
Parthian Books works with the financial support of the Books Council of Wales
British Library Cataloguing in Publication Data
A cataloguing record for this book is available from the British Library.

Acknowledgements

This book is the result of a broader research project called *Refugee Wales: the Afterlife of Violence* which began in 2019. We are grateful for the support given to this project by the Arts and Humanities Research Council [grant number AH/S006400/1]. The research is directed by Professor Radhika Mohanram, School of English, Communication and Philosophy in Cardiff University in partnership with St Fagans National Museum of History, which is part of Amgueddfa Cymru – National Museum Wales. More information about this project is available at https://museum.wales/refugee-wales/.

We would also like to acknowledge the advice and support of our third sector partners in this project, Oasis and Diverse Cymru. These organisations and many other charities across Wales work tirelessly to fulfil Welsh Government's ambition for Wales to be a Nation of Sanctuary. Our thanks also go to Alison Lochhead for her permission to use her paintings, to Jehan Bseiso for her poetry and to Parthian Books for their support in getting this volume so quickly.

Most of all, we would like to thank those who participated in this project and shared with us experiences and feelings which were far from easy to relate. The recordings will be archived at St Fagans National Museum of History and become a part of the national collections. They will be a learning resource for present and future generations.

شكر وتقدير

شكراً لكم يامن فتحتم لنا أبواب قلوبكم وبيوتكم ومنحتمونا ثقتكم ووقتكم لتشاركونا ذكرياتكم ونجاحاتكم ولحظات يأسكم. شكراً من القلب لفناجين قهوتكم ولكرم ضيافتكم وعذراً لكل دمعةٍ سالت مع حَكايا الحرب والرحيل والفقدان والحنين.

هذا الكتاب عنكم وأليكم فلولاكم لم يكن ونتمنى أن نكون قد نجحنا في سرد قصصكم وأيصالها كما هي للعالم

نشكر جميع من شارك في المقابلات المسجلة وكل من ساهم بأرسال الصور الشخصية الينا. وشكرنا الخالص للانسة أمل حلّاق التي كانت عوناً حقيقياً في أيصالنا للكثير من المشاركين والمشارِكات في هذه المقابلات. كما نشكر الدكتور سامح عطري, سليمان عثمان, ريمان ساداني وجاكي بيج على جهودهم ودعمهم لنا.

No Search, No Rescue

BY JEHAN BSEISO

Misrata, Libya... How do we overcome war and poverty only to drown in your sea?

Habeebi just take the boat. In front of you: Bahr. Behind you: Harb

And the border, closed...

Augusta, Italy

Where is the interpreter?

This is my family

Baba, mama, baby all washed up on the shore. This is 28 shoeless survivors and thousands of bodies Bodies Syrian, Bodies

Somali, Bodies Afghan, Bodies Ethiopian, Bodies Eritrean

Bodies Palestinian...

Alexandria, Egypt

Habeebi, just take the boat

Behind you Aleppo and Asmara, barrel bombs and Kalashnikovs.

In front of you a little bit of hope.

Your Sea, Mare, Bahr. Our war, our Harb

Maps on our backs

Long way from home

Contents

"Home is a sanctuary, safety, settlement. A place where you feel free and can express yourself freely. This is home. Syria is my first home, but the place that offers you all these elements is your real home."

RONAHI HASSAN, 2021

Why Stories Matter

If you ask the right questions and listen carefully, there is no one who does not have an interesting story to tell. Life stories engage us in a way that history textbooks never can. They can help us understand on a personal level the effects that world events have on people's lives.

There are many people in Wales today who have settled here after escaping war and violence in their home countries. For them, telling their story can be both difficult and life affirming. Listening to refugee stories cuts through the empathy fatigue produced by 24-hour news. Individual stories tell us how it feels to become a refugee, to lose one's home and the life one has known. They tell us what it is like to deal with a traumatic past and an uncertain future. They throw light on the many obstacles to creating a new life in an unfamiliar environment. They also reveal the positive contributions that refugees make to Wales today and how we can help smooth the process of settling in.

This book revolves around the stories of Syrians who have found refuge in Wales. They have been recorded as part of a joint research project between Cardiff University and Amgueddfa Cymru-National Museum Wales. Moving away from their country has resulted in a break from their past lives and a rupture from their histories and cultures. Our aim is to allow refugees to connect their past to their present and give them a sense of belonging. We want them to know that people are, indeed, witnessing their trials.

And those of us who already live in Wales, how will these newcomers change our lives? By hearing their stories, we will help them through their transformation and initiate new ways of being and becoming Welsh.

Knowing more about the lives of others is vital in shaping the kind of society in which we wish to live.

The War in Syria

"The Syrian situation is very much complicated."

Since 2011, hundreds of thousands of Syrians have been killed and half of Syria's population has been displaced. It is one of the greatest humanitarian crises since the Second World War. But how did this complex war start? How did it escalate into such devastating chaos, drawing in other countries and external forces?

Background

For many centuries, Syria was part of the Ottoman Empire, which at one time ruled most of the Middle East, North Africa and parts of Southern Europe. When that empire collapsed after the First World War, its territories in the Middle East were arbitrarily divided up between Britain and France. The borders between the French and British spheres of influence later became the borders between Iraq, Syria and Jordan.

These divisions cut across a region which is rich in ethnic and religious diversity. Syria's population is majority Sunni Muslim but has large minorities of Christians, Druze, Shia, and a Shia sect known as Alawites. Ethnic Kurds, who have their own language and traditions, have no country of their own as their traditional territory was divided between Syria, Turkey, Iraq and Iran.

"Syrian dynasty" (CC BY 2.0 by amerune)

The Asad Regime

Syria became an independent state in 1946. A period of instability followed, until Hafedh al Asad seized power in a bloodless coup in 1970. The Asad family came from the Alawi minority, a Shia sect that had sided with the French and had been elevated to privileged positions. Hafedh ruled Syria with an iron fist, suppressing opposition with brute force and binding people to the regime by handing out patronage.

When Bashar al Asad succeeded his father as President

Propaganda poster featuring Syrian president Bashar al Asad.
(CC BY 2.0 by watchsmart, 2007)

"In the National Education lesson we used to memorise the Sayings of al Asad which were as important as the Qura'anic verses…"

of Syria in July 2000, there were hopes for a brighter future. His previous role as head of the Syrian Computer Society suggested an outward-looking moderniser. At his inauguration, the president called upon 'every single citizen to participate in the process of development and modernisation' and asked for 'constructive criticism' towards this end. He rejected 'Western' democracy and favoured Syria's own type of 'democratic thinking'. Before long the international media was talking of a 'Damascus Spring'. The Damascus Spring did not last long. The regime used violence against a group of Syrian activists accusing them of having a foreign agenda against the country. In September 2001, media censorship intensified and critical bloggers and journalists were targeted. The torture of dissidents was highly systematic. It was particularly widely practised in the detention centres of the security services, where people would be held, often without anyone's knowledge, for weeks and months of interrogation.

Youth unemployment reached a high of 48 per cent, with young women four times more likely to be unemployed than young men. The education system discouraged free thinking, schoolchildren were made to join the Baath's Revolutionary Youth Union, and textbooks endlessly celebrated the virtues of party and president.

The economy was in a mess. Corruption was rife, enabling the regime's close relatives to gain substantial assets and occupy high ranking positions in the government. Fifty per cent of the country's wealth was concentrated in the hands of five per cent of the population.

In 2006 the situation was made worse by the severe drought plaguing much of the country. Rural areas such as the Jazeera (in the east) and the Hawran (in the south) suffered the most. By 2010 the drought had pushed between two and three million Syrians into extreme poverty. Hundreds of thousands of farmers lost their livelihoods and were forced off their lands. Food was in short supply because of crop failure and the death of livestock. The effects of the drought were exacerbated by poor water management and wasteful irrigation practices. The regime's failure to deal with these economic and political challenges inevitably led to an uprising against the government.

The Uprising of 2011

Demonstrations increased in number, demanding regime change and an end to structural violence and inequality in Syria. They were violently repressed by the regime.

Demonstrators were described as 'armed gangs', 'Salafist terrorists' and 'foreign parties' aiming to destroy the security and sovereignty of the country. Protestors were detained, killed and their corpses returned to their families bearing signs of torture.

On 28 January 2011, in the north-eastern town of Hasakah, Hassan Akleh set himself alight in protest against the regime. His final act mirrored that of Mohamed Bouazizi in Tunisia, who sparked a transnational revolutionary uprising known as the Arab Spring.

On 6 March of 2011, fifteen young people were arrested in the town of Dara'a for writing anti-Asad graffiti on a wall. They were tortured under arrest and this prompted their parents and relatives to take to the streets in protest.

The protests were met with a heavy response from the government, leading to the deaths of some unarmed civilians. A few days later, a group of people mourning the dead were fired at, leaving one dead. In the aftermath of the toppling of Bin Ali, president of Tunisia, and the Egyptian president Mubarak, Syrians took to the streets shouting '*Selmiyyeh, Selmiyyeh*', or 'Peaceful, Peaceful', words that would soon be heard across Syria.

The response was anything but peaceful. The demonstration was violently dispersed and the Mukhabarat, Syria's Military Intelligence Division, made several arrests. The regime launched campaigns aimed at creating dissent between Sunnis and Alawis, using a strategy of divide and rule. Armed gangs named Shabeeha were seen in Latakia, a heavily Alawi populated area, shooting from their cars, screaming and threatening Sunnis with rape and murder. In Sunni areas they presented themselves as vengeful Alawis and in Alawi areas they were acting as vengeful Sunnis.

Crowds demonstrate against the Asad government in the city of Baniyas. (CC BY 2.0 by Syria-Frames-Of-Freedom)

People search for survivors in the rubble in a damaged area in Al-Suwkkari neighbourhood in Aleppo. (REUTERS / Aref Haj Youssef – stock.adobe.com)

An internationalised civil war

What began as protests against President Asad's regime in 2011 soon escalated into a full-scale war between the Syrian government (backed by Russia and Iran) and anti-government rebel groups (backed by the United States, Saudi Arabia, Turkey, and others in the region).

By the end of July 2011, some members of the Syrian Army had defected to form the Syrian National Coalition and began fighting against Asad. The Kurds, in the northeast of Syria, saw this unfolding civil war as an opportunity to be armed and demand independence from Syria.

America, Saudi Arabia and Qatar had been supplying arms and funding to the Syrian National Coalition, channelling them through Turkey and Jordan. Later in the war, the USA undertook direct attacks on Asad's forces. The USA's justification for this was the alleged use of chemical weapons by the regime.

The Asad regime barrel-bombed and launched air raids on the liberated cities of Homs and Aleppo. Backed by Shia militias in Iraq, Asad's regime succeeded in taking over all the liberated cities by threatening to cut off food supplies. In 2013, during the festival of Eid in eastern Ghouta, the regime imposed a complete siege, sealing the borders.

People were reduced to eating stray animals, leaves and animal fodder. Without water, electricity, or landlines, they had to dig wells to find a water supply. Later the regime used gas attacks and chemical weapons. People were left without sufficient help or medical aid. Paramedics entered houses to find whole families dead in their beds from gas suffocation. Many were gassed in their basements while seeking refuge from the shelling.

In 2011, the regime freed 1500 extremist Salafi Muslims from prison. The Salafis were well connected with al-Qaeda and ISIS. This was a calculated move by the regime. Asad wanted to present to the world a stark choice between his rule and the jihadis.

In the meantime, defectors from the Syrian Army formed the Free Syrian Army (FSA), which was mainly a resistance group aiming to destroy the regime and form a democratic state. The FSA was struggling for funds.

As funds were available from Salafists in the Gulf region and Saudi Arabia, many members of the FSA drifted to the Salafi Jihadists/ISIS to survive. Following their successes on the battlefield, ISIS started enforcing sharia law through their own sharia courts: stoning, crucifying, attacking shrines and churches and causing Christians to flee.

In 2014 battlefield events and media reports were often dominated by the atrocities of Sunni Islamist militias (Al Qaeda-linked Jabhat al Nusra or ISIS). However, the regime had an undeclared non-aggression pact with ISIS. They bombed everywhere apart from ISIS headquarters. Asad even bought oil from ISIS.

His strategy was to scare people into believing that it was better to back the regime than the jihadists. He also succeeded in convincing western powers that his dictatorship, despite its savagery, was the lesser threat.

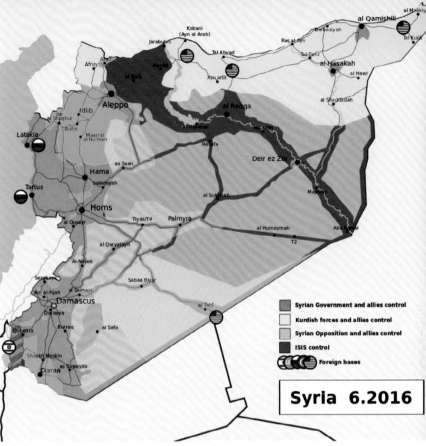

Syria in 2016: a snapshot of a constantly changing conflict. (Still from animated map by Alexpl, CC BY-SA 4.0, via Wikimedia Commons)

Many factors have driven and complicated the conflict in Syria: violence between Asad's regime and opposition forces, efforts by an international coalition to defeat Islamic State, Kurdish aspirations for independence and military operations against Syrian Kurds by Turkish forces.

"We were dreaming of change, but it was all in vain…"

The Human Cost

"I was nine when I lost my mum. It was bombs shelled on the town from the government. Then my father was killed by an airstrike..."

SINCE THE
WAR IN SYRIA
STARTED

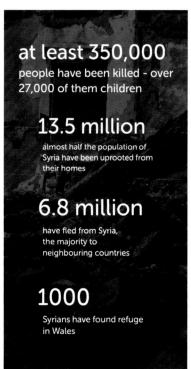

at least 350,000
people have been killed - over
27,000 of them children

13.5 million
almost half the population of
Syria have been uprooted from
their homes

6.8 million
have fled from Syria,
the majority to
neighbouring countries

1000
Syrians have found refuge
in Wales

As the regime continued bombing, starving and torturing its citizens, a humanitarian crisis unfolded. By February 2015, more than 220,000 had lost their lives and four times this number were wounded. In other words, six per cent of the Syrian population had been killed or injured since 2011. More than 150,000 were incarcerated in Asad's dungeons and 11,000 were killed in prisons.

Cities turned into wastelands of ruins. People deserted their houses and neighbourhoods looking for shelter, food and safety. Schools were destroyed and half of Syria's children were not being educated. More than half the country's hospitals weren't functioning. Diseases spread because of lack of medical care, water and sanitation.

Activists in local communities distributed food, beddings and medicine. They tried to dig wells for water supplies, to help people remain in their homes. Doctors set up private hospitals in their homes and teachers gathered children for schooling. External aid was very slow to arrive for the activists to distribute. Asad restricted humanitarian organisations' access to besieged areas. Some of the convoys were subjected to mortar attacks.

By July 2015, half the population of Syria were no longer living in their homes. Four million had fled the country and 7.6 million were internally displaced. The rich were able to transfer their money or business to Lebanon, Turkey or elsewhere. The middle classes, who initially fled to Lebanon or Turkey, used up all their savings in these countries and returned home to find their homes and belongings taken by the militias.

The families who remained in Syria lived in the houses of friends and relatives, in half damaged schools or in camps run by Syrians. These camps are not under the

A refugee camp at Azez, Syria in 2019. Since the civil war began in 2011, 12 million Syrians have fled from their homes. (By hikrcn/Adobe Stock)

control and supervision of the United Nations. They consist of plastic tents pinned on rocky ground, leaving them to flood in winter and bubble under the sun in summer.

Tens of thousands of people are crammed into these camps. Women face sexual harassment, abuse and rape. Battles take place between smugglers and Turkish police, ISIS and opposition militias. Camps have been raked by machine gun fire from Asad's helicopters.

The speed with which Syria emptied itself of nearly twenty per cent of its population shocked the world. The number of refugees fleeing from Syria has now reached 6.6 million. They are the largest refugee population in the world.

Neighbouring countries have each responded differently. There are over a million Syrian refugees in Lebanon. Lebanon's residency policy makes it difficult for Syrians to gain legal status. Seventy-four per cent of Syrians in Lebanon risk detention for being in the country unlawfully.

In 2017, the Lebanese authorities stepped up calls for refugees to return to Syria, despite the ongoing dangers. A small number of refugees have indeed done so. Some have said they are returning because of harsh policies and deteriorating conditions in Lebanon, not because they think Syria is safe. Municipalities in Lebanon have evicted thousands of refugees in mass expulsions.

By 2018, Turkey had registered almost 3.6 million Syrian refugees in the country. During that year, Turkish security forces intercepted and deported thousands of newly arrived Syrian asylum seekers at the Turkey-Syrian border. They deported them to the war-ravaged Syrian province of Idlib. Turkey has stated that it will not open its border to asylum seekers fleeing from Idlib. Instead, Turkish authorities have opened several displacement camps in areas under their control in Syria.

As of April 2021, Jordan has registered around 665,000 Syrian refugees. They have categorically refused to open

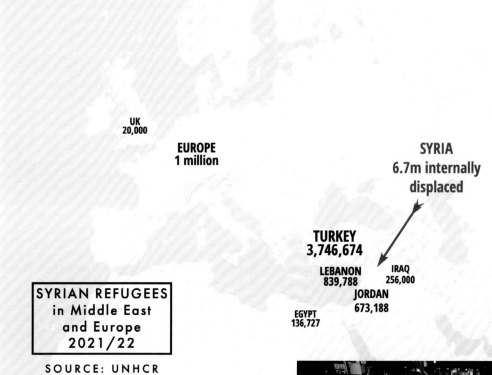

UK
20,000

EUROPE
1 million

SYRIA
6.7m internally
displaced

TURKEY
3,746,674

LEBANON
839,788

IRAQ
256,000

JORDAN
673,188

EGYPT
136,727

SYRIAN REFUGEES
in Middle East
and Europe
2021/22

SOURCE: UNHCR

Syrian refugees resting on the floor of Keleti railway
station, Budapest, Hungary, 2015. (Mstyslav
Chernov, CC BY-SA 4.0, via Wikimedia Commons).

the border to incoming asylum seekers fleeing hostilities in the southwest. However, Jordan did help evacuate members of the Syrian Civil Defence, a humanitarian emergency response team. Germany, the United Kingdom and Canada, among others, had agreed to resettle them. In 2018, Jordan began regularising the stay of refugees without residency permits.

By April 2021, Iraq housed 245,953 Syrian refugees. The majority are Kurds and live in Kurdistan, a territory controlled by the Iraqi Kurdish regional government (KRG).

In response to the large outflow of Syrian refugees, the UK government launched the Syrian Vulnerable Persons Resettlement Scheme (SVPRS) in 2015. This gave a commitment to resettle up to 20,000 Syrian refugees in the UK by May 2020. As part of this plan, close to a thousand Syrians were resettled in Wales.

The US renewed its grant of Temporary Protected Status (TPS) to almost 7,000 Syrians living in the United States but did not extend the status to any new Syrians. It also maintained a ban on Syrian citizens entering the United States.

The European Union's response to the Syrian refugee crisis continued to fall short, with its emphasis on preventing arrivals from Turkey and confining those who do in overcrowded, unsanitary camps on Greek islands.

Syria is a humanitarian tragedy. The 2011 uprising was the culmination of long-standing conflict brought about by political players in the region. The Asads played on Syria's internal divisions to maintain their rule. In doing so, they created deeper sectarian, ethnic and class divisions between people. The torture and killing of activists, growing unemployment and the curb on individual freedoms finally led to the uprising. As the conflict descended into civil war, outside powers – Iran, Turkey, the USA and Russia – funded and armed different sides of the conflict.

The victims at the centre of all this are the people of Syria. What began as a temporary refuge in a camp in Turkey, Jordan or Lebanon has become a search for a new home and a better life. These people are seeking to find for their children the peace and security which most of us take for granted.

"We were ready to sacrifice and endure whatever hardships we were facing for the sake of our families… for their safety."

The Storytellers

The Syrians who generously shared their stories with us came from a wide range of backgrounds and different parts of Syria, all badly affected by the war. We are deeply indebted to the people listed below for not only sharing their experiences with the project team, but also for allowing us to share them with you. Each of them has a different story to tell: their journeys to Wales have taken place in various ways and at different times.

The interviews took place during the Covid-19 pandemic, in challenging circumstances. All but one were conducted in Arabic. Angham Abdullah, a native Arabic speaker with personal experience of being a refugee, was both interviewer and translator. We hope that what is published here is as true a reflection as possible of the original Arabic testimonies.

'Looking for Exile' – calligraphy by Abduljaleel Olayyane, inspired by an article written by Ali Zain.

A M was born in Damascus in 1993. With the start of the war AM was doing a university course in Architectural Engineering and he was also an activist. When the political situation worsened, AM was forced to leave for Lebanon with his family. He had a chance to continue his studies here and later in the UK in 2015. AM got his master's degree in Architectural Engineering from Cardiff University, and he is currently pursuing his PhD studies in the same field.

Ali Zain is a poet and a writer in Arabic. Ali was born in Al Hajar al Abyadh, in the Aleppo governorate in 1988. He lived there for ten years before moving to Al Ratoniyyah with his family. Ali was a university student and an activist when he was forced to flee Syria for Lebanon. Ali took the sea route to Europe in 2015. He now lives in Cardiff with his wife and two small children.

Baher al Abed was born in Damascus in 2002. By the age of ten he was an orphan, having lost both his parents in bombing raids. Baher lived with his foster family in Lebanon before coming to the UK. He came to Wales in 2019 to study in Atlantic College, having been encouraged by Save the Children, Lebanon to apply for a scholarship. Currently, Baher is doing a university course in political science at Bristol university.

Bashar Mousa was born in Al-Raqqa in 1992. Bashar was badly injured when he took part in the peaceful demonstrations against the Asad regime. Bashar arrived in Europe on a rubber boat in 2014 and Wales was his first place of refuge in the UK. Despite his injury Bashar was determined to learn street boxing techniques, judo, and karate. He also ran up to 15 Kms a day for 365 days, as a message of determination and hope to young refugees. He now runs a small media company in London.

Dona al Abdallah was born in Manbij in 1988. Dona has a diploma in dental implants and worked in a dental lab during the war. She was newly married when her husband fled Syria. With her husband's family, she escaped ISIS-controlled areas to Lebanon and finally joined her husband in Cardiff in 2017. Dona gave birth to her two small children in Cardiff.

Halah al Shami was born in Damascus in 1960. In Syria she worked in a managerial role at the ministry of health. When her safety and that of her children were threatened, Halah decided to flee to Lebanon. Left on her own when her grown up children scattered all over the world, Halah decided to join her two sons in the UK. She applied for asylum at Heathrow airport and then settled in Cardiff.

Hussam Allaham was born in Damascus in 1983. His work as a surgeon during the war was both traumatic and dangerous due to his heavy involvement in activism. When his life was endangered Hussam fled Damascus in 2013. He arrived in Europe on a rubber boat. Hussam now lives in Wales and works for Oasis, a refugee aid organisation which is a partner in this project.

Khalid al Saeed was born in Dara'a in 1974. Dara'a is located in the south of Syria, on the border with Jordan. When the war started with no end in sight, Khalid, his wife and three small children, fled from Dara'a across the border to Jordan in 2012. The plan was to take the family away from the conflict until the situation improved, but they spent eight years in Jordan, waiting for the war to end. Their fourth child was born in Jordan before they were resettled in Cardiff in 2019.

Latifa Alnajjar was born in 1988 in Homs. In 2011 Latifa, her husband, daughter and her parents left Syria for Egypt after losing one of her brothers in the war. While waiting in Egypt for a decision to resettle in the UK Latifa had her second daughter. The family came to the UK in 2016 and were settled in Aberystwyth. Her third child, a son, was born in Aberystwyth while Latifa was starting her own food business, the Syrian Dinner Project, with other Syrian women.

M H was born in the city of Jedda in Saudi Arabia in 1987. In 2012 MH and his wife NS came to the UK to pursue their higher education at Cardiff University but decided to stay in the country as the political situation worsened in Syria. In the Middle East MH worked as a Dental surgeon. Currently, he is going through a complicated process to get his licence to practise as a dental surgeon in the UK. MH and his wife lived in Cardiff for seven years where they had their two daughters. In 2019 the family relocated to Birmingham due to a job opportunity for M.

Mohamad Karkoubi was born in Aleppo in 1982 and worked as a blacksmith. In 2012 Mohamad, his wife and his three children left Aleppo for Lebanon after an air aid had destroyed their house. In addition to the difficult living conditions in Lebanon, Mohamad's children were not allowed to attend school there. Mohamad and his family were resettled in Aberystwyth, Wales in 2015. Since arriving in Wales Mohamad has learnt Welsh.

Mohammad S was born in 2000 in Manbij to a family of seven siblings. In 2013, when Manbij was controlled by ISIS, Mohammad and his family fled to Turkey. In Turkey, Mohammad and his younger siblings were deprived of education and he found himself working twelve hours a day to provide for his younger siblings. In 2017 Mohamad arrived in Wales and resumed his studies. He is now studying for a degree in civil engineering.

N S was born in Damascus in 1986 and grew up in Kuwait. In 2012 NS came to the UK with her husband MH to pursue their higher education. The couple lived in Cardiff for seven years and had their first two daughters before relocating to Birmingham in 2019. NS specialised in speech therapy, but she couldn't practise her profession because of the high language requirements for her IELTS. However, NS is determined to keep trying and will never lose hope.

Najla'a Hadle was born in 1987 in Aleppo. She got married at the age of twenty-three and had her first daughter in Syria. In 2012 Najla'a, her husband and her family left Aleppo for Lebanon where they stayed for four and a half years and had their second child. In 2016 Najla'a and her family were resettled in Wales and have been living in Aberystwyth since then. She aspires to a future in the field of care.

Natali Hadad was born in Homs in 1955 but lived and worked in Damascus. She is a retired microbiologist. Natali loved her job and had a specialised lab back home. When her sons fled Syria for Europe, Natali and her husband travelled to Turkey hoping to meet with their sons but failed. Natali's husband passed away in Turkey and Natali was resettled to the UK. She now lives in Cardiff with her daughter and grandchildren.

Noor was born in 1999 in Manbij. When ISIS took control of Manbij, Noor wasn't allowed to continue her high school education. Noor was sixteen when she fled Syria for Turkey with her family. Later, Noor and her mother took the sea route to Europe and had a risky journey through the borders of Europe until they made it to the UK in 2016. Now Noor lives in Cardiff with her husband and her baby boy. She teaches Arabic at a school in Cardiff.

Ronahi Hassan was born in 1974 in Qamishli, a Kurdish majority city in northeast Syria. As a proud Kurd and a human rights activist, Ronahi couldn't endure the Asad regime's brutal crackdown on Kurds from 2004 onwards and left Syria for Europe with her three children. The family were first settled in Swansea, then lived in Cardiff for ten years. Arriving with hardly any English, Ronahi managed to get a bachelor's degree in Media Studies in Wales. She now lives in London with her family.

Salih Hamza was born in 1966 in Qazani, a Kurdish subdistrict of Ayn al-Arab in northern Syria. Salih worked in Ayn al-Arab as a barber where he had a barbers' shop. With the onset of the war Salih's children became refugees in Europe while Salih and his wife fled to Turkey. Due to his severe physical disability, Salih was resettled to the UK in 2019, accompanied by his wife. The couple lives in Cardiff, longing to be reunited with their children.

Sulaiman Sulaiman was born in Manbij in 1993. Back home Sulaiman studied electrical engineering for two years but didn't continue for financial reasons. When the war started Sulaiman volunteered to help people and was an activist too. When the situation worsened, Sulaiman fled Syria and almost drowned on his sea journey to Europe. In 2014, Sulaiman arrived in the UK and now lives in Cardiff. He runs a restaurant, studies electrical engineering and has two children.

The Stories

Aleppo by Dario Bajurin

Before the War

*"Sometimes I sit down at night and contemplate and remember.
I feel it, I smell it and feel like my soul is still there."*

Latifa Alnajjar

My name is Latifa Alnajjar, born in 1988. I am from Homs. I was born there, lived and got married there and I even had my first daughter in Homs. I got married at the age of twenty-two. My daughter was born shortly after. I was married in 2010, had my daughter in 2011 and left Syria in 2013.

I did a Diploma in Women's Arts where we learned embroidery, knitting, and sewing. I also did a course in nursing. In Syria we usually join summer courses, and I did a course in nursing. I worked in a health centre for two months and then got engaged and married and stayed at home.

I will always miss the neighbourhood, my house. I mean my parents' house not my husband's because I only lived for one year at my husband's. After marriage, I lived in the same neighbourhood because I loved that neighbourhood a lot. I miss the neighbourhood. I miss our house. I even long for the noise which used to annoy me. I really miss that noise. The family gatherings, my brothers and all of this.

In Syria it is considered a must to every young woman to learn how to cook and help with cooking at home. This was usually done throughout the summer school holidays. Also, in winter we had a cooking lesson at school which was an essential lesson! When I got married, I used to visit my mother and help her with cooking. When my mother travelled to Saudi Arabia for *Umrah*, she handed me the responsibility of the house. She trusted me with the food and since then I have been cooking.

"Homs – Syria" (CC BY 2.0) by Beshr Abdulhadi

Esh Al-Bulbul, a Syrian sweet.
Image: Syrian Dinner Project.

I was in the first year of my Diploma, around nineteen years old. When I got married, I was top in cooking. My dad used to compliment me for the dishes I cooked saying: 'Your dishes are even better than your mum's!' And my mother used to tell him: 'I taught her this!' And yes of course, she taught me all the skills of cooking. In Syria it is essential for any young woman to know how to cook. Even in cities, it is a must for every young woman to study and go to school in winter and to learn how to cook in summer.

We in Syria are very much into visits and gatherings. This means we must make desserts. We must make desserts daily in case a guest comes for coffee. It is not nice if we have nothing to serve besides the cup of coffee, like a piece of *Ma'amoul*, a piece of *petit four*. This is a must. We love to have bites. By the way we never buy ready-made desserts. We've never bought *petit fours*, biscuits etc. Everything is handmade. So we are used to making things ourselves. Even our *Mooneh* [seasonal food supply]. We used to spend almost all our summer creating a food supply that we saved for later: *Romman* [pomegranates], *Laban* [yogurt] and *Makdous*. Lots of things to work on.

My parents used to live in a flat where there was no space to grow things. But in the village areas you find all kinds of vegetables and fruit. Also if you have an Arabic house, Arabic houses are designed to have a wider space to grow your own trees, flowers etc. As you know, most of these houses have a *Bahra* [fountain place] in the middle of a yard. Vegetables are grown in villages. Whereas in other areas you find bigger houses with space large enough to grow whatever you like.

Tomato paste was handmade. We used to dry it under the sun. We also used to make dried aubergines. Even the pomegranate sauce, we used to make it at home. We'd never bought it from a shop. We'd never bought such stuff – loads of hard work! Back home I used to grumble a lot about it. I used to murmur about spending the summer drying sweet peppers followed by pomegranates and so on.

Yes, an ongoing food labour! But when I came here, I honestly missed that kind of labour. We used to gather at our neighbour's house. We did all that hard work from the flat rooftop of her house. Peppers, *Makdous*, all this. There was that spirit, a sweet spirit, teamwork. Of course, there were difficulties. Life wasn't all positive. It wasn't that beautiful. There was poverty. But we used to support one another. We were together. I miss Ramadan in Syria, the call to prayer, the dishes, the aroma of food in the building, in the neighbourhood. Going back from school and the smell of food. Oh, I am hungry! The smell of food! I remember that lovely childhood. The first of September used to be a return to school day, like here. The image of my mum storing our summer clothes and bringing out the winter ones – this image is always connected with a dish my mum used to cook on the same day. A very sweet memory. Sometimes I sit down at night and contemplate and remember. I feel it, I smell it and feel like my soul is still there.

Raqqa. (CC BY 2.0) by Beshr Abdulhadi

Bashar

Raqqa lies on the Syrian borders between Deir al Zur region and Aleppo. The people of Raqqa are kind and simple people. There is only one hotel in Raqqa, because it is not acceptable for a guest of one of the families to stay in a hotel. It is against the traditions of the people of Raqqa to allow their guests to stay at a hotel. The hotel is just for politicians who come for a visit and perhaps some tourists.

There are oil mines in Raqqa, *Nahr al Furat* [Furat river] and the Furat Dam which is famous for providing electricity to most parts of Syria. I come from a family of farmers. We lived a simple but rich life. At the age of eighteen, I had my own house on the family land. My family supported me to build my own house. There was a house built for each one

of my siblings on that farm. Raqqa was very kind to me. I learned how to be patient.

My house overlooked a very nice and wide landscape. It was a sunny place. I was very happy over there. As a little child, I would accompany my uncles on their fishing trips to *Nahr al Furat*.

I long for those days. Swimming, fishing, barbeques afterwards. I was so loved and cared for by my uncles. I am the fifth child in my family. A spoiled child. My cousins were also my best friends. One of them died during the war. He was my best friend. We studied and played together and had our best time together. He was hit by an air raid. Some of my friends are still there. Others became internal refugees or left the country like me.

A typical traditional Syrian courtyard with fountain. "Azimhof" (CC BY-ND 2.0) by captain.orange

Halah al Shami

I come from an educated family. My dad was a university professor and a medical doctor. We moved a lot between houses. My parents' house was so big, and the walls were all covered with wood plates. That was nice in terms of decoration but very dangerous if there was a fire accident. I remember that there was a fire accident in the opposite house which engulfed our house and the other houses. The whole neighbourhood was evacuated, and we had to move to an area farther away.

We then lived in a smaller house, but it was convenient enough for us. When the fire happened, I was around two to three years old. My aunt used to carry me and place me on a chair to look at the children playing outside the window. I have several nice memories of this house – such

as the *Bahra* [fountain]. There was a big *Bahu* [lounge area] and my dad had his clinic in the same lounge downstairs. Our bedrooms and living rooms were upstairs. The *Bahra* and the trees were in an open space at the centre surrounded by the lounge. So, my dad's patients used to sit in the lounge close to the consultation room.

Ali Zain

I studied philosophy at the Lebanese University for two years and tried to continue studying for my third year at Aleppo University but had to stop because of the war. I arrived in the UK in October 2015 and I have leave to remain – refugee status. I am married with one son and we are expecting our second child five months from now.

My childhood is divided into two parts. The first part was in the village of *Al Hajar Al-Abyadh* [The White Stone]. I lived in that village for ten years. My uncle's house was next to our house and so were all our relatives who were around. After I became eleven, we left the village house and moved to live in the wilderness. There was no one around in the wilderness. We moved to the area of Al-Ratoniyyah in 1998 and I spent my life there until I left Syria in 2015.

The shift from the village to the wilderness was a crucial stage in my life where I moved from having several friends, relatives, and acquaintances to being a completely lonely person. After moving to the wilderness, I couldn't stop thinking and dreaming of our house in the village, in particular the yard in the middle of the house, and I still feel nostalgic for that village house. My best and worst

Al Hajar Al-Abyadh, where Ali was born.
Photo taken by his sister.

memories were in that house. I used to play with my brother, who died in the war, in that house. Also, I was slapped for the first and the only time in my life, by my father, in that same house. My dad slapped me when I was only four because I insulted the president Hafedh al Asad in front of the policemen in the village.

I still remember how my father treated me as a friend. A father-son friendship didn't exist in my rural culture at all. But our relationship was exceptional. My father married at the age of thirty-seven which was unusual in that culture and when I was born, he was thirty-eight and mature enough to treat me as a friend when I grew up. Over time we became so close. He had a distinct scent that I could smell even when I was asleep. When my father was to travel for his business, he avoided seeing me before leaving as I used to cry on his departure. That close relationship and his constant encouragement to me to read and to

write strengthened my sense of who I was. When my father died, I felt as if the whole world had fallen away.

After finishing high school, I took a gap year and worked as an Arabic language teacher on an hourly basis. I taught students aged fourteen and fifteen for four months. My dream of being a journalist did not contradict that of teaching as my aim was to leave a mark and influence my students. I will tell my son about all the teachers who taught me and had an impact on my life.

In October 2008, at the age of twenty, I was admitted to a Lebanese university for a self-funded study in Philosophy. Lebanon has a different culture, a more open and secular society. It was a drastic shift from a rural and conservative environment to a totally open society. University fees in Lebanon were affordable and I managed to pay by working while studying. In my free time, I used to attend Arabic literature classes and seminars which I enjoyed a lot.

Ali's parents' home in Al-Ratoniyyah

Lebanon resembles Europe in its openness to differences and freedom of speech to some extent. Beirut is closer to my heart than Damascus in terms of the freedom one can experience.

Natali Hadad

I was born in a city called Homs in 1955. I went to school there and then moved to Damascus for my university studies in medicine. In Syria I worked as a microbiologist. I have been in the UK for one year. I entered the UK via the United Nations' Refugee Resettlement Scheme, and I am currently living with my daughter's family. My daughter and her husband have been living in Cardiff for many years and they have four children. I have three sons who are in Europe.

I have three sisters and we all lived at my parents' house, a rented property, which was very large with a very big garden full of fruit trees, jasmine flowers, and roses of different colours. My dad used to take care of this garden and in the middle of the garden there was a small fountain. My best time was when I was asked to fill the fountain with water. After filling it, I always used to paddle in it.

In summertime, my parents and my siblings used to take a nap, but not me as I couldn't sleep during daytime. So my dad made me a DIY tree swing by attaching ropes to our garden trees. That was my best time ever in that garden.

My other favourite game was making a tent out of a big piece of cloth by placing it over the washing lines. I used to visit the countryside where my aunt was living. There, I used to play with my cousins on a cart pulled by a horse. But I didn't like the countryside a lot as the other children were reluctant to play with a child from the city.

I miss my childhood days, the schooldays in particular and how we used to live. I always remember how I used to go to school and back with my friends. I had three close friends from whom I was never parted. The four of us were inseparable and we are still in contact with each other through Facebook and WhatsApp.

We were neighbours, so our families knew each other and trusted each other. I was always allowed to play at my friends' houses, and they could play in my family's garden.

"Khalid ibn Al-Walid Mosque, Homs" (CC BY 2.0) by Beshr Abdulhadi

A rose growing in an Aleppo garden

We were the same age, same class and knew a lot about each other. When my family moved to a new house, we still saw each other at school. Our relationship continued until after university. What makes those friends so special is that we share stories, secrets, names. We simply share one history.

My primary school, where my mother was a teacher, was called Al Fatat. When I was four, I used to accompany my mother to school. My best teachers were my mum and my mum's friend. We were never hit or bullied by any teacher, the way some schoolchildren are nowadays. My favourite subject in school was maths. I didn't like Arabic language and its grammar.

During our secondary education we studied the locations of European countries, their borders, population figures and the exports and imports of each European country, so we had the basics. But we also used to watch TV channels that introduced Europe to us. There was a programme where we were introduced to a different western country each time. That programme helped us to form an idea about most western countries.

At high school, I scored high marks in science, biology and physics and was able to join a medical school in Damascus University. I was so excited about having to move away from my family and my hometown Homs to study in the capital city Damascus. It was a very new stage in my life. Fortunately, most of my friends from high school were admitted to the same university in Damascus. So we were together and lived in the same university halls. Those were very good days. They still resonate in my memory. I specialised in Laboratory Diagnosis and I studied for six years. I opened a private lab in Damascus where I lived. From time to time, I used to visit my family in Homs, but I was already settling in Damascus. I got married at the age of twenty-eight and stayed in Damascus.

Salih Hamzah

I spent my life between my village and Kobani. I lived in Qazani and worked in Ayn al-Arab as a barber. I had a barber shop there.

I did four years of primary education and had not continued my study. My mother died when I was six months old and my father died when I was ten years old.

You know, I experienced orphanhood from a very early age and was responsible for my family.

So I left school and trained to be a hairdresser for men. I later opened my own shop in Kobani. Three to four years in school. I learned the basics. I learned Arabic alphabets, some basic Arabic writing plus some basic maths. My Arabic was developed by mixing up with Arabs. Almost all of my customers were Arabs. And as you know, there are Arabs and Kurds in Kobani.

Mohamad Karkoubi

My name is Mohamad Karkoubi from Aleppo, Syria and I live in Aberystwyth with my family, my wife Ishraq and four children: two girls and two boys. I was a blacksmith. I worked in this field since 1993 or 1994. My eldest brother and my father both worked in this profession, and I loved it. I used to work after school. And I succeeded as a blacksmith.

We lived in a good environment with very kind parents. Very friendly people. Just like the way I am bringing up my children, being friendly to them. I love life like my parents did. Sadly, my parents were poor, and you know my dad was hoping that we would be the best. He wanted us to become doctors.

My mother was very clever. My sister is now. *Mashallah* [what God has willed] she is a teacher. She was very clever to become a teacher. We couldn't continue with our education because we had to help our father. As you know, in Syria there were some benefits for parents, but it wasn't enough.

We loved ironwork. My dad used to work in the same field. We never made him feel we sacrificed because of poverty. If we had studied, it would have been financially difficult. But *Alhamdulillah* [praise be to God] my sister became a teacher, and my eldest brother was a master blacksmith. He was well-known in the city. He is so skilful.

Noor

My childhood was spent in Manbij. I still have relatives, uncles and grandparents from my father's side living there today. Manbij means the neighbourhood where I lived, my best friends, my relatives, and my best and worst days. My best days, the memory of which is closest to my heart, were those spent with my father, *Allah Yerhamu* [May he rest in peace].

A photo of Aleppo taken by Mohamad Karkoubi

Panorama view of Latakia. By Jadd Haidar, CC BY-SA 4.0

My father used to arrange our family gatherings with all the other close relatives each Friday. The best day for me was when my father took us to the seaside of Latakia city where I met my uncles, grandparents, cousins and their extended families. I was about nine years old and the gathering felt like a great big family.

I also remember a very special family tradition which was held at my grandparent's house. When a little child took their first steps, we had a special celebration called *Qate'a al-Ahjar* [stone breaking]. They used to attach a thread with sweets at one of the little child's legs and the other children would gather opposite the child. When asked to start, the children run towards the child to cut the thread off their leg. My grandmother and the child's mother would be present at the celebration. We also used to celebrate the emergence of the first tooth of the baby.

My primary school was very close to our house. The best days of my life were at my primary school when I had so many friends. Every morning before lessons, we used to queue in the school's open yard to sing the Syrian National Anthem and to witness the Syrian flag-raising ceremony.

Mohammed S

Manbij is a small town in *Reef Halab* [the Aleppo countryside]. The population is around 500,000-600,000 people. I left Manbij at the age of fourteen in 2013, which was two years after the war in Syria began.

The best thing about living in my parents' house in Manbij was my primary school. The school was less than thirty seconds walk from the house. I used to spend my fifteen-minute lunch break at home and some of my friends used to accompany me there. It was also great waking up in the morning. I didn't have to wake up early to prepare at all as I could always make it to school within a few minutes before 8:30 am.

My parents' house had two floors and we had a small

green space on the second floor. We filled that space with potted plants and flowers, and we made it feel like a garden really. Springtime was the most pleasant season for us. The place used to be filled with the fragrances of Damascene Jasmines and *Ward al Joori* [Damask Roses]. It was so beautiful. Those plants and roses on the second floor gave our house a pretty look from the outside. Adults smoked *Shisha* and had coffee. I was too young for *Shisha*! We used to have breakfast there when the weather was good. Also afternoon teas in spring and summer.

Sulaiman Sulaiman

I was born in Manbij which is the largest city in the Aleppo district. About thirty-five kilometres from the Turkish borders and eighty kilometres from Aleppo. Before the war the government was planning to turn Manbij into a governorate, but this plan stopped because of war. Manbij is a very big city inhabited by one million people. Before the war a huge M4 Autostrada was constructed to connect Manbij to Aleppo, Raqaa, Deer al Zoor and Hasakah. The city has witnessed waves of immigrants, so it is relatively safer than other cities in terms of security.

My primary school was called Abu Firas al Hamadani. Al Hamadani is a well-known established Arab poet who was born in the city and the school was named after him. I studied for six years in this school, which was my primary education. My secondary education was in another school called Manbij secondary school for boys. Manbij is actually known as the city of poets as it is the birthplace of established poets like Omar Abu Reesha, al Buhturi and

Jasmine growing on the garden wall – one of the few photos Mohammad has of his home in Syria. Jasmine is an unofficial national symbol of Syria and its people's resilience.

Abu Firas al Hamadani. During my schooldays I was so organised. I used to arrange my clothes and things the night before I went to sleep. I used to wake up on my own and was so excited about going to school. I was so happy to go and meet with my friends and teachers. My favourite topics were Maths and Arabic language. Teachers did their best to push us to achieve great results. We used to respect our teachers a lot. If a teacher happened to pass our way while we were playing or joking, we used to avoid looking them in the eyes out of respect and appreciation.

I miss my close friends. Four or five of them were so close to me. We were always checking on each other and helping and supporting one another in good and bad times. We used to play football on the weekends in a very big field behind the school's backyard. The field was full of pomegranate trees, walnut trees, damask roses and other types of flowers. During schooldays, we used to visit the field with our teacher when we had a planting lesson which I was fond of. I still remember how excited I was during that lesson. The teacher used to train us in how to prepare the land for plantation which required wearing gloves, cleaning the field, carrying waste bags and using tools for digging. The most pleasant part was planting and seeding because it was always accompanied by watering the plants with hoses, which I loved. These were joyous moments and happy days, indeed.

During the fasting month of Ramadan we, the people of the neighbourhood which comprised twenty-five houses, used to exchange food, cookies, and sweets. When the call

A Manbij street scene, by Jacky Lee CC BY 3.0

for the sunset prayer starts and we began breaking our fast we were amazed at the variety of food and the number of dishes on our dinner table. Arabs, Kurds, Turkmen and Circassians used to be friends. Same with Muslims and Christians. During Christmas we used to have a day off to celebrate the day with our Christian friends who did the same during our Eid celebrations.

During our seventh, eighth and ninth grades we studied English and French. I still remember the hardcover of my English grammar book with the photo of the London Eye and Big Ben on it. We learned about England, Wales, Scotland but we didn't know much about names of cities. We learned about Germany, Italy, Spain etc and were dreaming of visiting any of them one day as tourists. It never occurred to us that a day would come when we would be refugees in these countries.

In the fifth to the ninth grade, we studied National Education where we learned about the Palestinian-Israeli conflict and that Israel is the biggest enemy. However, we later realised that if the Syrian government wanted to fight Israel, they would have done it many years before. They were actually fighting us, the people, instead of Israel.

In the National Education lesson, we used to memorise the Sayings of al Asad which were as important as the Qura'anic verses! Before each exam we had to memorise and discuss two or three of these sayings which I personally believe were nonsense. Why on earth do we have to memorise a sentence or a line that al Asad has said in a conference or in a meeting? We all thought that National Education was a waste of time and we wished that we were learning about more important subjects like maths, science, or physics.

In the 1970s and 1980s there was a lot of military training, and this stopped somewhere in the 1990s. When I was at school in 1998, there were the Ba'ath Party Vanguards who used to represent the party in events and elsewhere. If you are a member of the vanguard, you would get a better chance to find employment, regardless of your qualifications. There was no justice for people and there was a lot of favouritism and corruption.

Ronahi Hassan

Qamishli is the centre where I was born. It is my childhood – *al Seba* [youth] as they say. Schooltime, marriage, building my family. Everything was in Qamishli. Life is summarised in Qamishli. It is a period of more than thirty years of my life before leaving the place for the UK. It means so many things to me, many things. I wish that life could take me back to those moments again. They were the best moments, the best days.

I feel so homesick to the extent that I am sinking. I sometimes meet people from other communities getting together with their relatives and family. I crave this kind of getting together. I wish that I could have my big family here. For instance on the weekends. Friday was a family day where we visited members of the family, parents, relatives, or in-laws. We lost all of this. In Syria we used to meet up with friends but no more now! This loss, the longing! Sometimes I walk in the streets here in the UK and I suddenly smell certain food aromas which take me back. My life has turned into recollections of memories especially those of my childhood. Those memories have been occupying a larger space in my mind. Perhaps if you asked me now about what I did yesterday, I might easily forget recent events. Yet, I remember the past very well and especially in Syria. Childhood in particular.

I remember things from the age of four. I remember that stage before even being admitted to primary school.

A view of Shukri al-Qiwatly street Qamishli. By Arab Salsa, Public domain, via Wikimedia Commons

I wonder how this memory works. If you ask me about yesterday's or today's details, I might forget. I might forget what happened some hours back. I feel that there is a mystery behind the reactivation of memory. I find it very strange indeed. Details about a time when I used to play with the neighbour's children. There was a lot of fun in that. There were no differences between us. Girls used to play with boys freely. We were equal. We were friends, friends of the neighbourhood. There were many games to play. We used to play in the evening until a late hour.

Honestly, it was a safe environment. I still remember the level of safety, closeness, and kindness among the children of the neighbourhood. Neighbours were like a family to us. There were no formalities. I feel so sorry for our children. I feel that they haven't been enjoying their childhood the way we enjoyed ours. We used to play until eleven or twelve o'clock at night on the street. Old and young women from the neighbourhood were all around us outside. We the kids played, ran, and had lots of fun. Life was so enjoyable and simple. It was a stress-free life. It was safe. When we were in the first and second year of primary school, our parents didn't walk us or give us lifts to school. We used to walk to and from school on our own. You'd find one school serving several areas which meant that children had to walk many kilometres to arrive at their school. It was so safe for us to walk on our own and that was never an issue for our parents at all. Our families brought us up to be self-dependent.

I am a Kurd and Qamishli is a Kurdish majority city. Kurds constitute around three million people in Syria. It is the

Children carrying flag of Kurdistan at a procession in Qamishli. Photo: "Al Qamishli" (CC BY 2.0) by Beshr Abdulhadi

second largest ethnicity in Syria but sadly it did not receive any recognition. We grew up in an atmosphere of persecution and a denial of our identity. If they realised you are a Kurd you were not only going to be treated as a second-class citizen, but you would be badly treated.

I was born under Hafedh al Asad, the father of the current president Bashar al Asad. The Kurdish language was prohibited. No one could use Kurdish, ever. Also, Kurdish cultural and social events were banned. Our National Day, the Newroz day where we celebrate the new Kurdish year on the 21st of March – for years and years celebrating this day was banned and those celebrating it were arrested.

I grew up in a family that has a high sense of Kurdish national feeling. There were several activities at our house. Kurdish groups used to meet up in our house. There was a

KURDISTAN

Location of the Kurds on the map of the Middle East

period when the Kurds of Iraq had to flee the persecution of the late Saddam Hussein. My family hosted most of those who fled from Kurdistan to Syria. My parents' house was like a refuge. Many families had to seek refuge in our house. We looked after them and were responsible for them from A to Z. We provided housing, food, and clothes. When the authorities knew about it they arrested my grandfather. We were sharing our house with my grandparents. My grandfather was imprisoned and was severely punished. His punishment led to a permanent physical disability. I simply grew up under these circumstances – a nationalistic Kurdish family who always suffered from persecution.

However, this tense atmosphere didn't affect our interactions with the other ethnic groups in our neighbourhood. We were living in peace with everyone around. There was no difference between a Kurd, Arab, a Christian etc. We all lived in an age full of contradictions. Sadly, the regimes have participated in creating such rifts between communities. Yet, as a society we were living in harmony. My uncle's wife is an Arab from Deer.

Newroz at Girê Tertebê, near Qamishli, in 1997. Photo : MikaelF, CC BY-SA 3.0, via Wikimedia Commons

Intermarriages, Christian neighbours celebrating each other's religious events etc – unfortunately, policies played a dirty role in messing up that unique experience. For instance, in school we were not allowed to use the Kurdish language. Can you imagine a little kid on their first day in school prohibited from using their first language? I had to use Arabic. I didn't have a single Arabic word! At home we used Kurmanji Kurdish and at school we had to use Arabic. Almost all our teachers were Arabs. Kurdish teachers were a rarity. Kurdish teachers were not allowed to work in schools. The policy was to appoint Arabic speaking teachers from the coastal and local areas of Syria and to place them in the Kurdish areas. By the way, this didn't apply only to education but to almost all other organisations. The regime's policy was to appoint Arabic speaking employees. To bring Arabic speaking people from different parts of Syria and place them in the Kurdish majority cities and towns. The regime's policy was to Arabise the region. No employment opportunities for Kurds. We didn't even have universities in our areas. The whole Jazira region had no university. Universities or advanced colleges were banned.

Some Syrian Kurds were stripped of their Arabic nationalities and were not considered as citizens. Just imagine you are born somewhere but you don't have a nationality, a passport, or an ID card. Sadly, thousands of Kurds were persecuted by this law. They had no right to education. They couldn't even dream of studying at a university. We couldn't even travel internally. If we were to travel to Damascus or to Aleppo, we had to stay in a hotel that would eventually require an ID card. Kurds had no right to own a house or land. Had no right to employment. It was a prison. I personally describe it as a slow death in life. We were lucky. My family had a Syrian ID card, but this doesn't mean we were better off. There was a lot of discrimination going on.

There were two groups: one without a Syrian nationality or ID and another with a Syrian ID but they were always considered Kurds. So they had the same treatment. Yes, we were allowed to go to universities, but the government had imposed limitations on that. I am considered a second generation which experienced relatively better treatment compared to the first generations who had to travel to other governorates. They could spend eight to ten hours travelling to and from Qamishli to those cities and that was costly in terms of accommodation etc. This was a big burden on the Kurdish families who didn't have the financial means to support their children in their university journey. As to employment, Kurds were the last to be given a chance to work. Kurds were banned from occupying sensitive positions in the government. No one could ever argue about it. The general atmosphere was one of injustice.

I still remember a scene I watched when I was in the fifth grade of my primary education. As I said before, Qamishli is a Kurdish majority town. Pupils were mostly Kurds. But teachers were all Arabs. I remember a day when a teacher asked a girl in my class a question which she didn't answer correctly. The teacher grabbed her hair and began hitting the pupil's head over the table once, twice, three times. A brutal punishment which might have caused the girl a lifetime disability.

There were two things which saved me from all that hatred from teachers in school. First, I was clever, and I used to participate a lot in lessons. Second, my name. Most pupils have Kurdish names. New teachers used to ask each pupil to introduce themselves in front of the class. My Kurdish name is Ronahi but in the official documents – when my father wanted to register me in the school, he gave the authorities an Arabic name: Lonaee to save me future hassles. And this name has no specific meaning apart from the Arabic letters. So, when teachers heard Lonaee they never realised that it was a Kurdish name.

Insecurity in the place where I lived has nothing to do with war. I grew up in an atmosphere of trust and security. When I became a young woman and I got married, that sense of security began to disappear slowly. Despite the general sense of security, young women walking in the streets were frequently harassed by young men and this became a common phenomenon in the Middle East. Perhaps because of globalisation, the internet, and the access to hundreds of satellite channels. We began to hear about harassment cases a lot. So there were certain hours when a young woman could be out. And, of course, the war and the conditions which led to the war played a role as well.

In 2004 a big demonstration started from Qamishli and later spread to the other cities in Syria including Damascus. Those demonstrations were called the demonstrations of the millions. Those protests were not talked about in the media. No one outside Syria was supposed to know about the protests. No one knew that they took place. I believe that the protests of 2004 were the beginning of the revolution. The events that happened in 2011, were not the real beginning of the revolution. Yes, it began in Qamishli and led to millions of demonstrations and protests.

Unfortunately, if all the ethnicities, including the Arabs and other ethnicities, had united we could have witnessed a new Syria, a new country. If they had united, the regime would have made compromises.

Yes, the Kurds suffered a lot and the political system participated in increasing that suffering. The whole story of the protests started with a football game that quickly turned into protests, demonstrations, killing, shooting. Thousands were imprisoned. It was a dark year indeed.

An incident took place in Dara'a. Some school teenagers painted some words against Bashar al Asad. That incident arose from the difficult conditions under which Syrians were living. When those incidents happened, we the Kurds realised that it was not just us who were persecuted. The Syrian Arabs were persecuted as well. Only later we realised we are all equal in being victims of this regime. If someone doesn't comply with the regime's principles, they will be persecuted. I am saying this because we were living in the Kurdish majority areas which were very isolated from the other areas inside Syria. Of course, we had an idea that there were Arab political prisoners – members and leaders of communist parties and members of parties who called for freedom and democracy etc. We knew about them.

However, we had no idea about the big numbers of Arab political prisoners and other ethnic groups in other Syrian cities. The regime has adopted the policy of divide and rule. Sadly, the regime created and enriched this policy which led to widening the gap between us and the Syrian Arabs in the other cities.

The regime considered Al Jazira an underdeveloped area. It was totally isolated from the other parts of Syria. We have always suffered from the lack of developed hospitals. We

A later demonstration in Qamishli against the Syrian government in 2014. Photo by KurdWatch.org, CC BY 3.0, via Wikimedia Commons

had no universities. Al Jazira had not been visited by any Syrian official in the government. I remember when I started my university course, Arab students were surprised to know that we have ever existed. When we introduced ourselves as Kurds, they were surprised. Just imagine. They used to think that Kurds were Bedouins or something! It was a surprise for them to know that we were like them. We talk, think and we live in houses like them! I got the same attitude here when I moved to the UK. Some people were surprised to know that I came from Syria. They thought that any woman from that part of the world must be veiled, living in the desert! Sometimes when I compare the two situations, I feel like the same scenario is being repeated.

As I said, we were persecuted to the extent that we tried to adapt to the level of persecution and marginalisation. In 2004, when those demonstrations took to the streets, it was a turning point in the life of the Kurdish communities in Syria. Unfortunately, after the protests the regime's attitude shifted from bad to worse. When the father Hafedh al Asad was in power he never mentioned us. He didn't even think of visiting the Kurdish region during his lifetime. Bearing in mind that al Jazira region is regarded as the breadbasket of Syria because of the petrol, the agriculture. Al Jazira is the major channel of resources to the whole country. Sadly, the inhabitants of al Jazira are the poorest groups in Syria. It is a contradiction, isn't it? In 2004 the regime sent military troops, tanks and turned the region into a war zone!

I had never seen weapons, tanks and shootings before 2004. It became clear that we had to cope with that 'military situation' around. During Newroz day, killings and shootings at people were so common. Many young men got killed by the regime. Racism reached its highest level. Bashar al Asad went even further to issue a decree that prohibited Kurds from buying, selling or owning a house or land. I think it is called the '49 decree'. He realised that if any other ethnic group would support the Kurds, the whole regime would collapse.

"I had ideas on democracy, coexistence, and anti-racism etc. These were all considered threats to the regime's ideology."

So in the beginning he tried to silence the Kurdish nation for the first time in the history of the Kurds. Even cultural activities were banned. My husband and I used to organise some of those cultural events. But we felt that organising them would put us at a great risk. I personally did not join any Kurdish party. But being an activist, being active, having some ideas to change the status of things was considered as working against the grain. I had ideas on democracy, coexistence, and anti-racism etc. These were all considered threats to the regime's ideology.

Intelligence forces were all over the Kurdish region. They were growing and spreading everywhere like cancer. At some stage I was planning to establish a charity to help and support poor and needy people. I got a phone call from a friend warning me against a lady I trusted to work with me to establish the charity. I found out that she was working with the Syrian intelligence forces. My husband's financial situation was very good, and we were planning to buy a bigger house in the centre of the city. We couldn't do that because of the prohibition. How could anyone function in an atmosphere of fear, humiliation, and marginalisation?

We had children and we were in a constant fear for their future and their safety. My children were so little, and I wasn't working. I was studying from home. I was doing a degree in Economics at Aleppo university. Sadly, I couldn't continue my studies because of family responsibilities, pregnancies etc. Later, private studies at universities were opened and I signed up to a distant learning course in Agrarian Reform Engineering. So I studied from home and did my final tests in person in Homs. My family and kids didn't stop me from studying this time! I always loved to study. I was into reading from a very early age.

The education system in our region was suffering a lot. We didn't have highly qualified staff to teach our children. I used to teach my children at home. Almost all my time was for my children. This is the reason I couldn't work. My children were very clever, and I couldn't rely on the education they were given at their schools. So, I had to do my part. Even if I was lucky to find a good school for my children, I had to supervise their learning. All those reasons, pressures. The authority, the intelligence etc. The political situation worsened in our region tremendously.

I lived in a flat in the town centre. When Sheikh Khaznawi Allah Yerhamu [May he rest in peace] was assassinated at the hands of the Syrian authorities – he was an-open minded sheikh, so brave and so outspoken. He used to preach against the regime and against injustice. This led to his assassination. As a result, Kurds organised several protests and many people were imprisoned.

There were Arab gangs. Those Arabs who had been transferred to our region as part of the policy of Arabisation which the regime adopted, those groups were so spiteful to Kurds. When the protests took place in the aftermath of the assassination, those gangs were the first to hit the Kurds. They hit young men harshly, looted the shops of Kurds. They broke their belongings and stole their stuff.

I remember that day when I was sitting on my balcony, overlooking the main street. I saw a white van in the middle of the road. Masked men holding sticks and weapons. They captured a few young Kurdish men. They

began hitting them on their heads. They hit them spitefully. I I quickly pulled my children into the living room as I didn't want them to watch that violence. But they saw most of the scene and they still remember it.

I lived amid all that violence, humiliation, and fear. I took the decision to leave without even giving it too much thought. It was a very crucial decision that I made. It was December. At the end of 2008. I took my children and left.

M H

I was born in the city of Jedda in Saudi Arabia. It is a very complex story. I mean the Syrian situation is very much complicated. Since the change of the ruling system in Syria back in the 1960s, I think. When al Asad, the father, took over by force and cemented his place as the leader of the country, it started to be brutal and very difficult to cope with for most people in Syria except for a few groups who were benefitting from that regime. My father was in his early twenties and so were his younger brothers and friends. They started to realise that living in Syria was becoming very difficult.

My father was sent from Syria to study in Jordan. He did a degree in foreign political studies. He moved back to Syria after graduation and got a job there. As a result of his hard work, my dad was offered an opportunity to work in a start-up business in Saudi Arabia in the mid 1980s. At that time, this area was a great place for investment. My father ran the business and eventually became a shareholder in one of the major firms after thirty to forty years of service. So the family had lived in Saudi Arabia since the mid 1980s,

Houses and farms in Zabadani Valley. Wesamt, CC BY-SA 4.0 via Wikimedia Commons

but we were always back and forth to Syria. My grandparents, uncles and extended family were all in Syria.

There was a period of time back in the 1990s where we couldn't travel to Syria and used to spend our time and meet relatives in Jordan. The ruling regime was suspicious of all Syrians who left the country in the 1980s regardless of their political affiliations and background. It was a scary six to seven years when we avoided going to Syria. As the situation became a little bit better, we started to visit Syria more often. This might explain to you why we lived in Saudi Arabia. My father's place of residence was in Jedda. I was born in 1987 and my twin sisters Layla and Salma were born in Jedda in 1991. My brothers were born in Damascus.

The last time I was in Syria was I think in January or February 2011, during the first eruptions of the Syrian uprising and when people were becoming fed up with the whole situation. It was before the innocent uprising was hijacked by militias and radical groups who unfortunately gave the revolution a bad name, which is frustrating to be honest. When I was there, I knew. I knew it was the end of it. I had a feeling that it was the last time that I would be walking the streets of Damascus, my beloved home city. And that was it – I haven't been there since.

I saw in the Syria of 2011 the hardships, the tight security fist on people's heads, chests, necks, and throats. I am speaking metaphorically here. Actually, not just metaphorically, because it was really like that and even worse. It was clearly going downhill although in 2009 and 2010 the country was getting to a level of becoming very open, very active with a very strong economy and healthy social life and community. But it was a ticking bomb because people were just running away from the truth to that Utopia, which wasn't there in reality

I remember seeing family – and we are not talking about grandparents, uncles, aunts and cousins but even cousins of your grandparents, cousins of your father and mother. So it was massive, huge. It was great seeing all those children, the beauty of the land and the trees. We used to grow our own fruit and vegetables in our backyard. We have a countryside village house in an area called Zabadani that is a rural area on the outskirts of Damascus where you find pure water and fresh air. Even though the place could only accommodate ten people, we used to have thirty people squeezed in and having fun. My grandma used to make marmalade out of fresh oranges, strawberries and cherries. I remember the cherry tree at the corner of the house which they chopped down years later. It was a massive cherry tree. On one of its branches we hung a handmade swing and we used to take turns on it. We ran around to the backyard, playing football and when we grew up, we started playing cards at the front of the house. There was a little fountain downstairs and a bigger one upstairs. We had a vine plant. We grew different types of grapes. It was heaven on earth!

When we were partly living in Damascus and Zabadani as children, we didn't realise the darkness behind that natural beauty. It is not because of the country itself but because of the people who are abusing its wealth, strength and exploiting the best of everything in the country for years and years.

The Umayyad Mosque, Damascus © ali/Adobe Stock

We are still seeing this going on. Apparently, our parents were living that hell and were dealing with it every time they went there. I remember my dad and my uncles were called by the security department every time we were in Syria, to declare things or to clear up a few things and it was over nothing. It was a repetitive type of extortion. So it was honey mixed with bitterness. It is still a beautiful country but with a heavy darkness looming around it. You sense death is coming from it and to it from all different angles.

I remember, my grandpa had a nice flat in central Damascus. He is over seventy now and he still has it in an area called Ein al Kersh which in slang Syrian Arabic means the eye or middle of the tummy or the navel. The place is called that because it is located just in the middle of the capital city of Damascus, a very vibrant and lively area.

If you walk ten minutes from my grandpa's house to the left, there is the Umayyad Mosque which was St. Paul's Church before the Umayyad Caliphate controlled Damascus. And if you walk to the right you get to the famous squares and gardens made even before the French rule in the 1920s or the 1930s. It is an amazing place to live in.

I remember going down with my cousin Zaid to the mini market, a traditional market that is completely different from what you would see here, even back in time. The market is very different from any other market I saw in Amman or elsewhere as it is very basic, but we still loved it. Nice commodities for very cheap prices, a very friendly man selling stuff who could easily turn grumpy if you haggled about the price! I have a very strong attachment to those childhood memories and to the place. An interview

Damascus Old City (CC BY-ND 2.0) by Marc Veraart

would never be enough to describe Damascus and its memories.

Eid, New Year and Christmas were all special times. We always closed the streets in that neighbourhood and used to bring homemade wooden swings and a hand-operated one where a man stands by it, with little live ponies which we used to pay something like a pound or less to ride. Lots of candyfloss and sweets being sold. A very simple and cheerful atmosphere for anyone passing by. It was fascinating.

At the age of eleven I fell in love with my wife. Although she was born in Kuwait, she was also like me living between Kuwait and Syria. And it was very normal to see Syrians going back and forth to Syria from the 1970s and 1980s onwards. It was a very common thing to see Syrians living in the Gulf region and visiting Syria. Most of those people back then needed to leave a foot outside Syria in case of a sudden run. That was the way Syrians lived and that is due to the ruling regime who made people prepare to run away at any stage unfortunately. I believe six or seven Syrian families out of ten have always been back and forth to Syria until after the eruption of violence in Syria – whether in the Gulf, Saudi Arabia, France or Canada etc. This explains why even before the uprising we always had dual nationality Syrians in the country: loads of American Syrians, Canadian Syrians, British Syrians.

Qasioun Mountain, where you can see the whole of Damascus from the top, has a special memory, as it is where Nisreen finally accepted me as a sweetheart. We used to hang out at Hadeqat al Jahez, a public park named

Damascus from Mount Qasioun. ZCU, CC BY-SA 3.0, via Wikipedia Commons

after a famous Arab writer al Jahiz in a very posh area of Damascus. I still remember the fresh carrot-orange juice we drank. We even imagined our current family, we imagined having our first daughter. We used to have the famous Syrian *Sahlab* drink [a drink made up of milk, corn flower, sugar, cinnamon, coconut flakes and nuts] and I remember the names of places and shops we visited.

During those pleasant days there were also some difficult and challenging moments. When I was applying for a Syrian national ID card – we had to get one at the age of fifteen, or sixteen at the latest, or we would be in big trouble. We normally had to start preparing documents and going through the process by the age of fourteen. You would be asked questions like 'Where do your political allegiances lie?' and 'Why do you live between two countries?', 'Why is your dad working there?' And questions about my uncle

which stressed me out. I have an uncle who was beaten by security forces because of another uncle in the family who had different political views. So they harassed me and my dad for that reason, to be able to arrest that uncle and shut him up and shut up his beliefs. My uncle was badly hit on his face by a Syrian security force officer with the back of a Russian machine gun and he lost his front teeth. He was jailed for few days as well. I have another uncle who was so badly harassed by the government that he eventually fled the country because he couldn't stand it. So memories bring a lot of mixed emotions.

At the age of eighteen, every Syrian man has to get a military ID because in Syria serving in the army is compulsory. But if you live between Syria and other countries, you are permitted to pay a fee without serving. This is another reason why many Syrian families choose to live between Syria and another country – to save their sons from serving in the army. My dad served in the Syrian army and he knows what it is like. He was jailed during his service over nothing. He was put in a hole for three nights, not because he disobeyed orders or anything – it was just jealousy. That superior was from an underprivileged family in the village and not well-educated, whereas my dad was educated and from a well-known family in the capital city of Damascus. It was all about misusing power because of jealousy and envy. So my dad knows how terrible and how unfair military service in Syria can be. He sacrificed living in the country he loved the most, near his parents, for us. And at the same time, he kept us in contact with the country.

I was doing my undergraduate course in dentistry in Jordan and the capital city Amman is very close to Damascus. If you take out the border stops it is just a matter of a three-hour drive from Amman to Damascus. During my study, I used to visit Damascus whenever I had the chance to do so. I was feeling homesick and missing everyone there, so I visited my grandparents.

One of my cousins suggested we go to our favourite Qasioun mountain. We went there and were having a good time. A friend who was studying at Damascus university was explaining how difficult life could be with his Maths degree and so on. I was telling him about my university – how disciplined it is and how hard the curriculum is and telling him that I was struggling because Jordan is expensive. Without my dad's financial support, life would have been impossible.

Apparently, we were overheard by someone from an intelligence security department in that part of Syria. The guy assumed I was talking about Syria and we had a confrontation. I was nearly about to be dragged to his car, which is very common in Syria in such situations. Men are dragged to somewhere unknown! I explained that I was complaining about Jordan where I was studying and luckily I had my Jordanian student ID card that was still valid. That card saved me.

"It was honey mixed with bitterness… a beautiful country but with a heavy darkness looming around it."

We Syrians became used to the bullying and harassment of the border officers every time we crossed the borders from Lebanon or Jordan to Syria. Imagine going to your own country and a border officer extorting you to pay him money to prevent him from making something up against you, just because you are living away.

Yes, Syria is our country, and yes Damascus is our beloved city but not like this. We realised that we could not make it better. We couldn't do anything to make it better in terms of safety and security because you can be imprisoned and tortured for political views, religious affiliations, or nothing at all. There is always the chance that you might be picked up in the middle of the night from your bed or from the street and that's it – you disappear forever. Every time we went out in Syria, our parents knew there was a chance we might not get back. Even during times of peace and prosperity.

Syria was very open and prosperous in 2009-10. We had American restaurant chains. Even in the remote parts of Syria we had malls, we had brands and lovely things. You'd think the country was turning around. But in depth and in reality, the country was a dark place.

Damascus by Dudarev Mikhail

"Above or Below – Never Safe" by Alison Lochhead

Our War

"We longed for a long, peaceful and quiet sleep.
At night, we used to wonder whether we would still be alive the next morning."

Sulaiman Sulaiman

In July 2012 the Free Syrian Army [FSA], groups of soldiers and low-ranking officers, began to defect from the regime forces when things started to take an unpleasant and ugly turn, as the regime began to repress the uprising more and more. As the FSA members were already armed the revolution turned from being peaceful into an armed struggle and that was exactly what the regime wanted.

On the 19th of July 2012, my city Manbij was liberated from the regime's hold to fall under the FSA's control. We were so pleased that the FSA was ruling, and people demanded reforms, change and basic rights. The FSA continued for about two years in Manbij, during which the city witnessed heavy aerial bombings, barrel bombs – oil drums, fuel tanks or gas cylinders filled with explosives and metal fragments – from Asad's regime. For instance, you might be shopping in the city centre and suddenly an oil drum or a gas cylinder would explode somewhere close to you. The government used to kill innocent people and spread lies on the state TV channel that the bombings had targeted a group of terrorists and had killed twenty of them. I personally witnessed passers-by being killed by shrapnel hitting their heads, and elderly men who had heart attacks as a result of the terrible noise of explosions.

At this stage, I tried to help as a volunteer with the ambulance team. The city was suffering from a severe shortage of ambulance staff. I personally had no idea about how to offer first aid or any of that. So I volunteered with a group of young men and women and had an intensive month of training on nursing and first aid with a female doctor. We learned several essential things about how to draw blood, inject, evacuate people and help the injured and the wounded etc. In the meantime, we decided to form a small society for young men which we called Future Youth Society. The society was located in an office which formerly belonged to the Asad regime. We started with a hundred members from different educational and professional backgrounds and gradually we expanded. We were basically offering services, raising awareness about the best ways to avoid shrapnel and stay safe, helping people fleeing their homes and finding temporary refuges for them. For instance, we used to locate deserted schools, clean classrooms, ensure that water supplies were available, provide bedding and essentials and simply make temporary places ready for people after evacuation.

A man with bloodstains on his face carries a boy after what activists said was shelling by forces loyal to Syria's President Bashar al Asad in Aleppo's Bustan al-Qasr district, August 16, 2013.(REUTERS / Aref Haj Youssef – stock.adobe.com)

We approached pharmacies and asked them to donate medicine, bandages, necessary drugs for those who needed them the most. Later on we initiated another campaign called Syria is Bleeding. The aim was purely humanitarian and had nothing to do with politics or the regime. We, young men and women, simply wanted to help people survive. We collected blood to help children with a blood disorder called thalassemia who were in need of a blood transfusion every now and then. We used mosques to call people to come forward and donate their blood after heavy bombings on the city. During peaceful intervals especially on Friday mornings we used to visit remote areas and ask villagers for blood donations during the Friday's prayer and through the Imams. In each visit we used to collect over 150 blood bags and handed them to the blood bank. And things went smoothly for some time, and we were so happy that we were able to help as many people as we could through these Friday visits to rural areas.

The regime's agents filled the walls with slogans like 'Asad or we burn the country', 'With soul and blood we redeem you, Bashar'. We, the youth, had a deep love for Syria and we all hated the notion of having to glorify a person – Bashar! For instance, here in Britain, people have never glorified a particular prime minister like Cameron, Blair or May. We have never seen a poster or a statue of any of these prime ministers in the UK or in Europe. Whereas in Syria, we grew up with photos of the Asad sons everywhere in schools, offices, streets, hospitals etc.

As part of our volunteering role, we initiated a campaign called 'My city, my home' and we washed and painted the walls of Manbij's city centre. We replaced the president's photos with lines from poetry or famous sayings encouraging young people to study and gain knowledge and education. We were trying to focus on our love of Syria rather than sect, religion and politics.

Baher al Abed

I don't have the best memories of Syria. I lost my mum. Twenty-one days exactly after her, my dad and a year after, my brother. I lost so many relatives and cousins, even friends. Then my house got destroyed. I have two sisters, but I don't really talk to them because I was raised away from them. So I don't have the best memories. I don't really remember my house properly. I remember bits of it, you know. I remember very, very simple things. Personally, I don't remember much from Syria. I was ten. Yeah, I was actually younger when I lost my mum. It was in 2011 so I think I was nine when I lost my mum. It was bombs shelled on the town from the government. Then my father was killed by an aeroplane strike.

Noor

We witnessed bombings, explosions, and air raids for a while but there was no way to get out of that situation. We were so scared of the sounds of explosions and the news of families that had been buried under the rubble of their houses. But we had no choice but to leave our fate to Allah and be patient. One day, while I was hanging the laundry

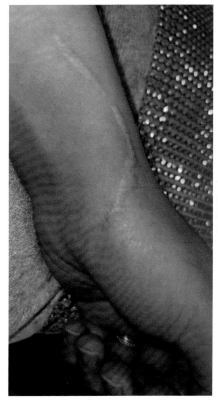

The scar on Noor's wrist from where she was hit by shrapnel while hanging out the laundry.

on the washing line on the roof of the house, I got injured by shrapnel that came from distant air raid bombing. The shrapnel hit my wrist. Normally, such wounds would get stitched but because the hospitals were overwhelmed by far more dangerous and serious cases, my wound was treated as a minor case, and I got it dressed in a bandage only. So it left my wrist with this clear, deep mark.

I remember a day in 2013 when there were fierce bombings from a plane. Without thinking, I sat cross-

Women wearing full face coverings or Niqab. By Grzegorz Japol

on Saturdays only and there was a school bus that used to take students from home to school. Even though we were already covering our heads with a headscarf, we had to wear an extra cover. Black *burka* was compulsory. There were sudden raids from ISIS members on schools and classes to check on the female students and to make sure they were fully covered. But we couldn't cover our faces during lessons as it was so hot during summer and we could hardly breathe. Our male headteacher was supportive and kind and there was a secret code shared between the head teacher and the students. Once ISIS members came to the school, a teacher's assistant would ring the bell to warn us to cover our faces and hands. We know that this is not what Islam is about. A true Muslim woman should only cover her hair, not the face and the hands. But we had no choice.

On my third week in that school, we noticed a new female student wearing black *burka* entering the class for the first time. We all wondered who that lady was as she looked suspicious and didn't say a single word to any of us. On the same day, we were all taken by surprise when an ISIS member dashed into our class while we were uncovering our faces. It was such a scary scene. He was fully armed when he asked the teacher to get out of the class. At that moment we all had to cover our faces and hands. He started rebuking us and telling us off with phrases like 'You must wear a Burka and if your parents have allowed you to go without a face cover, it is now our responsibility to impose it on you.' So, it was a long lecture which he ended by writing our full names on a piece of

legged on the floor hugging my three-year old sister, trying to protect her. I wasn't aware how scared I was until after the air raid, when my neighbour noticed I was actually trembling. We had no shelters at home to move to during an air raid. There was an underground shelter at school which we used when air raids took place on schooldays.

It wasn't just the regime's bombings. We witnessed the Free Syrian Army. who had its grip on the city of Aleppo and the surrounding villages, followed by ISIS. In 2014, when my city was under ISIS, I joined a private school for girls to study for my year 12, which is the last year in high school before entering university. The school used to open paper. He told us he counted the headteacher responsible for this mess and that he would deal with him later. Some of my colleagues asked him 'What are you going to do with the headteacher?' He replied with a sign movement that refers to killing. We all became emotional and were scared to death. It was a dreadful feeling and a very difficult day. When I told my family, they advised me to stay at home and to postpone my study.

At some stage, ISIS prohibited female students from seeing male teachers face-to-face. They warned headteachers that if they didn't obey the rules, ISIS would force schools to close. The new ISIS rule was that lessons were to be offered by downloading the material on a computer and only audios of teachers were allowed.

After a few days, we noticed ISIS cars in our neighbourhood and some members were standing at the door opposite our house. When we asked our neighbour what they were doing on her doorstep, she told us they were looking for girls aged fifteen or over for marriage. Just imagine how easily they could force families to give them their daughters! I was fifteen by then and this incident drove my mother mad as our house could be their next target. We heard several stories of incidents like this with other families and girls.

They are a group of brainwashed and programmed people who could do anything by force. At the beginning we were allowed to wear black *niqab* [a head and a face cover with an opening or a see-through cloth around the eyes] and a long and wide coloured coat.

Later, that coloured coat was prohibited. A friend of my mother was wearing a coloured long coat plus *niqab* and was beaten by an ISIS member with a bamboo stick telling her 'What you are wearing is *Tabarruj* [elegance that attracts men] and *Tabarru*j is religiously illegitimate." Women were really confused about what was a legitimate dress code as they were already wearing long, wide coats that were not revealing or body defining.

Also, during that stage, the price of black clothing soared, and some people couldn't afford to buy a new piece every time ISIS wanted them to. I had to pay 5000 SYL for my long coat which was very expensive. Sadly, it was not black, and I had to purchase other pieces like black gloves, a black cloak and black cover. Shop owners were not allowed to let female shoppers in unless they were fully covered with a black *Burka* and long-sleeved gloves.

When the situation got worse under ISIS, my mother decided to put an end to the suffering, the fear and uncertainty and leave. Sulaiman, my eldest brother, along with my other brothers supported my mother's decision to leave. They could endure anything but seeing me or any woman in the family abducted by ISIS. Not only my family, but almost every family who had young women in their house left the city. We wanted to live in peace even if it was for a short while. Back home we longed for a long, peaceful and quiet sleep. At night, we used to wonder whether we would still be alive the next morning. The fear was not just for the young women but was also for young men who were dragged off to join ISIS by force. Danger was all around.

Destroyed neighbourhood in Raqqa, Bashar's hometown. Mahmoud Bali (VOA), Public domain, via Wikimedia Commons

Bashar

I finished my high school and applied for Beirut Arab University. I studied Media and Journalism for two years in Beirut. But when the war started, I had to stop my studies and return to Syria. It was hard to stay in Beirut away from my family in wartime. I could not stay away and watch my family suffer from a distance. I stayed in Raqqa and things got worse between 2012-2014. ISIS came and I was badly injured. The Syrian army targeted ISIS and we the people had to pay the price. I was hit on my legs. Two bullets penetrated my legs. A bullet for each leg. I was badly injured and couldn't get proper medical treatment. I only had first aid. Gradually that injury got worse and affected my right leg badly. I needed urgent surgery. Once I recovered and was able to walk normally, my family suggested that I leave the country.

"I used to take off my sweater, scarf or some of my clothes to cover the bodies of women and children killed and left on streets."

I was taking part in a protest and the Syrian forces began firing at the protesters. They fired randomly at anyone. I was against the Syrian regime and against ISIS and I was a very vocal critic of the two horrible groups. So, I was targeted afterwards. I was targeted by both forces. I had to flee Syria to Turkey and then to the UK.

I volunteered with a group of young men to help people in the affected area. In the aftermath of air raids, I used to roam around, and pick up the remains of corpses to help families identify the bodies of their loved ones. Yes, those were horrible memories. I used to take off my sweater, scarf or some of my clothes to cover the bodies of women and children killed and left on streets.

Ali Zain

When the Syrian revolution broke out in 2011, I was working, studying, and mobilising my fellow young Syrians through my writing on social media and other platforms. I was an activist working remotely from Lebanon. The revolution was a dream that came true. When it began, I was torn between staying and working in Lebanon and going to Syria to take part in the revolution.

Taking part in the revolution became impossible after my father's death. As the eldest son, I had to take care of my family and earn a living. If I joined the revolutionaries and got killed, my family would be lost. Also, my younger brother was a soldier in the regular Syrian Army of Asad's regime which is the state's army. So I was torn between my revolutionary feelings and my inability to take part in the demonstrations. I was also torn between being a revolutionary and having a brother fighting in the army against the demonstrators. I had to leave for Lebanon and was studying and working to support my family in Syria. A year later, my brother was killed and was buried before I could see him.

I was twenty-three when my father died. My brother was just twenty. After two years in Lebanon, I had to transfer my studies and to move out from the Lebanese University of Beirut to Aleppo University to be closer to my family. Also, the revolution devolved into a war, and it all started in Aleppo which made it even worse in terms of safety and in commuting from my house to Aleppo. But with the war getting fiercer, I had to stop studying.

In Lebanon I participated in demonstrations against the Asad regime and was posting revolutionary texts on Facebook daily. I was following the events in Syria from afar. The Shia'a communities in Lebanon are followers of Hezbollah which is a pro-Asad. The Sunni communities supported the Syrian revolution. Even though I am from a Shia background, I used to go to the Sunni neighbourhoods to demonstrate, as they were against the Asad regime.

There were clashes between the pro-Asad groups and the anti-Asad demonstrators. One day while delivering a restaurant order, my employer called to tell me that I should hide for a while as some members of the Syrian National Party in Lebanon, which supports Asad, came to arrest me because of my social media activism. I had to hide for a while in Lebanon. It was then that I heard about my brother's death.

On my way from Lebanon to Syria to attend my brother's funeral, the Syrian authorities found my diary in which I recorded my thoughts against the regime. That was a disaster that could lead to imprisonment or to a field execution. I'd heard about several field executions at the borders. My Shia'a name, family name and Shia'a background helped me in that fearful situation. The fact that I was going to attend the funeral of my brother, a soldier in the regime's army, saved my life after a long investigation session. I went home and spent two years with my family under severe war conditions, during which I got married.

Four months later, ISIS controlled our village and that was another dark chapter in our life. I've always believed that the Syrians' real issue is the Asad regime and that ISIS is just an outcome of the ruthless ruler who killed his people in cold blood. ISIS men were roaming the neighbourhoods wearing their explosive belts while intimidating men, women and children. The situation got worse when they started recruiting young men by force.

I was always against serving in the Syrian army as I have always considered it a criminal regime. Asad the father killed 42,000 civilians during the Hamah massacre of the 1980s. He had ordered regular army units and special forces to besiege Hamah, the country's fourth city, and bombarded it. The aim of the assault was to respond to a revolt led by the Muslim Brotherhood movement based in Syria. Air strikes and mortar fire caused the death of several thousand civilians. Hamah was to be the scene of torture, summary executions and privations of every kind.

Even before the revolution and the war began, I was ready to flee the country in order not to join this army. Unfortunately, almost all those who worked for the regime as high ranking officers and generals have turned into criminals intimidating people and exercising power in its ugliest forms. All the higher ranks in the Syrian army were allocated to the Alawites. Alawites who work for the regime are ruthless. For instance, the infamous Tadmor prison, run and managed by the Alawites, was known for harsh conditions, extensive human rights abuse, torture and summary executions. The army is infamous for its corrupt officials. It is widely known in Syria that if you want to avoid military service, you can do it by bribing officials.

When the Free Syrian Army took hold of my city, we experienced a time of freedom in all aspects of life. We enjoyed freedom of speech, we were free to discuss political and religious views. New newspapers were introduced and I was so excited about writing in those newspapers. It looked like we had discovered a new life compared to the previous life of abduction and intimidation. I was introduced to poets, to educated elites, Marxists, atheists – to ideas and ways of thinking that no one had ever dared to express before. Unfortunately, that short-term freedom was turned upside down once ISIS took hold of our city.

In 2015, Manbij and the surrounding areas where I lived were taken by ISIS. Life became really difficult under ISIS's rule, especially when they started forcing young men from all backgrounds to join their forces as their motto was "You are either with us or against us". All the young men who were aspiring to create change had to escape Manbij and Aleppo when ISIS entered these cities. We could never argue with ISIS members or their followers. One day I was walking out with my wife, who was already veiled, and an ISIS member stopped us as he believed that she should put on extra layers of *Khemar* [a black cloth that covers the face and the body of women]. When I asked him on what grounds he was asking her to use *Khemar*, he replied that there is a verse in Qur'an named *Surat al Hijab* [the verse of the veil] and that all Muslim women should abide by that verse. I told him I know all the verses in Quran and there is no one verse that is called *al Hijab* verse. He insisted on that idea. I realised that I was talking in vain with an ignorant person who was brainwashed to force people into believing that there is a holy verse addressing Muslim women to commit to *Khemar*.

When the situation under ISIS escalated, my mother was so frightened that ISIS might target me as they started recruiting men by force. After losing my brother, my mother couldn't afford to lose me. She persuaded me to leave for Lebanon and then to be joined by my wife until the situation improved enough for us to return to Syria.

My journey started with crossing the border from Aleppo, where ISIS was ruling, to Damascus where the Syrian regime ruled. I travelled with my forged ID. My panic when an officer took my ID card to check was indescribable. I was scared that once they realized that I hadn't served in the Syrian Army, they would conscript me immediately. Conscription meant that I would be fighting with the regime's forces against the revolutionaries. The second time I panicked was on the sea journey from Turkey to Europe.

Dona al Abdallah

While I was studying at the college, I met an old colleague from my schooldays. He was a friend of my husband and he told me that Ali was writing lines of poetry about me. I talked to Ali over the phone and wanted to find out what was he writing, and I wanted to listen to him. The first time we met, there was an air raid! My friend accompanied me to that first date and while I was talking to Ali an air raid

took place. It targeted a nearby hospital and we started hearing the noise of ambulances and people and it was a scary time indeed. We met again and we decided to get engaged. Our engagement lasted for eight months.

When I started working in the lab, Manbij was under the grip of the Free Syrian Army. ISIS controlled the city during the last five months of my work at the dental lab. When ISIS first came, they were not very strict about women's dress codes. But they were very strict about couples meeting outside. I mean a man and a woman alone. They created lots of trouble for us when we used to walk out. ISIS men used to raid workplaces and schools.

They were targeting the mixing of men and women. They used to come to the lab during our working hours to check if women were working alongside men. They asked the lab's owner to place a curtain in the lab to separate men from women. Like a borderline between men and women where we were not allowed to mix with each other and talk face-to-face. Ali used to visit me in the lab during my lunch breaks and this created lots of trouble for us from ISIS. At a later stage, things got worse with ISIS and life was hard, really hard. They became very strict with our dress codes. In the beginning they were OK with women wearing a long cloak of any colour with a coloured headscarf. Later, they became very strict about that. Everything should be black – the headscarf and the cloak. We were not allowed to show our faces. Faces had to be covered. I mean a full-face cover. Even the eyes had to be covered. Those who didn't adhere to that law could easily be arrested.

Every time they saw us walking or sitting side by side,

Women in *niqab* in the old city of Hama, Syria. Vyacheslav Argenberg (CC licence 4.0 International)

they used to start an interrogation. For instance: 'Who is this woman?' 'Are you related?' One day during our engagement, two men from ISIS stopped us and asked Ali, using modern standard Arabic, 'Who is this lady?' Ali replied: 'She is my wife,' the man asked: 'Do you have proof?' Ali answered: 'Do I have to carry my marriage certificate wherever I go?' and they left us. Ali was intolerant of such questions. He used to argue with them. But their minds were closed. I used to be so scared. There was no way to argue or to debate things with such people. To avoid trouble, I suggested that we maintain a distance between us when we walked out. Owners of clothes shops used to employ their wives or sisters to deal with female customers. The women's section had to be run by a female employee and the men's section by a male employee. They made things very tough for women. The black fabric had to be of a very heavy quality. The body of the woman should not be seen through it. Some fabrics can define a women's bodies, like Lycra. Lycra is a highly elastic fabric. Such fabric was prohibited. Imagine yourself inside a black sack. It was like that. Having a full-face cover made from a harsh material was tough. It was suffocating. I was forced to put it on for over a year.

When Ali fled the country the only way to get in contact was to use an internet café. Wi-Fi wasn't available for us to use at home because it had to be censored. There were only two internet cafés in Manbij and those cafés were heavily censored and guarded by ISIS men and women. So if you wanted to use your phone for social media, or for a WhatsApp text or call, you had to go to one of those cafés in town. There were opening times for women separate from those of men. So I went to that café wearing a black face cover and a black *Abaya* [cloak]. I even had black gloves covering my hands. I texted Ali over WhatsApp and was about to leave the café. I had two mobile phones with me, one for myself and the other was my sister's. My phone was full of comments against ISIS which I texted to Ali, to friends and to relatives here and there. There was a history of written and voice texts which could have criminalised me if they had found them. You know, WhatsApp was a venting medium and I vented on it a lot! On my way out, I heard some women whispering: 'Al Hosbah [the supervision team] is here.' I didn't pay attention because I was fully covered and to my knowledge, I wasn't breaking any dress code law. Suddenly, a veiled woman grabbed my arm pointing at my cloak, angrily using modern standard Arabic, saying: 'What's this you are wearing *Amatu Allah*? [female slave of God]' 'You mustn't wear such a cloth. Go into the truck.' She dragged me to a truck. She was a big-bodied woman. I was so scared. She was scary. I think that was how they selected them. I was petrified and I even lost my balance. She dragged me to a truck and there was a big man standing at the rear door holding a thick stick and forcing women into the truck. I didn't know what to do. Many covered women were inside the truck and luckily, I had a couple of ladies from my neighbourhood who had also been caught and pushed into the truck with me. They were caught because they were wearing a Lycra-fabric cloak. The truck moved

and we had no idea where to. Later, it stopped at a familiar street. They pushed us outside the truck to the basement of a flat or a house.

"What's this you are wearing Amatu Allah? [female slave of God]"
"You mustn't wear such a cloth. Go into the truck."

The whole situation was scary. Also, I was holding two phones with me. My sister's phone was fine. I mean I was sure there was nothing threatening on her phone. But my phone was loaded with anti-ISIS statements, complaints and swear words. I thought of getting rid of that mobile. If I left it in the truck, they would recognise it and I would be in a critical situation. I think that was the most difficult situation I had ever been in. I have heard stories of women who were dragged onto vans and trucks because of the way they dressed. I was aware that I would be told off, rebuked and forced to attend religious classes to learn about Islamic Sharia law. But I was more concerned about my phone. I was sure they were going to check the contents, texts, photos on my phone. For ISIS such content is a big threat and that would threaten my life. Because we were crammed into that truck, I was able to turn the phones off.

We were asked to get off the truck and were dragged one by one. I was shocked to find an elderly woman among us. I guess she was in her eighties or something, a very old woman. The old woman was accompanied by her daughter-in-law and the two women were dragged there. The poor old woman was using swear words and was shouting and crying at their brutal behaviour. I was wondering what that old woman had done to deserve such treatment. We were lined up in a big hall. There were so many of us, all covered with black and not allowed to uncover even amongst other women. There were other rooms full of women and I thought that perhaps the whole city was there. Most of the women who happened to be in the marketplace or the city centre on that day were dragged in with us.

"To be able to recover your phone," they said "you must sign in for a Sharia course to teach you how to dress properly according to Sharia and how to grow the hair on your eyebrows."

Before getting into a closed room for inspection/ interrogation, I had to think quickly of a way to hide my phone. I wasn't sure if there were CCTV cameras around. Then I thought they wouldn't dare fix cameras because that would be against Sharia. I saw several women going to the toilet. There were many toilets. I thought the women were facing a similar dilemma to mine. I wasn't sure whether it would be a good idea to hide my phone in one of the toilets and recover it later. I was hesitant about doing that.

Luckily there were some cushions on a sofa in that hall room, so I threw my phone under the cushions and asked a lady I knew to recover it after her interrogation ended. She was ahead of me in the line. We agreed on that and it worked. I went into the room. There were two of them there – ISIS women. They immediately asked about my phone, so I handed them my sister's. Before entering the room, I realised that my sister had uploaded a digital coffee cup reading app on her phone. I knew if they found it they would consider it blasphemy or polytheism, so I deleted the app. After checking the phone, they couldn't find anything against them. They began rebuking me and criticising the cloak which, in their view, was defining my body. And they thought that my face cover was not thick enough and that my face could be seen through it. They scrutinised my eyebrows. They thought I had plucked them. 'Don't you know that plucking eyebrows is against Sharia?' one of them asked. I couldn't persuade them that my eyebrows are naturally thin and arched. I had never plucked them. But they rebuked me. They insisted that I had plucked them. They checked and listened to every single voice or written text on the phone and luckily everything was fine. But I couldn't recover my sister's phone from them. 'To be able to recover your phone,' they said 'you must sign in for a Sharia course to teach you how to dress properly according to Sharia and how to grow the hair on your eyebrows.' They examined my Islamic religious knowledge and I succeeded in that tough test. Later, I had to attend a twenty-day course at a mosque that was too far from where I lived.

Yes, we fell victims to the several powers that controlled our cities and villages. People were scared, so scared by every new ruling power or group. So most Syrians were afraid of saying anything to anyone or about any of the ruling groups. Our situation was like the Arabic proverb: 'I don't hear, I don't see, and I don't speak.' We wanted to stay alive. That's it. Many people paid with their lives for silly issues like a song against the Asad regime on their phones or a revolutionary statement in a text. I know a nine-year-old boy who had a song about the Syrian revolution saved on his phone. When the Syrian authorities checked his phone, they arrested him for that song and then he disappeared. They terrified us. An innocent text about the regime, the revolution, ISIS could lead to catastrophes. I always advised my youngest sister to delete any text or voice message on her phone when she travelled from Manbij to Aleppo, as a precaution.

Halah al Shami

When the Syrian revolution began everything changed and it was so tense inside the workplace. People's attitudes changed a lot. For instance, I used to work in an office with people from different ethnic backgrounds: Druze, Christians, Arabs, and others, and we were getting along very well with one another. As a conservative Muslim woman, it was very difficult to deal with a person from an Alawi background bullying me and directly referring to me as '*Musanedah lil Thawra*' [supporter of the revolution].

At that stage, I was juggling two departments at the same time, and I was overwhelmed and overloaded with responsibilities. So I asked for someone to help with these tasks and we announced a vacancy, and there were around seven candidates from whom I chose someone who was described as a hard worker. Suddenly, it turned out that the new candidate was an activist, a revolutionary who used to take part in the protests and demonstrations against the regime. He was absent most of the time and I had no idea where he used to go. 'How did I know?' During that period, I took a month leave to prepare for my daughter's wedding which we had planned in Lebanon. So, I was away from work for almost one month.

When I returned to work, that employee was still absent and the senior staff members were investigating his absence. I was accused of supporting him because I was veiled and was a conservative woman! They accused me of selecting him in the first place to work with me because I supported his revolutionary activities. I was also accused of medicating the demonstrators who were hit and injured in the protests. I explained that I was attending my daughter's wedding, but they didn't believe it. Coming from a Baath background, the manager could easily believe such an allegation against me from an Alawi colleague who used to be at his office most of the time. So, I was put under strict surveillance.

On the home front, it was a different story. As I mentioned before, I am a single mother and I was responsible for my children. My eldest son had just graduated from university and was looking for postgraduate opportunities abroad. He got offers from Arab and western universities and he wanted to pursue his studies in Lebanon, but I thought Lebanon was very close to Syria. With the upheavals and uncertainties, I didn't want him to be close to Syria in any way. So I suggested the UK because of the high standard of research. Besides, we had a relative who travelled to the UK often for business and he would be a great help. My son got admission to the UK and was the first in our family to enter the UK, for his master's.

My other son was in the first year of his BA in architectural engineering in Syria when the revolution began in 2011. I had such a horrible time when he was studying. He was frequently trapped behind barriers on his way home from university whenever an explosion took place or a demonstration erupted. He would spend hours behind the barriers unable to return home or even to use his mobile for security reasons. You cannot imagine the state I was in whenever I heard the news of explosions or shootings close to the university and had no idea where he was, or whether he was alive. I had hours and hours of fear and uncertainty. As my son is a young man and the youth were joining in demonstrations, he used to support his colleagues and friends. My third son had just finished his high school and was trying to apply to universities outside Syria when the revolution started. He got admitted at Ain Shams University in Egypt. But borders with Jordan, Turkey and Iraq were closed and the only travel route open was through Lebanon.

I took the decision to leave the country because I feared for my sons and my daughter. It was in Ramadan the holy month of fasting. Protests were organised every evening after the evening prayer, and my house was in a central

Anti-riot police in central Damascus, Jan. 16, 2012. Photo: Elizabeth Arrott, Public domain, via Wikimedia Commons

location which used to be frequently closed. By that time, my daughter was engaged and was preparing for her wedding. News was circulating about awful things done by the Syrian regime's forces – how they used to break into people's houses 'to check' and how they would mess with young girls' private possessions and photos. There were stories of some officers asking women to put on nightgowns or revealing pieces of clothes. Also stories of officers breaking into houses and bedrooms and enjoying looking at personal photos of young women. This happened to my cousin, a newlywed young woman, who was out when forces broke into her house and scattered her wedding photos and clothes all over her bedroom. You know, those forces were from all sorts of backgrounds. I was so worried that the same thing might happen to my daughter who was so excited about her engagement. I could never stop her living her life. It was my responsibility to keep things under control.

A M

In 2012 the situation worsened, and the regime simply failed in stopping the protests. In the capital city of Damascus, the Syrian regime's army used to hit the demonstrators with rubber bullets. The regime did not use live bullets for fear that this might agitate the protestors further. Bashar al Asad was aware that if any of the Damascene protestors was killed, the tribe would avenge the killing which would eventually lead to the overthrowing of the regime. I think he did not want to lose his city. So, rubber bullets and tear gas were used against the demonstrators. Many people were arrested. Everyone was aware that partaking in the demonstrations was a life-threatening action. So demonstrations didn't last longer than five minutes. Sometimes, intelligence forces were informed of a protest even before people had gathered. It was a really critical time.

Once demonstrations grew and became frequent, the regime resorted to the use of live bullets. With live bullets we entered a new perilous stage which was a red flag for most of us. We decided not to take part in the protests. As demonstrations grew in number, the intelligence centres were multiplied and were found in every neighbourhood. Our neighbourhood has four intelligence centres. Our concern was that once Free Syrian Army made progress in taking over these centres, our neighbourhood would turn into a battlefield. In no time, the Syrian Free Army was in our neighbourhood and the exchanges of shootings were taking place daily.

My mother had to go to work daily because she was in a senior position. Luckily, it was during the summer holiday when the situation in Damascus came to a peak and we found ourselves under constant showers of bullets from all corners. My mother encouraged my younger brother and me to leave the country for Lebanon. This would not have been possible without the help of relatives who live in Beirut. They did all they could to facilitate our departure and arrival in Beirut. The plan was to stay for a short time in Lebanon until the situation back home became clearer. So, we rented a house in Chtaura at the Syrian Lebanese border. As the regime was on the verge of collapse, we thought that a month away would help us stay safe and observe the situation from afar. My younger brother and I did not want to leave our house in Damascus because we thought that Damascus was not going to be bombed the way other places were. I could watch the bombings and the shelling of the Syrian regime over rural Damascus from my balcony. My mother succeeded in persuading us to leave Damascus and to head towards Lebanon to attend our sister's wedding in Lebanon. When my brother-in-law came for a visit from Canada to propose to my sister, he was targeted by a sniper who missed him. He vowed not to return to Syria and the couple decided to have their wedding in Lebanon instead.

Because it was a temporary visit, we left everything behind. I still regret not taking a photo of our house there in Damascus. Sadly, I do not have any photos of the place.

In Aleppo, Karm al Jabal. This neighbourhood is next to Al Bab and had been under siege for 6 months, 4 March 2013. Credit: Basma

Mohammad S

Before the air raids, we fell short of things to meet basic human needs. The essentials of life were absent. The Syrian regime punished Manbij by imposing a siege. No clean water, no electricity, no phone lines, and basically no Wi-Fi. So, people were unable to connect. My eldest sister was living in the city centre with her husband and children, and we were unable to contact her. At some point we had no idea if she and her family were still alive! Then firing began. We were not only concerned about the firing and the shelling, but we were badly affected by the blockade. The Syrian government prevented the supply of gas, electricity, food, and water. These services were deliberately stopped by the Syrian regime as a form of punishment to Manbij and Aleppo. Actually, the blockade preceded the shelling.

The regimes planned it all. A blockade followed by shelling and firing to punish the people of Aleppo because they revolted against the Syrian regime. At that stage, most people couldn't endure the siege and the firing, and they began fleeing their homes.

We are a big family, and we had our own house, and we were not ready to leave as it was a very difficult decision to make. We saw whole families leaving and sometimes only one or two members fleeing. Matters got worse when ISIS controlled us. They used to target young men and recruit them by force. They didn't care about the age of young men. All they wanted was to recruit as many men as they could for their purposes. I decided to flee on my own. I was fourteen years old. My eldest brother Sulaiman left us earlier. He fled Manbij six months before me, and by 2014 he arrived in the UK. For one long month we had no idea where he was or whether he was alive. My other brother was badly injured in his leg and was in a hospital in Turkey on his own. The plan was to cross the Syrian borders and to head to Turkey to stay by my brother's side. My first attempt to reach the Turkish borders failed. I could not do it. I was led by a smuggler who guided me to a point and left me there to try crossing the border on my own. I entered a tunnel but couldn't get out to the other side as it was too high to climb to the Turkish side of the border. I returned to Manbij and stayed for a month.

Life became intolerable under air raids, ISIS and the Syrian siege. Some families considered fleeing despite the dangers and the uncertainty of the journey from Syria to Turkey. Other people preferred to stay in their houses and

Explosions at Kobani, Saleh's hometown.
© Ali/Adobe Stock

to endure the hardships of life as they believed that this would be wiser than leaving everything behind for an unknown destiny. For some families with an elderly or a disabled member, fleeing was not an option at all. To plan to flee one must be able to walk for long distances, to run and sometimes to run very fast to cross the borders etc.

For instance, my mother was able to walk for long distances. We had an elderly female neighbour who was disabled and couldn't flee for her life. Her sons had to leave her behind. My family and I were forced to take the decision to leave. My eldest brother was in the UK, my other brother in Turkey and my eldest sister fled to Turkey with her husband and children.

My cousin, who was my age, and I were approached by a guy from ISIS who offered to recruit us for $100 a month. He said he would take us to visit countries and that we would be driving our own cars etc. But of course, we knew he was an ISIS member. We tried to avoid him and stayed at home for some time. My mother was so worried that I would be forced to join ISIS and was also worried about my sisters. So, we decided to leave.

Salih Hamza

I have six children, three daughters and three sons. My eldest son and my eldest daughter are married and living in Turkey. The other four are in Bremen in Germany: a married daughter, two single sons and a single daughter. Yes, we are all out of the country now. Our houses were completely destroyed in Kobani, most of our belongings were either looted or burned.

As you know, problems started in 2011. We lived in the area until 2015. That year things really got worse and we decided to flee. When the revolution started, the city of Dara'a was badly affected and gradually the upheaval developed. Eventually, ISIS took control of Kobani and destroyed the city. People lost their belongings, sheep, cows, houses, cars. It was a total destruction. We were threatened. We had no idea what was waiting for us. What should one expect after all that destruction? We were forced to leave. To leave for our lives.

Hussam Allaham

I am a doctor. A medical doctor. I left Syria when I was a fourth-year medical student at university. I was studying general surgery. I personally wasn't into medicine at all. During my high school education, I wasn't working towards medicine and I tried to avoid going that route. But my father wanted me to study medicine. My father didn't force me, but it was his wish. My brother was studying electrical engineering in Syria. He changed his studies. He accompanied me to Ukraine and we both did a degree in medicine.

I was more into General Internal Medicine. I always felt that surgery was a manual profession. I didn't want to be specialised in surgery. But when I returned to Syria, I was given two options: to serve in the State Syrian Army or to enrol into specific medical specialisations which were very much needed at that period. Otherwise I had to serve in the military. Surgery was one of those available options and I had to choose it. Better than the army! I think I was destined to be a surgeon. So, I used to travel between Damascus and al Quneitra in Golan. I lived in Damascus and

Hussam Allaham.
Photo courtesy of Oasis Cardiff

worked in a hospital in Damascus. And I also had to work at a hospital in al Quneitra which was 60 Km from my house in 2010.

As you know, in 2011, in March the revolution started. And things changed afterwards. When I began working in surgery at al Quneitra's hospital, al Quneitra had been a destroyed city and it is still destroyed. The city is uninhabited. But as a governorate, there are villages around it. The hospital serves the surrounding villages. The hospital wasn't highly developed like the ones in the major cities. In my early days at the hospital, my supervisor told me that the hospital staff were supportive and that the work would go smoothly. He explained to me that what was missing was the emergency facilities. Which means that there was a shortage of surgeons to undertake certain urgent surgical operations. For instance, a casualty from a car accident or a shooting.

And for a new surgeon that was a challenge. Rarely ever would a new surgeon interfere with such cases, in an early stage of their career. The supervisor told me that I would be lucky to work on only one or two of such cases throughout my whole career. However, after 2011 and after the revolution, we came to a stage where we had between ten and twenty such surgical emergencies, from shootings, weekly. It got to the stage where I had to work without a supervisor, because when it is an urgent case, you have to act quickly. There is a procedure which is known as a chest drain in English. It's a complicated procedure where a pipe has to be inserted in the patient's chest to drain it of air or liquid. I was in my first year of training. I had read about the chest drain procedure in books. I read about the way the procedure should be performed. I only had the theoretical side of it. My field was general surgery, and such a procedure was for specialists in chest surgery or emergency surgeons. But when a case was admitted to us there were no other surgeons but me. I found myself imagining a book in front of me. I had to apply the theory I had read about but had no practical experience of it before. *Alhamdulillah*, I made it. It was a delicate surgery where I had to make sure that the pipe I was inserting wouldn't touch the lungs. It was so stressful and when it was all finished and had gone well, it was such a relief! It was an emergency procedure. A question of life and death, indeed. Any mistake would finish someone's life in less than a second. There were so many cases.

I worked in field hospitals. I used to work in the government hospitals. I was back and forth between governmental and field hospitals. You know how people in our region think. They think that a doctor is a magician. For instance, I was once called to a house to treat a kid who was in a terrible condition after being shot. No facilities to help. The family brought me bandages, antibiotics, scissors etc and they were expecting me to operate on him and save his life. There were times when I saw... Patients were dying in front of me and I couldn't do anything to help. Nothing was available. When a patient had been shot they needed anaesthetics, instruments. Bandages and antibiotics won't save a life. I tried my best. But there were times when patients died in front of my eyes and I couldn't do anything about it. And that was so hard.

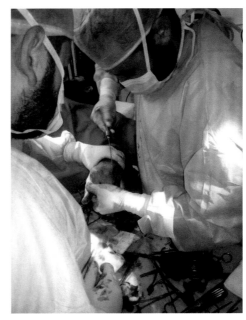

Surgeons in Syria, 2014. Photo: Savesyria, CC BY-SA 3.0, via Wikimedia Commons

At the checkpoints, it was much better to present yourself as a garbage collector than a doctor. If I told them I was a doctor I could expect hundreds of questions. Where have you been? Where were you heading to? Those checkpoints from my house to my work were a real hassle. If they found any medical instruments on me, they would immediately confiscate them. This would be followed by a long list of questions. Some of my colleagues disappeared because of a bottle of steriliser found in their car – a steriliser which was there by mistake. But I continued working in the government hospitals. When the revolution started, I stopped working at Damascus and worked at al Quneitra hospital. It was quieter there. It was a small hospital with a small team. Regardless of our political views and affiliations, we were there as medical staff. We had different views, with and against, but we were there to save lives. I loved working there because there were medicines and tools which you couldn't find at other places. For instance, anaesthetics were only to be had in hospitals. There was no way you could get them at pharmacies. They were monitored. So I preferred to work at these hospitals so that I could use such medical substances in field hospitals. I had a big bag in which I used to hide the medicines to use them in the field hospitals.

At one point the number of checkpoints between my house and the hospital reached around thirteen. It was only about 50 Km, but it took a doctor two hours. Some checkpoint staff knew some of us and they used to facilitate a doctor's passage. But thirteen checkpoints were difficult. I experienced situations where I thought I would be caught. But Allah protected me.

Damascus Checkpoint, 2012. Elizabeth Arrott, Public domain, via Wikimedia Commons

Many times, we witnessed shootings at the checkpoints or while we were waiting. When we used to pass through those thirteen checkpoints, it felt like a war zone. The army was on both sides. You heard gunshots followed by military aircrafts. All this was within the regime-controlled zone. The problem arose if a person crossed from the regime's zone to the other side – to the areas of the revolution. This was the main difficulty. Some of the field hospitals which I used to visit were under the regime's control. But they were hidden in certain houses. It was a risky situation. I had colleagues who disappeared because of that. They were caught. People might inform the authorities about a doctor visiting one of these houses to treat a patient. Also, if you ventured to cross the border to the side that was out of the regime's control, you might be targeted by a sniper. I once survived a sniper's shot. There were no barracks and checkpoints in areas that weren't under the regime's control. But there were bombings and clashes. I spent two days in these areas and there was continuous shelling. I realised that people were setting their own rules to protect themselves. It was a very difficult stage. I worked like this for around two years till the end of 2012.

I lost many of my colleagues. We, the doctors, were focussing on treating people regardless of our differences. Gradually we experienced a big shortage in doctors. Anyone with a medical background of any kind started promoting themselves. Vets provided services like stitching etc. When we got a call that there was a wounded person in a particular village, we used to look for a nurse or anyone with some experience to go and help. A nurse became a doctor and a doctor who had specialised in whatever field had to help with stitches etc. Dentists were helping in surgeries. People came forward to help. Because you can't just leave an injured person to die.

My family was around and my brother, another doctor, was working with me. But my family was based in al Sham. They lived in an area which wasn't hit by any violence. The area has been relatively safe. We used to travel, and my other siblings were studying at university. My family was so supportive, but they knew that the risks I was taking could also affect them. When we started, we formed a web – no, not a web because if we had formed a web, it would have been a disaster. It could put all the members at risk if one of us was caught by the regime. So, we formed a chain where each one of us knew just one member in the chain. I

had no idea about the other members. The maximum was two people knowing one another. If I was caught and put under pressure to disclose names, I would only disclose one name and by the time the regime found that name it would have allowed the other members to flee. We followed this procedure because it was better and safer than a web of members who knew one another.

We continued like that until the suburb of Daraya had been overrun by the regime. The invasion of Daraya resulted in several casualties and members of our chain were captured. They were anaesthesia technicians. Step by step, the regime started identifying members of the chain, including the doctors. At this point, my brother the doctor fled Syria to Jordan. Gradually all doctors tried to flee as it became so hard for doctors, even if they were not taking part in revolutionary activity. Just being a doctor would put them under scrutiny, especially at the border checks and the barracks.

After two years, when the revolution became armed, doctors found themselves in a position where they were forced to interfere. There were many doctors who didn't want to be involved in politics. They just wanted to do their jobs and nothing else. They wanted to work and live in peace amid that chaos. But if a doctor had a clinic in an area that was under shelling or an area overrun by the FSA ... And when shootings and shelling caused injuries, everyone would look for a doctor. In this case, the doctor wouldn't say no to them. Regardless of whoever controlled the area, the doctor would be called to help the wounded.

This put doctors in a critical situation. Most doctors preferred to flee that situation. Some found jobs in Jordan and abroad and fled for their lives and for their safety. Many doctors left. I stayed. Most of my colleagues had either left the country or been imprisoned. No one remained. The most difficult situation I had when I worked at al Quneitra hospital was, there was a security centre for the Syrian regime in the nearby area. An officer used to take us, doctors, to a prison in the centre. To check the prisoners... to assess if they could endure more grilling and torture. The regime didn't want the prisoners to die. They wanted to torture them. They tortured them until they lost consciousness. They asked us to treat them so that they could endure more torture. These were the hardest moments. The hardest to remember. The idea of entering those centres was... It was intolerable ... I wish... I wish I could forget this thing. It was so hard to watch and see how brutal man can be against man. I witnessed horrible

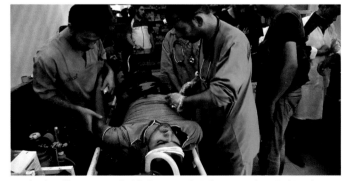

Medical staff treating rebel fighters and civilians at a hospital in Aleppo. Scott Bobb, Public domain, via Wikimedia Commons

scenes. I saw bones coming out of bodies. I saw flesh. I saw how cigarettes had been extinguished on the human body. And the voices. The sounds I heard while walking in the alleys. Indescribable. All this was an act of man against a man. At that moment you would feel like... you would wonder what would drive a man to act in such a brutal way against another man. Whatever they did.

Yes, anyway – there was a doctor, one of my colleagues. He treated a person. He took a wounded patient to his house because there was no suitable space for treatment. The patient was in the military. He got better afterwards. During his leave from military service, he headed home and decided to flee the army. When he arrived at his family's house in northern Syria, in al Hasakah close to the Iraqi borders, his father forced him to re-join the military and made him inform the authorities about the doctor who cured him. The patient had fled the army and been wounded by a gun shot. People took him to that doctor to save his life. We then arranged for him to go home. But his father forced him to go back to the army and informed the authorities about the doctor. The regime's forces raided the doctor's house and luckily he was not at home. The doctor was informed and managed to flee to Jordan. But the fleeing doctor was so close to me. So, the authorities started watching me. They came to the hospital where I worked. They started enquiring and checking on me.

When my brother fled to Jordan he started coordinating with committees and aid organisations to send aid to Syria. The brother of a colleague from al Quneitra was also working with my brother in the field of Syrian aid.

Currently, he is in Birmingham with his family. But his brother, who was my colleague, remained in Syria and supported the revolution. And he was wanted. He was caught. He was invited to his sister's house, and someone saw him and he was caught. They raided the house and there were gunshots and explosions. Eventually they killed him inside the house. They brought his corpse to the hospital where I worked. There were over ten shots in his body. They threw the corpse on the floor in front of me. They jumped on the corpse. They abused the corpse in front of my eyes. They started hitting the corpse with a rifle. They looked at me. It was like a warning to me. They were indirectly passing a message that no one would protect me and that this would be my end. I knew the person, but... I couldn't do anything...

Later, the staff in the hospital – even those who knew me – I was almost isolated. Everyone realised that I was against the regime and that my capture and killing was a question of time. Even those who sympathised with me, they abandoned me. Besides, there were others who opposed my political views. As my brother was coordinating aid to Syria, I was in contact with the youth of the FSA. At that stage there was a power balance in the state of things. At night the youth of the FSA were stronger and in a much better place. When night fell, the Syrian soldier would rather protect himself. The soldier's priority was to protect himself. The FSA members knew more about the area. Therefore, they were in a better position. At that stage, those who worked with the regime were a bit cautious because they knew I had connections with the

FSA. So I was abandoned. No one approached me or talked to me as they realised that I would be caught and liquidated soon.

I tried to leave Syria. I had no one with me. Even my family. I had forced my family to leave Syria earlier, since the Daraya events. I was aware that to arrest a wanted person, the regime would arrest women. In such cases, that would force the wanted person to surrender. I was concerned about my sister and my mother. I forced them to leave as the situation got worse. I couldn't endure. So, my family travelled to Egypt. They lived in a city called Damietta and my brother had left earlier. So, I was on my own in Syria. I was aware that I could be caught and killed at any moment and at any checkpoint.

"I saw how cigarettes had been extinguished on the human body. And the voices. The sounds I heard while walking in the alleys. Indescribable…you would wonder what would drive a man to act in such a brutal way against another man."

"Maybe Over the Horizon" by Alison Lochhead

Long Way from Home

"I will tell my children about Syria and why we left.
But I am not going to talk about the pain and the humiliation I faced."

Ronahi Hassan

The world is aware of what has happened in Syria. You hardly find a Syrian family or person whose relatives haven't left Syria. My sisters, brothers, and my mother all left Syria, but I still have one sister living in Damascus. This happened in so many stages. Each member of the family left Syria at a certain time based on the circumstances and the situation of the country. The last one to leave Syria was my mother, three years ago. After my father passed away there was no one left to take care of her and be with her. She had to leave. Sadly, she was smuggled through a very difficult, risky, and tiring route. We couldn't believe it when she arrived safely in Sweden where my brothers live.

Bashar

When I bade farewell to my family, I wasn't sure if I would be able to see them again. I had a dreadful feeling that I might not make it. I was literally leaving death behind and was heading towards another deadly journey. *Tarikk al mawt wa rakib markab al mawt* [leaving death behind to get on the boat of death]. My mother told me: 'You are leaving as a young man and will be returning as an old man.' It was so difficult. It was hard to hear those words. It was a difficult moment. I travelled to Turkey and took a flight to Algeria, then smuggled to Libya through the desert. That was the worst part of the journey. We were kidnapped by a group of outlaws in Libya and were humiliated. We were blackmailed by human traffickers. They threatened us and imprisoned men on one side and women on another side and tried to steal our money and precious belongings. They simply took advantage of the bad situation we were in.

From Libya we were smuggled to Italy through the sea. That sea journey took about one and a half days. We were 250-300 people. We were about to drown and were covered by water. We were jammed on that boat and we didn't realise that it would take us all that time. Passengers were desperate to urinate. I was holding a little girl who urinated on me. The boat was swinging right and left. We drifted in another direction and lost our way, and we ran short of water and food. Amid that frustration, horror and starvation, I reached a point where I didn't care about anything. I was ready to die at any minute.

We finally reached the Italian coast. We remained in that coastal area for about nine hours before we were rescued by the Italian navy. We stayed on board their ship for two

Photo taken from the Calais Jungle, 2016. (CC BY 2.0) by malachybrowne

days. Later, we were placed in a camp and then we travelled from that Italian camp to Calais camps in France on the British borders. I stayed one day in Calais. The second day, I smuggled myself to the UK. I was lucky to make it.

I met refugees who were in that camp for six months, others were there for two months and there were some families who were there for longer. I was so disappointed when refugees in Calais used to tell me that I had to wait for ages to be able to make it. I had to plan it carefully. I realised that I had to jump over a four-metre fence and then head towards the line of cars. Usually, you know, cars, vans and trucks are lined up for checking or for rest. I jumped over the fence and was caught twice. The third time, I hid in the toilet and walked out pretending I was a cleaner at the border point. I acted confidently and held my phone as if I was talking over the phone. So, the security

man didn't suspect me. I was heading towards the van acting as if I was the driver of one of the vans. So I hid underneath a van, clinging to the pipes underneath. The van moved on. It then went onto a ferry and stopped there. I had to wait where I was. The plan was to get out from under the van once it reached the port. To my surprise, the van didn't stop at the harbour. It just continued moving. It moved for about an hour on the highway.

My arms and legs went blue as they were both numbed. They were cramping and aching. I then managed to get off the van when a security man found me. I immediately asked him to call the police who came and took me. They just wanted to make sure that there was no arranged agreement between me and the driver. Then the routine procedures. I was transferred to Newport in Wales.

Sulaiman Sulaiman

In 2014 the situation got worse with the rise of ISIS who intimidated people and forced them to join their forces. We found ourselves between the hammer of ISIS and the anvil of the Syrian regime which was also intent on conscripting us. In either case, we would be conscripted to cause more damage and more massacres against our own people.

My friends and I decided to migrate when we realised that staying would endanger our lives and our families. We could never join the Syrian army, ISIS or let ourselves be manipulated by any other group, as each of these options was equally fatal. There was no other way but to leave. The closest routes were either Lebanon or Turkey. I decided to travel to Turkey and live there and then bring my family to join me. I stayed in Turkey for around fifteen days, but it was so difficult to settle in Turkey as everything was different: language, customs and life in general.

A friend of mine suggested that I had better travel to Europe as the political situation was getting worse with the recent developments in Syria. The plan was to travel to Lebanon, North Africa and then Europe. I preferred Britain because I had basic English and I knew I would manage with English and get better at it. Since an early stage of my life I had loved Britain and the image of the London Eye and Big Ben was always present in my mind.

From Turkey I travelled to Lebanon where I stayed for six months working in a supermarket from 8:00 am to 11:00 pm to be able to earn a living. I saved around $3000 and travelled to Algeria without a visa. Then, we were smuggled to Tunisia through the desert, which took us three days, and then to Libya. In Libya, we met a smuggler who asked for $1000 to take us to Italy by sea. The smuggler told us that the boat could take 200 people, which I thought was a big number. We paid the money and were asked to wait for four days. On the fifth day, that was Saturday 24th August 2014, we were taken to a beach to start the journey with over 500 people in a miserable old boat. That was a very difficult day in my life.

We were jammed into this boat with 500 passengers of different backgrounds and nationalities: Syrians, Afghans,

Mstyslav Chernov/Unframe, CC BY-SA 4.0 via Wikimedia Commons

Iraqis and Sudanese. There were families, young people and children, mothers alone with their children and some elderly people. The boat journey started smoothly and at some stage the smugglers handed us over to another boat and left, as it was illegal for them to sail any further.

The new boat was even more miserable than the first one. I and hundreds of others, families and children, were placed on the deck, and around eighty people with really big bodies from Bangladesh, Sudan and other parts of Africa, were placed in the engine room below deck. Under the pressure of the large number of passengers, the boat leaned either to the right side or to the left side leaving the people struggling to keep it balanced. In the meantime, the people were hearing sounds of wood logs falling off the

Refugees on a capsizing boat in the Mediterranean, 2016. Ggia, CC BY-SA 4.0 , via Wikimedia Commons

boat or breaking under the heavy weight. Everybody realised that this was an abnormal situation and that the boat would break up at some stage.

I saw women crying and praying to God for mercy. I was so scared but was trying hard to comfort the families while feeling the end approaching. Everybody was thirsty and there was just one gallon of water to use, so we had to prioritise the children, women and old people. The boat then stopped completely and we were left in the middle of the water for six hours with no idea of where we were and what would happen next. Luckily some of my young companions had some mobile signals and they used them to ask for help.

Then a ship and a helicopter appeared from afar and people used their lifejackets to wave to them for help. Everybody was happy thinking that it was an end to this frightening journey. The crew on board the ship told us that they were going to send us lifeboats and rescue one family at a time. They did rescue two families.

Suddenly the engine room below deck was opened allowing eighty or so people to come out onto the upper deck, causing chaos and panic and the boat to turn upside down. We were in the water! I could feel people treading on my head and shoulders when I was thrown deep in the water. Luckily, the life vest I was wearing helped me to float to the surface. I managed to swim towards a wooden beam hanging from the upturned boat and found myself clinging to it firmly. A young man was shouting for help and held my arm in desperation begging me not to let him go. In front of me a woman was struggling to swim and stay afloat while her daughter was drowning. Unable to help her daughter, the woman was crying desperately and shouting for help. At that moment I felt so helpless, so paralysed, and ashamed that I wasn't able to move to help the drowning girl. I was aware that if I moved any further, I would not only endanger my own life but that of the young man gripping my arm. The girl drowned and no one could help her. The rescue team were doing all they could to rescue the elderly, the women and the children. After remaining in that position for a while – it felt like years – we were rescued. We were taken to the shores of Italy where we heard that 160 people had lost their lives in that tragedy.

Later, I travelled to around six or seven countries until I was able to be illegally smuggled to the UK in a refrigerated truck full of lemons. Along with a few other Iranians and Syrians, I was hiding in the truck when we suddenly got a British phone signal on our mobiles. Only then did we realise that we had finally made it through to the UK border. I was taken to the border agency's office for investigation and then I was transferred to a very good hotel in London and stayed for about a month. During that first month I felt alienated, having very little English and horrible memories. In the meantime, my family were facing severe bombing and dire conditions, so I advised them to travel to Turkey, which they did.

Noor

My mother, myself, my two brothers and my youngest sister left Manbij for the Syrian-Turkish borders where we were not allowed entry into Turkey. We spent two days at the border crossing, waiting for the border to open but we lost hope and returned to Manbij. Two days later, someone called us to tell us that there was a way to enter Turkey. We spent three days in a forest at the Syrian-Turkish border.

These were very hard times in summer when we had to walk for about 2-3 km to get water from a spring. After three days a smuggler arranged to take us to Turkey via a valley which we had to cross to be able to reach to the first city in Turkey. We travelled to Ankara where my eldest sister lives with her husband and children. The plan was to stay in Turkey, observe the situation back home and return to Syria once things got better.

After two months in Turkey, my mother decided to leave my younger brothers and sister at my sister's house and to take me on the sea journey to Europe to join my brother Sulaiman, who by that time had arrived in the UK and was living in Cardiff.

In Turkey, my brothers and younger sister were not allowed to go to school. Even if they were allowed, the Turkish language was a big problem. The political situation in Syria was getting worse and worse, the financial situation in Turkey was even worse for a big family like ours. My brother Sulaiman was urging my mother to leave for Europe for a better future for the family – especially my siblings. After two months, my mother made up her mind to take the route to Europe. It lasted for four months until we made it to the UK.

It was a very long journey. We left Turkey at 1:00 pm. There were twenty-eight people on a pathetic, small dinghy. My cousin and my brother-in-law were with us. We arrived

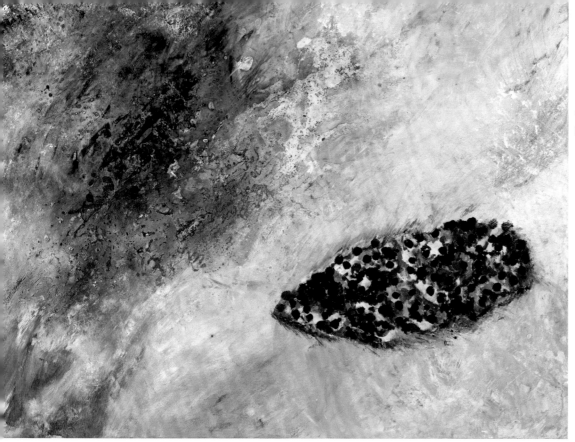

'All at Sea 2'
by Alison Lochhead

at the Greek shores at 5:00 am and it was so dark. The sea looked too dark. It was black at night. I had seasickness and was so scared by the darkness all around us.

We had no idea who was behind it. Everything was arranged through an agent who called us, asked us for a certain amount of money, decided the date of the journey and the place to meet them. Smugglers don't usually accompany refugees on the boats. On the day, they ask if any of the passengers has an idea of how to steer the boat. If no one is available, they ask a volunteer to be the leader and they give that volunteer some instructions as to how to operate the boat and the direction the boat must take. So, we set off with clear instructions on the direction of the boat. We were heading to the Greek island of Mytilene.

Suddenly, one of the passengers lit a cigarette and a fierce argument started about his behaviour. We were all very concerned that his behaviour might lead the inflatable boat with the twenty-eight people to certain disaster. The argument developed into a fight between him and some passengers, which made us lose our way in the middle of the sea. Because the boat went in a different direction, it took us over five hours to arrive at a different Greek island to the one we were supposed to reach.

It was 28th of August 2015 when we arrived at the other Greek island. Once there, we were received by a Greek lady whose house overlooked the coast. The house had a big farm attached to it. She greeted us, took our lifejackets, and asked us inside her house and offered us tea and snacks which was a heartening and warm welcome to us at that desperate stage. As it was 5:00 am, we spent an hour at her place and headed towards our next destination, the island of Metyline which we were supposed to arrive at earlier.

We walked a long distance from 6:00 am to 8:00 pm. It was so hot as it was in the end of August. Because we had no legal status in Greece, we were not allowed to hire a car and nobody was allowed to give us a lift. However, Greek people were so kind and nice as many cars stopped by and offered us water bottles. Some of the drivers were very apologetic because they couldn't offer us a lift.

We formed a group of nine people, among which were my cousin who had a good command of English, and my brother-in-law. We bought one Sim Card and used it for Google Maps. Before arriving to our destination, a car with two women stopped by and offered a lift for three people as their car couldn't take more than that. The group asked my mother, myself and my brother-in-law to go with them and we did. Once we arrived at Metyline, we put up a tent and stayed for one night. Next morning, we walked for three hours to get us an exit letter from a border camp.

The queue was too long. It took us two days to get that letter which would allow us to go on board a ship to Athens. It was exhausting to stand in the queue in high temperatures. It led the refugees to start a fire, to protest against the inhuman behaviour of the Greek authorities towards the refugees. There was a heavy media presence and the scene went viral that day. As a result of the protest, the Greek border police directed us to a field where we had to join another long queue to get our letters. We did get them in the end.

All that effort was about getting from that island to Athens on board a ship. From Athens we continued walking in heavy rain towards Macedonia, where we found tents which we used to rest and wait for a train to Serbia. There were no vacant seats on that train for us. So we sat on the floor of an overcrowded train. In Serbia, we spent two more days in a tent. Then to Hungary through a cornfield and a valley which would take us to the safer side. Then to Austria, which was the best part of the whole journey.

Austrian police treated us with respect and kindness and they were so nice to us. They took us to a camp which consisted of two parts: one part for men and the other for women. They allowed us to stay there until we decided on the next step. The humanitarian attitude of the Austrians, the smiles on their faces and their extraordinary kindness made our lives easier at that difficult time. We met other Syrian refugees in the camp who were heading to Germany. When we arrived there, our clothes were worn and in tatters. The Austrian authorities provided free clothes banks which we used to take what we needed to keep warm in that cold winter. After Austria, the journey became easier as we could take trains and travel more easily.

When we arrived in France, we found ourselves very

Group of refugees on their way to EU via the Balkan route.
Thousands of refugees on border, autumn 2015.
By Ajdin Kamber

close to the Eiffel tower. We sat in a garden through a very cold and rainy night. I wasn't able to see the beauty of all those countries because I wasn't a tourist, you know. We sat in a train station because we were looking for a warm and covered place to spend the night before taking the train to the Calais camps. At 2:00 am the officers in the station asked us to leave the station as they were closing.

So we had to sleep on benches in the garden near the Eiffel Tower in heavy rain. We used pieces of cardboard to cover our bodies. There were big rats around us in that garden. We were also very hungry. Luckily, we found a mobile canteen where we bought some hot drinks and snacks. We also found a spot on the ground, perhaps for a bakery or a restaurant, which was producing some warm air and we were taking turns to warm ourselves. We spent the night in the open under the rain and we were completely drenched and wet.

Next morning, we decided to look for a café or a place with a toilet to change our wet clothes inside. While climbing stairs towards a coffee shop, I felt a heavy blow on my chest from a passer-by who hit me fiercely and ran away when I cried for help. My first thought was that it was racist behaviour because I was veiled. I cried out loud and was so devastated by that attitude. But we continued walking to the coffee shop to change our wet clothes. Unfortunately, we were not permitted inside. I wondered whether it was the law of the country or was it just racism? We returned to where we were before. We had no choice but to use our coats and veils to cover one another and to change our wet clothes in the open garden.

We were getting instructions from Sulaiman, who warned us that the Calais camp route would be very difficult for my mother and me. So, we had to travel to Belgium by a train and we stayed at a friend's house for over twenty days. But we still had to go via Calais and the Jungle. We lived in a tent in that muddy and cold Jungle for a week. We had no idea that there was a camp for women in the Jungle with big warm tents, rooms, better facilities and three meals a day. We went there and were guarded by security forces outdoors and felt safe there. Every day we used to walk for three hours back and forth to try to find a way to enter the UK. We heard stories of people who got injured or even lost their lives while attempting to jump on a moving train. We saw a lady who had lost her leg in the attempt. She warned us against trying that risky jump. Refugees used to jump and cling to a moving train that was too fast. We heard of many refugees who made it that way and one of them was my cousin and his friend. Sulaiman warned us several times against trying that dangerous jump.

In Calais Camps, we used to wait for the 'Dougar' every day. The Dougar is a traffic jam caused by refugees who deliberately block the road for trucks and lorries entering the UK, forcing them to queue so that refugees can jump into the trucks and hide. Once a person shouts 'Dougar', all the refugees run towards the line of trucks for a chance to get into one of them. However, the way to the Dougar is blocked by a barbed wired fence which we had to cross through. I was told that the French authorities had doubled the height of the fence by two metres and had added intruder deterrents to prevent refugees from jumping over to the other side. But barbed wires did not deter refugees from trying, as they used their sleeping bags to cover parts of the fence so that they could jump over. As for my mother and me, jumping over that fence was not an option at all. One day, while we were standing behind the fence, the French police used tear gas against the refugees who were gathered there, and I fainted. I was only sixteen years old at that time.

We had to find another way. We walked for four hours to reach a truck. We were very happy that someone helped us to get into a truck that was loading energy drink cans. It was freezing cold inside that truck. It was 7:00 pm when we got into it. We sat on our sleeping bags and were shivering from the cold. But the truck didn't move until next morning. We spent thirteen hours or so inside the truck.

Finally, the truck moved and we were so pleased that we had finally made it! Sadly, the truck stopped again and the truck door was opened by the driver who was so polite to us. He told us 'No UK. Belgium, Belgium'. We had to get down and try again. This time we got into a lorry with some beddings. We were eleven people inside that lorry which we thought was heading to the UK when it was heading towards Denmark. When the lorry stopped, we had no clue that we had arrived in Denmark. The driver was taken by surprise when he found eleven people inside his lorry. We tried to run away but it was too late as he immediately called the Danish police.

The driver was filming us with his phone when the Danish police arrived. They took us to the police station and called for an interpreter. There was a female Lebanese interpreter there. We were told that we needed to choose between returning to Syria via the first available flight or to

Migrants stand on roadside in hope of hiding inside trucks in Calais. (REUTERS / PASCAL ROSSIGNOL – stock.adobe.com)

have our fingerprints taken in Denmark. If we let them take our fingerprints, we wouldn't be eligible to apply for asylum in the UK and returning to Syria after all that suffering was the biggest punishment. It was a big blow for us as the plan was to head to the UK. We didn't know anyone in Denmark. We had no friends, or relatives there. They shut us in a cell-like room and took our belongings. Later, we were moved to another centre and were asked to wait for our names to be called.

As I was only sixteen, I was the first to be called to their office, while my mother and another lady were still waiting. I was scared and overwhelmed by the whole situation. The moment I entered the office, one of the officers grabbed my arm and started cleaning my fingers for the fingerprints. He said something in Danish that I couldn't understand and I asked for an interpreter. The interpreter told me that I had no option but to give my fingerprints. I refused as I was aware of the consequences of giving my fingerprints.

When I insisted on not giving my fingerprints, the officer grabbed me by my neck and held my hands fiercely, forcing me to give my fingerprints while I was crying. I still remember that scene. I hate Denmark so much. I hate them. After that, they sent me to the room where my mother was waiting. She was so concerned when she saw me crying. I felt guilty and powerless. I thought that my mother would be angry at me for giving my fingerprints. I explained the situation to her and there was no other choice for my mother but to give her fingerprints as well.

We were led to a prison-like room to spend the night. Our bags and belongings were taken from us. Sadly, my phone was in my purse because both my mother and I were dying to call my brother to let him know that we were safe. We also wanted to know where we were on Google Maps. I knocked at the guard's door and asked him to let me have my purse to get some tissue papers. When the guard handed me the purse, I had to act fast as I was aware of the ceiling security cameras. So I quickly took the tissue papers and threw my phone behind the sofa cushion and returned the purse to him.

Luckily the phone was partly charged and I was able to use WhatsApp. Yet I was very cautious about using my phone. If the guards knew about it they would immediately take it. Fortunately, the blankets they provided saved me as I used to cover my whole body and use my phone from under the cover. I traced our location on Google Maps and sent it to Sulaiman who was so worried.

We were taken to accommodation where we were told we would spend two to three days and then be released. There was a Syrian lady with a baby there who told us she had been there for over two weeks. They gave me and my mother a room upstairs with bunk beds and offered us meals three times a day. When I Googled the location of the house, I realised that it was in a remote area surrounded by a forest and a river. After three days, we were taken on an overcrowded bus to the Danish Red Cross headquarters. When we arrived, an interpreter welcomed us and told us that we were at the department for asylum applications in Denmark. My mother asked for a lawyer and an interpreter. My mother asked the lawyer how long the reunification process might take if we applied for asylum in

Denmark and she was told that it could take two to three years. We were taken to a hostel and were given a bag with some necessities. There was a guy that we had contacted earlier for help, and he told us to wait till 4:00 am in that hostel and then flee. We walked a long distance to take a train back to France.

We stayed in the Calais Camps for a while but failed to enter the UK. We returned to Belgium and it was on the night of the seventh of January that we paid someone to help us to jump into a lorry going to the UK. My mother, myself and my brother-in-law had lost hope as we had tried several times and couldn't make it. However, we thought it was worth trying. We had only one bottle of water with us as we were sure that we would fail. We didn't want to overload ourselves with unnecessary stuff.

There were footballs inside the lorry. We were sure that the lorry was heading from Belgium to Britain this time. No problem as long as footballs were not as cold as the energy cans we had last time! The three of us hid between the balls all night as the lorry wasn't moving. We had to keep quiet. We had interrupted sleep as we were concerned the driver might open the truck door any minute. Next morning, we realised that the lorry had already moved. We could see a sea scene through a small opening. Later we realised that the lorry was on board a freight ship. We were so pleased that we had finally made it. We thought that it would be a short distance from Belgium to the UK. But it took the ship fourteen hours to land at Hull. So, we nearly spent three days inside that lorry. Unbelievable!

We got a mobile signal for Britain. We had to stay still in the lorry because if someone found us while we were on the ship, we would be returned to Belgium again. The lorry was left at Hull harbour and no-one came to open the door. It looked like the driver had left the lorry. We ran out of water and were so scared, exhausted, thirsty, and hungry. We waited patiently, but no-one came. I had a set of nail clippers and a nail scissors which I used to cut through the thick wired cloth covering the sides of the lorry. It was so difficult to make an opening and to get through to the open air. Once we were out of the lorry, three police cars were following us.

They took us to an investigation centre and were very nice to us. They offered us water and snacks and were wondering how we survived without food and water for three days! I told them how the Danish authorities had forced me to give my fingerprints. They were joking with me and asked if I was willing to give my fingerprints to the British authorities this time. Of course, I would! We were transferred to a hotel and then to Birmingham where we stayed for eleven days. Later we were taken to Huddersfield where we stayed at a house. It was a four-month journey for us to make it to the UK. An unforgettable journey.

Hussam Allaham

I tried to get out. At first, I tried to travel legally but they refused, because my medical profession was written on my passport. They wouldn't allow doctors to leave the country as they needed doctors. So I was denied exit. A couple of times I tried to travel illegally. But it didn't work for some reason. Things got worse. At some point al Quneitra hospital phoned to inform me that the regime was looking for me. I was advised to disappear. I stayed in Damascus. I was hiding for a while and had no idea how to get out. Someone suggested to me that I should leave the zone controlled by the regime and head to other areas like Al Ghouta which falls outside the regime's control. Damascus airport was closed because a conflict area was very close to the airport, so it was closed for two weeks. Later, it was opened but no one would dare to go to the airport. The road leading to the airport was a conflict zone. Someone asked for around $200 or $150, not sure how much, in return for helping me to travel to the airport. I agreed. I bought the ticket and my uncle travelled with me. My uncle wasn't comfortable with that arrangement as he didn't want to put himself in any sort of trouble. I remember we were on the road to the airport and my uncle was talking to his wife over the phone. He was telling her: 'Look, we are safe so far. We are still OK.' He was afraid because I was accompanying him. Luckily, the way to the airport was so empty. We could hear shooting from each side of the road. We could see some smoke as well. But we were the only people driving. We had a taxi which took us to the airport. The airport was so empty.

I met a person and he asked me 'Are you Dr Hussam?' 'Yes, I am.' and then everyone around was saying: 'Oh, Dr Hussam' and they wished me a safe flight. My uncle was surprised to see people paying their respects to me and helping with the luggage. They didn't even focus on the weight. Yes. Allah helped me. It was a small aeroplane that was heading to Jordan. When the plane took off, I felt such

'Did People Live Here?' by Alison Lochhead

internal conflict as to whether to stay or leave the country. I was wondering how useful I was to the country. I treated people and I tried hard. I wished I could have remained to witness a better situation, to see things to conclusion. But...

When the plane took off, I looked out of the window and all I saw was smoke. Areas were burning. It was an unforgettable image. I was flying while the country was burning. And it is still burning. Since the very beginning, no one expected that the situation would come to this. We were hopeful. We used to say this month, the next month, the next year. Two years... Sometimes I wonder whether this thing, the revolution... I know it is a violent regime, but the blood! There is always this persistent question about arming the revolution. Also, people had no option but to protect themselves. On the one hand, you wonder if the revolution had continued to be peaceful, would things be better? On the other hand, people were fighting against armed forces. I remember the revolution started in Tunisia, Egypt and other places. We were hoping that things would turn out the way they did in those countries.

We had several unarmed confrontations, but it looked like the regime had planned for bloodshed from the very first week. In a way, it was like Saddam Hussein's way. Both regimes were based on a sadistic Baath ideology. They both adopted the policy: if you slap one person, two hundred others would be intimidated. They always believed that killing one would teach the rest a lesson. So, from the very beginning the regime confronted the revolution ruthlessly. By killing, by blood, by persecution. Yes, they survive by killing and by persecution. For instance, imagine that Splott in Cardiff is controlled by the FSA and the regime's forces are out. The Syrian regime has a very clear strategy: OK, now the FSA controls this area. Regardless of who lives there, for or against, the regime doesn't care about the people and the inhabitants. Let them all die, be they supporters or opponents. The regime forms a security square in each big city. This square is well protected and secured. Anything that falls outside this square is worthless. The regime doesn't care. If they are looking for or targeting someone in a building they can take a whole building down, together with its inhabitants. If Splott falls under the FSA, the regime will bomb and destroy the whole area. By means of the bombing, they send a message to everyone that the destruction has happened because the

FSA entered the city. Furthermore, they would destroy all the surrounding areas. Any area around Splott, for instance, would be invaded. They did that in Syria. They raided houses, intimidated and abused people, searched and robbed houses under the umbrella of looking for revolutionaries or members of the FSA. They embargoed food and bread. As a result, innocent people would think that all the havoc and the chaos was because of the FSA. They began to accuse the FSA. We are bombed because of the FSA. We will die because of the FSA. The regime was showing people how ruthlessly it can act against the FSA or anyone who revolts. This was their strategy.

I went to Jordan and joined my brother who was working. He was working at the borders helping those who were fleeing. He was also working on aid to Syria. He turned his house into a rehabilitation centre for those who were injured back home. We lived in this house together. It was a big house where some other doctors lived with us too. Injured Syrians in the camps, who had fled the country, got some treatment at the hospitals in Jordan, but they were released earlier. And we helped with that. There was a seventeen-year-old boy who had lost his hands and leg in a shelling. You can't leave a person like that to live on his own. No one cared about anyone else. There was no support at all. We took care of him. Another person had lost one of his eyes. There was a person who was hit, they thought he was dead and placed him in the mortuary fridge. But he started banging after regaining consciousness and was brought out alive. I bet you there were people who might have been buried before being assessed. There was no assessment in that chaos. Anyway, we continued helping people. But it was very difficult to find a job in Jordan.

We had troubles with the Jordanian government. My brother and I had these problems because we used to facilitate medical aid from Jordan to Syria. To help people. The law in Jordan was that any aid to Syria, regardless of the source, any donations whether individual aid, aid from charities or countries in the world had to pass through the Hashemite Society. The society takes twenty per cent of the aid and distributes the rest. That is the Jordanian law. No one was allowed to send donations without the government's knowledge. It was so disappointing for us to know that twenty per cent of the donations and the medicines would be going to Jordan. It was a political move meant to control some political powers in Syria. Jordan was working with foreign countries to control the FSA and the political groups on the ground in Syria.

When I left Syria, there were two armies: the regular state army and the free army. In the southern part of Syria, we were aware that Hezbollah was active, but it was on a smaller scale. There were also other groups fighting but it was not so publicly announced. Whereas in the north of Syria, Turkey was there, as you know. And the borders were open.

In Jordan, my brother and I used to attend meetings about Syria and the political situation, which was our main concern. One of those meetings was with the Norwegian delegate to help Syrians. They held meetings with many people to understand what the Syrian people really needed, how to help and what to do. They suggested offering blankets, food, supporting women and improving the condition of the camps. In the break, there was a diplomat and a translator from the Norwegian embassy. He noticed that my brother and I were upset and disappointed. He wondered why we were so unsatisfied. We replied 'Because you are not delivering any real solutions to the root of the problem. Imagine someone who has been under fire, amid violence and bloodshed. You should offer a solution to the killing instead of offering them a handkerchief to wipe their faces.' He told us 'What you are witnessing in Syria nowadays is just the tip of the iceberg. A day would come when Syria would turn into a swamp for every sort of radical thinking. Syria would attract all sorts of radical and extremist thinking. All would come to Syria and only then would we be able to strike.' At the time, we didn't take his words seriously and we found them illogical. But this was what really happened. By opening the Turkish border everything became possible. The world got rid of the worst people. It was good for the world, but it destroyed Syria.

Now back to Jordan. After we had troubles with the Jordanian government, we were given a two-day deadline to leave the country or return to Syria. In Jordan there was a policy of sending someone who breaks the law to an area that neither belongs to the regime nor to the other side of the fight. I had some Syrian friends. They were wounded and were sent to that area. It was a sad situation. So, we left Jordan and joined our family in Egypt. I couldn't endure the state of unemployment in Egypt. I was blaming myself for leaving Syria. I stayed in Egypt for a couple of months. Then I decided to return to Syria. To go

Between March 2011 and February 2021

930 medical professionals have been killed in Syria

55% of these were killed in bombing attacks or shelling

21% were killed by small arms fire by ground forces

13% are suspected to have been tortured before being killed

7% were executed.

Source: Physicians for Human Rights
https://phr.org

by my brother. We had no idea what was going on in the northern part of Syria. When we arrived there, we realised that the situation was so bad. People were fighting one another. In the south there was a state army and a free army. People were either with this army or with the other one. Whereas in the north it was a different scenario. The Kurds were of several sects: Extremist Kurds, PKK Kurds, Al Nusra front. This group and that group and the tribes. All these militias. Even the regime was divided. I had no idea what was going on. The danger was because I was from Damascus, and the city was under the regime's control. So, I was looked at as a supporter of the regime. A seventeen-year-old boy is carrying a gun and walking in the street – if he doesn't like me, he could easily shoot me.

It was the whole northern region. Each village or town was under a specific group. If you move from one village to the other, you can easily endanger your life. In the south, where I was before, I was respected because of my medical profession. They respected me as they were aware that they might need my help at some point. Sadly, after three years, kids of fourteen years old who grew up with the noise of killing, the noise of arms became used to arms and weapons and considered arms as a means of protection. Everything changed – people, their ideologies, their values. The situation has become out of control. International ideologies – each country had a grip over a certain group or militia and policies. Money was the major player in all this chaos. If an area is controlled by a certain militia, say of 10,000 members, the militia leader has to look for a source to feed those members. And there lies the danger. When I

to Syria from the south of Egypt was nearly impossible because of the Jordanian situation. So, I went to Turkey, to Gaziantep where I tried to enter Syria. I was accompanied was in the south of Syria, I remember that the cost of cigarettes alone was around one million Syrian Liras. Money speaks loudly.

My brother and I spent a week in the north before deciding to leave as we were shocked by the reality on the ground. We returned to Egypt, but it was difficult to stay, and we managed to find a job opportunity in Yemen. Eighty per cent of Syrian doctors used to travel to Yemen as it was the only Arab country that allowed Syrians to work. We worked there for six months. Then, Yemen's situation got worse. Before leaving Egypt for Yemen, the political situation in Egypt worsened too. Syrians were accused of supporting the Muslim brothers party and the media was against Syrians. This was followed by a decision banning Syrians from entering Egypt. Egyptians are very nice and kind people. There is no racism or anything like this. Things can happen sometimes. But when things got worse, they would get worse for both the Syrians and the Egyptians. There was no discrimination among the people. But the policies...

If you ask me what is your wish? I would tell you: my dream is to visit my parents and my family in Egypt. I haven't seen them for seven years now. The last time I saw them was when I left Egypt for Yemen. Later, Syrians were banned entry to Egypt. Currently I have a travel document which doesn't allow me to travel to them. If I am to enter Egypt, I need to obtain a security clearance from the Egyptian authorities. I am looking forward to getting my British Citizenship to travel to my family. To travel as a British person not as a Syrian.

So, after we worked in Yemen the political situation worsened. Most Syrian doctors who were working there fled to the Saudi borders. I still have an image of Syria's top specialists, well-established Syrian medical doctors sitting at the side of the road close to the Yemeni-Saudi borders. Can you imagine this? At that moment my brother and I decided to migrate to Europe. Because I have good English and I have an uncle who lives in London. I believed that the UK would be my destination. So we decided to travel to Turkey and then head to Europe.

From Turkey we managed to get us Lithuanian passports by means of a smuggler. We took a Turkish flight to the Maldives. For the duration of the flight, we were watching the film *Les Misérables*. We arrived in the Maldives at 7:00am and to our shock the airport had been renovating its surveillance devices which detected our forged passports. We were interrogated. We pretended we were friends and that we were in the Maldives as tourists. Later we had a four-hour interrogation session. They wanted to check if I was a Lithuanian national. I had learned a few Lithuanian words and was able to read some information in Lithuanian. They searched our luggage, our pockets, handbags, everything. I was carrying Lithuanian currency and Lithuanian notes. Unfortunately, they found a piece of paper on which my Arabic name Hussam Allaham was written. Eventually, I had to confess and I handed them my Syrian passport. They gave me guarantees that they would never harm me. They decided to send my brother and I back to Turkey. So they took our Syrian passports, and we were ordered to wait for the Turkish flight for about twenty-four hours. We sat at the duty-free zone in the airport and couldn't buy anything because we had no passports. We sat there and watched the World Cup. Then we were escorted to the plane. The stewardess escorted us to our seats. Passengers thought we were VIPs! So, we flew to Turkey in a Turkish plane. And I had to watch *Les Misérables* all over again.

We returned to Turkey, were interrogated by the Turkish authorities, and had to sign some papers before being released. At that point, many refugees were heading towards Algeria, Libya, and then the sea journey to Europe. I tried to persuade my brother to take the route to Greece. My brother thought that the route to North Africa was much better. He was a bit hesitant because he has a brown skin and doesn't speak English well. So Greece would be a difficult option. So we ended up in Algeria. Algeria was the last place we entered legally as Syrian nationals. We then had a twelve-hour journey to the south of Algeria. We learned from Facebook that Syrian refugees used to head to an area in the south of Algeria. Later, they would meet up with a smuggler who collected them from a specific hotel. We arrived at that hotel and found it full of Syrians! An Algerian person came. He collected money from people and promised to get them to Libya the next day.

Syrians were banned from entering Libya. So we had to travel to Libya via the Libyan desert. It was another twelve hour journey during Ramadan. And during Ramadan, Algeria prohibits the selling of food and drinks. Not only eating and drinking but also the selling of food and drink was prohibited during daytime. No one would agree to sell us water on the way. It was banned. We travelled through a desert area and we reached the Libyan border. We moved into an abandoned house. We were about thirty-five people: families, children, and young men. We started getting to know each other. We were handed over to another smuggler, a Libyan smuggler. Libyan smugglers had pickup trucks and Jeep cars hidden behind a mountain. So, they took us to a mountain. When you trust a smuggler, that was it. It was a point of no return. We were worthless to them, and they could end our lives in a gunshot. We had to obey orders. The last point for us as legal Syrian citizens was Algeria. The moment we entered Libya no one would bother about us. We heard stories on the way of people who lost their lives, rape incidents and bandits because all those people were considered illegal refugees. We travelled in pickups and on foot and were led by one of the smugglers. We ended up in a two-roomed house guarded by two eighteen-year-old boys. They were carrying guns. We started to get to know each other. We cleaned the house and cooked us a meal. We gathered on the rooftop for a chat. The smugglers were happy because we were not a very demanding group. Some of us were singing. Others were telling jokes. It was like that.

Then we were taken to the most difficult part of the journey from the south to the north. To Misrata, a coastal city in Libya. The desert route was too hot and too risky. We were lucky though as the smugglers were experimenting with new land cruisers to transfer refugees. Land cruisers are faster and can cross the desert smoothly. The driver was from Zintan. He drove really fast because he didn't want to

Hussam and his brother with other refugees being smuggled through Libya.
Photo courtesy of Hussam Allaham.

miss the television series *Bab Al-Hara* [The Neighbourhood's Gate]. The driver was a young lad. He was armed and was driving at a speed of 120 mph in the desert to catch up on the series! And we were so pleased, as we just wanted to reach our destination. Then we were received by a new smuggler and were taken to a villa that accommodated around 350 people. There were different nationalities. Africans and Bangladeshis were placed in the corridors. They were seated in the corridors and were not allowed to lie down, whereas Syrians were placed in the rooms. They put the women and the children upstairs and men downstairs. We were asked to enter a room. People were sitting in queues. Some were wounded, others were injured and had skin burns on the journey. The place was too crowded and we could find our way out. Luckily, we found a corner in the backyard which we cleaned and tidied. We used some water from a nearby well to wash the backyard. We used to spend most of our time in that corner.

There was one toilet for the 350 people. There was one cook who used to prepare food for those people. So, my brother and I tried to minimise our food intake so as not to use the toilet frequently. We spent nine days in that house. The weather was bad, and the smugglers couldn't start the sea journey in such weather. It was such a tough time. Some women and children had food poisoning and another young woman had typhoid with a very high temperature. We managed to treat them with some medicines provided by the smuggler. When we helped with treating people, we were treated nicely by the smugglers. We had more food shares and were treated as VIPs!

The crucial moment came when they took a small group of six people. We were among them. They took us to a small house near the sea. They asked us to sit and wait for their orders. Once we heard the word '*Hayya*,' a Libyan word that means 'let's go', we were supposed to run fast. It was dark at night and there was some distance between the house and the sea. Once we heard '*Hayya*', we were supposed to run to the sea and walk into the sea and be received by someone. And we did. We heard that word '*Hayya*' and we ran to the sea. We walked into the sea and the sea almost reached our necks. I had a life jacket, inside which I placed my paper documents as we were not allowed to carry anything. It was dark in the sea, and we were nearly covered with water. Suddenly a hand pulled us onto a rubber boat. We helped one another to get on board the dinghy. I pushed my brother who was a big man. Then he pulled me to his side.

There were six of us. And we could barely see the others

walking in the sea and being helped the same way. We were told not to wear any light-coloured tops or shirts. Clothes had to be too dark to reflect the light. The boat moved for a while. We then came across another boat waiting in the dark. The boat was stacked up with people. We were literally seated on top of one another. It was a special boat which accommodated 150 people. It was a ten-metre-long boat. Bangladeshis were seated in the lower level close to the engine. I thought that the Bangladeshis were treated like that because they were paying less to the smugglers. I realised that they paid more than the Syrians. Syrians use Facebook to exchange information about the best smugglers to use and the ones to avoid. On Facebook people exchanged tips on the best way to be smuggled. So, smugglers prefer Syrians to get more online reviews. But Bangladeshis didn't have social media. Yes, they preferred Syrians for the reviews. Reviews like 'This smuggler was fast', 'We were comfortable with that smuggler' etc. The whole situation in Syria was affected by YouTube etc. Social media allowed the world to see what was happening. Social media made everyone realise that what was happening was different from earlier events in Hamah.

We were seated in the dinghy and the girl with typhoid was sitting next to me. She was trembling because of a high temperature. The dinghy set off at around 2:00 am. All we knew was that we were heading to Italy. Because that boat was considered a VIP, the smugglers had chosen a well-trained captain. A Tunisian guy with fifteen years of experience in deep seas. So we were in a better position than the other boats. Normally, the smugglers choose a refugee and give them a fortnight's training in handling the boat and that's it. We had families and vulnerable people with us on the boat. Our captain was knowledgeable enough to steer the boat. He didn't even use a compass. He immediately started the engine off and moved off.

The more the boat went into the sea, the farther the land appeared behind us. It was serious now and we were facing the sea. A boat stacked with people. We could barely move our bodies. At some point some people wanted to use the toilet. But no way. There were babies and children, and it was freezing cold. There were infants by our side. There weren't any covers over them. The father was arguing with someone over the space, leaving the babies uncovered. My brother and I took off our coats and covered the babies. I was left with only a shirt on me. I also offered some medicine to the girl with the typhoid. At this point, the land had completely disappeared and we were in the middle of the sea. Luckily it was a moonlit night. The moon made all the difference. It was a companion in the darkness. When you look around and see no land around, no words can describe that feeling when you realise that you are in the middle of the dark sea.

A dreadful situation. Those people who wonder why refugees come via the sea – if refugees weren't exposed to much greater dangers, they wouldn't put themselves in such a situation. Luckily, when the sun rose, we were able to detect a Libyan person on a yacht. He was on his own on a yacht the size of our boat. He saw us and he didn't ignore us. He came closer to our boat. The feeling of having a

Hussam with other migrants on the boat from Libya to Italy.
Photo courtesy of Hussam Allaham.

yacht by our side was a great comfort. He stayed by our side until we were saved. He just stayed by our side as a form of support. We saw an aircraft that watched us and left. Later, we found a ship that approached us, but they didn't save us. Our captain told us that the ship couldn't take us because we were still sailing in Libyan regional waters. Once we left Libyan waters, the ship would be able to take us to Italy. So, we spent around eleven hours on that dinghy. The aircraft was still watching us. The moment we came out of regional waters, the captain switched the engine off. He knew that the ship would come to save us. At that moment we saw a big ship coming towards us. That feeling! I can't forget that moment. Something was there to rescue us. A big thing coming fast towards you to help you. But that same moment was also the most dangerous. When you hear about capsized boats in the news, most of the boats capsize at that same moment. Normally, when the ship approaches, the refugees get excited and each one tries to get to the rescue ship before the other. People

usually move to one side of the boat towards the ship. Those who sit in the lower level of the boat near the engine try to rush out. This sudden movement causes imbalance and causes the boat to turn upside down. You know, it is just a dinghy, and such a movement would certainly capsize it. We tried hard to control the movement on our boat. We begged people to stay still until the ship reached us. We asked two big young men to control the movement of people near the engine. We even allowed them to use force in case anyone tried to get out. There was no other way to keep the boat balanced. We made it. The ship sent some rescue boats to us. We allowed the children and the women into the rescue boats first and it went on like that. Everyone found a place on those boats. My brother, myself and five others remained on the dinghy. There were seven of us who couldn't find a place on the rescue boats. We were told that there was no place left for us and that another rescue boat would be sent. Within a short while, there was a rescue yacht that took us.

It was so cold. During daytime the sun was unbearable. At night it became too cold. We were seated at the front of the yacht and not allowed to enter inside. We were even not allowed to use the yacht's toilet. We spent around six to seven hours on the yacht and we were then taken on board an Italian warship. It was a big ship. At that point we forgot we were on the sea. It felt like we were in a city! There was a military system on board of that ship. There was an armed military crew. They offered us two black bin bags: one to use as a cover and the other was to sit or to sleep on as it was raining heavily. There were around 3,000 passengers on board the ship. We could only see their heads. Just heads everywhere. Imagine a ship full of people – 3000 people. The crew got rid of all the stuff we were carrying and asked us to sit there. We spent twenty-four hours on that ship. That ship used to take four-day trips during which refugees were collected from different locations and taken to Italy. When we were on board the ship, we looked back at the dinghy we were on originally. We saw them burning the dinghy. It looked too small. We wondered how that dinghy had accommodated that number of people. It looked tiny compared to the ship we were on.

After the twenty-four-hour trip we arrived in Naples. When we saw Naples – I always refer to that as if I was in black and white mode and suddenly found the colours. It was such a relief. I couldn't describe that feeling. Finally, we made landfall. Yes, we had made it. The 3,000 people got off. We were all taken to a big hall where the UN began the process of documentation, names etc. This was Italy.

Ali Zain

I stayed for fourteen days in Damascus to be able to apply for a Syrian passport to travel out of Syria to Lebanon and then to Turkey. I was planning to stay in Turkey for a while and to return to Aleppo once things get better. Even though I couldn't get a passport issued, I managed to enter into Lebanon with my uncle's help. In Lebanon, I worked non-stop for long hours from 7:00 am to 5:00 pm daily. That job enabled me to pay my debts back, to support my family in Syria and to pay to get a Syrian passport issued

from Lebanon. At that stage, things had got worse back home with ISIS control which left me with no options of return. The only option available was to travel to Europe.

Normally the journey costs between $5000 to $6000. I had some savings, and I borrowed the money from friends and relatives and started planning for the journey. I was aware of its difficulty and risks. Before reaching my destination, which is the UK, I passed through eight countries. In 2015, when Europe opened its doors to refugees, people from different parts of the world gathered in Turkey aiming to reach to Europe. I took a flight from Lebanon to Turkey and that was the first time in my life to be on a plane. In Turkey, I met with people from Afghanistan, Syria, Sudan, and several other countries. At the start, I used to think that the number of Syrians seeking refuge in foreign countries was the highest. When I arrived at Turkey, I was surprised to learn that Syrians constitute around 7% only among the other nationalities of those seeking refuge in Europe and other places. People come to Izmir in Turkey, then to Greece by sea where they get a one-month residency in Greece. In 2015, getting that residency was easier for refugees as the Greek government was highly sympathetic to them because they were fleeing war.

In my first attempt to cross the sea borders from Turkey to Greece, I took a dinghy heading towards Mytilene, the capital of the Greek island of Lesbos. We set off at 2:00 am. The generator broke and we were driven by the waves which eventually led us in a different direction. The dinghy lost its way in the middle of the sea and we spent almost eight hours in the middle of the sea. I was among the four people who were conscious. All other people fainted. I had no idea if they had experienced fatigue out of seasickness or whether they lost consciousness out of hopelessness or perhaps they went asleep. We were surrounded by imminent death. I was aware that death was very close. It was like doomsday to me. I thought of all the wrongdoings I had committed in my life. As I cannot swim, I was a hundred per cent sure that I would definitely die if the boat sank. Slowly and gradually waves were getting higher and higher. We tried over and over again to call the lifeguards but got no response. At around 9:00 am, the Turkish lifeguards came to our rescue. Can you imagine how long we waited for them? From 2:00 am to 9:00 am next morning! When we were rescued, we thought that we had made it to Greece, whereas in fact we were still within the Turkish regional waters.

"A hundred and forty-six people on a pathetic dinghy surrounded by nothing but a borderless sea and a blue sky. Almost all the people had lost consciousness except four of us."

There were a hundred and forty-six people, among which were two families. An Iraqi family of five members, a father, mother and three daughters one of whom was a little child. And there was a Syrian family of a father, a mother and three kids. So, a hundred and forty-six people on a pathetic dinghy surrounded by nothing but a borderless sea and a blue sky. Almost all the people had lost consciousness except four of us: two young men from Latakia, a coastal city in Syria who had some experience in sailing and knew how to swim, a person from Algeria and me. Even though I was so desperate and couldn't swim, I thankfully didn't faint and hadn't any symptoms of seasickness. The worst part for me was when I heard the little ones crying. I couldn't imagine them drowning. They don't deserve to die. Then Faisal, one of the strong young men among us, also fainted and I almost lost hope to see him not responding to my calls.

The dinghy is designed to accommodate a maximum of ten people, and we were a hundred and forty-six people and there was no guide or leader. With such journeys, one of the refugees volunteers to drive the boat with some instructions as how to deal with the engine, where to head and whom to contact for rescue. In return, the leader travels for free. Each person pays 1300 $. I did not meet any of the smugglers. The deal usually takes place through agencies. I was asked to hand in the money to a second or a third party who arranges the journey and is the contact for details about the journey. You know it is very illegal. It is considered human trafficking. So, we embarked on the sea journey and within just one hour, the dinghy's motor failed causing the boat to cease moving.

I can't describe the fear and the frustration I faced. I was so distressed. Yet I refused to believe that this was the end. I tried to imagine a different end, a better end. When the water began to penetrate the boat from all sides, we had nothing but bottles which we used to take the water out of the boat. We were all drenched – our clothes, bags, blankets and everything. The water added extra weight to the dinghy which was on the verge of capsizing. So we tried to get rid of our heavy bags by throwing them into the sea. I was working with the other young men to keep the boat balanced, but I was haunted by the idea of drowning soon. I felt paralysed because I knew I won't be able to swim. Many years after that event I still have a frequent dream of myself not being able to swim or to scream in a deep sea.

In the middle of that hell, and the very high waves which were taking us up and down, I imagined a ship coming from afar and I shouted 'Look! A ship!'. Two seconds after, I realised that I was imagining. That was so embarrassing as I felt guilty of giving false hope to others. After a short while, I heard a distant boat. I couldn't believe my ears and I didn't say anything this time as I wasn't sure, and I didn't want people to think that I had gone mad. But it was true. I cried out loud, as did the other young men, and we used our lifebuoy rings to wave to the boat. At that moment, the people on the boat regained consciousness. It made me think that losing hope was the main reason for their losing consciousness. Hope brought them to life once again. I saw them all standing on the boat and that was a very dangerous moment as it might have turned the boat upside down. This is the reason behind many of the catastrophes that took place on such boats. Luckily, they sat down and we were able to maintain the boat on an even keel until we were rescued.

The Greek coast: a photo taken by Ali on his second attempt to cross by boat from Turkey, on a much calmer sea.

The rescue team, which belonged to the Turkish police, took us back to Istanbul in Turkey. I stayed at a friend's house for a while. Then we managed to go on another sea journey. But the sea was calm the second time. There were

Migrants in Hungary near the border with Serbia, 2015.
Photos: Gémes Sándor/SzomSzed, CC BY-SA 3.0, via Wikimedia Commons

three friends with me: two from Syria and another person from Afghanistan. We reached the Greek coast within five hours. From Greece we travelled to Macedonia, Serbia, Hungary, Austria, Switzerland, France and the UK.

When we reached the Greek coast, we had to walk for twelve hours to reach a refugee camp on the border where we had our papers stamped. It was on the eighth of September 2015 and the weather was so hot. Being in the sea for five hours had affected my feet, because of the salt of the sea water. Walking for twelve hours under the sun with my feet already aching was so painful. We stayed in that refugee camp for two days and it wasn't a pleasant experience at all. On the third day, we had our papers stamped and we travelled on board a ship from that island to Athens, where we stayed for two days. Then, we took a bus to the Macedonian borders where we were escorted by military officers into a military train that was heading towards Serbia. We arrived at the Serbian borders at 4:00 am.

I couldn't see the beauty of those places. Not just because I was travelling on a train, but I was so tired, exhausted, worried and above all I was cold. My friends and I were looking around for a surface, a corner or anywhere to sleep but we didn't find a chance to rest. On the contrary, we had to queue for fourteen hours to be able to get letters from the Serbian authorities to enable us to head for our next destination. I experienced all sorts of weathers in those fourteen hours and was so hungry. At 3:00am, we got our letter and took a bus to Hungary. Hungary was the worst and the most dangerous stage of our journey in Europe.

If refugees enter Hungary legally, the Greek authorities will take their fingerprints, and this procedure will prevent them from seeking asylum in the UK. Under immigration rules, once the UK authorities realise that we had our fingerprints taken in Hungary, they will ask us to return to Hungary. People who made the journey before us or those who had faced problems shared their experiences via social media and phones, which saved us. We were in constant contact with others for updates and directions.

So, the three of us met with another Syrian person and we travelled to the borders of Hungary. There was a stage where we had to stay away from the Hungarian border police, and it was at a railway near the borders. The railway offered two ways forward, one where we would have to give our fingerprints and then we could either stay in Hungary or go to Germany and seek asylum there. But we didn't want to go down that route. The other way was a corn field that we had to walk through cautiously to avoid the police dogs.

We had to wait for the sunset to enter the cornfield. Luckily, there was a heavy presence of European media all over that space. Cameras and news correspondents were around. One of my friends suggested that we took advantage of the media presence to cross the cornfield before sunset. He thought that the presence of the media was in our favour. If the Hungarian police would capture us, they wouldn't be harsh on us and would let us go without taking our fingerprints in front of the cameras.

Hungarian police are infamous for their harsh treatment and for assaulting and humiliating refugees. We entered the cornfield lying flat on our bellies while moving cautiously. While we were moving like that, there was a Japanese journalist accompanying us and taking our photos after he got our permission. It was a long way until we made it. After we got through the cornfield, we found an area with several taxis waiting for passengers. We were bewildered as to who those taxis were for and we were afraid they might belong to the Hungarian authorities.

Suddenly, we found a taxi driver heading towards us accompanied by a tattooed lady who looked suspicious. The situation felt like a scene from a gangster movie. The lady asked for 150 euros per person and she wanted the money in advance. She asked us to pay before entering the taxi which made us even more suspicious. But we had no other option but to pay. So we paid, one person at a time, and got into the taxi. Everybody was using us. They were all making profits out of our misery.

As the journey from that border area to Budapest took over an hour, we thought of getting ourselves ready for the next stage. I had two packets of wipes which we used to clean our faces, hands and shoes. We even changed our dirty clothes and put on clean ones which we were carrying in our backpacks. We did all that inside the car. I even wore my hair gel and we all looked so clean and tidy. The whole cornfield scenario was completely altered into a different scenario. The taxi driver asked us to get off at a different point from the one we were supposed to reach. We had to take another taxi to reach the railway station. At the railway station, we met a Syrian guy who told us that we could queue with several other refugees who already had given their fingerprints. And it worked! We booked our tickets and went onto the train safely. The train was heading towards Austria. So, we arrived at the Austrian borders.

Once we arrived in Austria, we realised that the rest of the journey would be smoother. Everything after Hungary was smoother.

The Austrian authorities were very nice and offered us food and clothes because the media was still talking about the seventy-one refugees whose bodies were discovered in the back of a lorry on an Austrian motorway. I have a friend who lives in Austria whom I called to come and collect us. Even though it was illegal, he couldn't say no. He was so kind and nice to host us and show us around Vienna. Next day, he took us to the railway station and gave me a coat to replace my worn coat. I still have that coat with me here in Cardiff.

We took the train to Switzerland. And on that train, a policeman discovered our Syrian identity and politely asked us to leave the train. We had to give our fingerprints only for security reasons, as the regulations were not as strict as in Hungary. We took another train to Zurich and it was so cold. We waited for our next train to France. We arrived in Paris. We were so excited to be in Paris. Sadly, we could not go out and about in Paris and had to book our tickets to Calais. I loved the French trains. Of all the trains I used, the French ones were the best. They also have a unique horn sound and tone. I recorded that tone and sent it to a friend who recognised it as he had had an earlier experience. It was a long trip as it took us fourteen hours from Vienna to Calais on the train.

Calais is a small, quiet, and nice city. Yet, we couldn't enjoy the place because we were so exhausted, uncertain and overwhelmed. We found a Turkish restaurant where we had our dinner. We met a Sudanese refugee who showed us the way to a Syrian camp in a park in the city. There were no tents and most refugees were sleeping rough. It looked like the people had become accustomed to living there like that. I couldn't imagine myself sleeping at that park. As we still had some money left, we booked a reasonably priced hotel for one night. Later, we moved to an area where there were camps for refugees.

I stayed there for twenty-nine days. Charities provided us with tents. Potato chips and baguettes was the main dish as it was the cheapest. We used to buy food from Lidl store and that was the first time for me to be introduced to Lidl. We had to queue for hours to shower. To avoid queuing, we booked for a night at the hotel to shower and have a decent sleep. As we were three people, we paid 30 euros each for a 90 euro one-night stay. The tent provided in the camp was designed for one person only. As we were three, we had to squeeze our bodies at night to fit in the tent. I got used to sleeping with a squeezed body. I am still unable to get rid of that posture. On the twenty-ninth day of my stay in the Calais camp, I managed to enter the UK.

Between the camps and the UK borders, there were wired fences which we used to climb daily in our attempts to enter the UK. If refugees succeeded to climb the fences, they would walk about three miles to the railway station to jump into a moving train to Dover. We used to watch the guards carefully and to wait for the right moment to jump over the fence. The worst thing was the wired fence which we had to cut through to make an opening to get to the other side.

"2016-01-17 13.02.06" (CC BY 2.0) by malachybrowne

Migrants enter a truck on the A16 highway that leads to the Channel tunnel crossing in Coquelles. By PASCAL ROSSIGNOL / REUTERS

Many refugees succeeded in jumping on a moving train. Most of them failed and either got electrocuted and died there or fell off the train and lost limbs or were badly hurt.

Desperate people usually don't see the risks. They only look at the points that can enable them to achieve their goals. As to me and my friends, we kept trying and didn't lose hope despite the many failed attempts we experienced. At some stage, the French guards enabled us to go through the gates of the camps. We walked to the railway station and stayed in a place close to the railway station for three nights. We were sleeping rough between the trees to evade the guards. The last night was the worst as I was so exhausted, frustrated, hungry, wet, and cold. It was raining heavily. So, I chose a spot between the trees and curled up into my sleeping bag where I could sense and hear dogs roaming around me. I woke up in the morning to find myself in a pool of mud from the heavy rains. It was a miserable scene. I felt so desperate and I was longing for warmth, rest, dry clothes, food and peace of mind. I gave up trying. I persuaded my friends to surrender to the English police and to return to the camps as it would be more humane there. And we did. The English police put us on a bus which took us back to the outskirts of Calais city. And here is where the last stage of my journey began.

At the entrance to Calais city there was a motorway verge called the 'dougar'. The word translates as 'traffic jam' where trucks entering into Britain form a long queue and can sometimes get stuck in that queue for hours. That dougar has long been the refugees' best chance of crossing the Channel to Britain. There were four of us at that spot. We found an unattended truck and we entered inside.

There was an item of furniture on which there were some bricks which I hid behind. I actually lay down behind it as I was so sleepy. Suddenly, the truck's rear door opened and the driver was standing there asking how many of us were there. As I was invisible, my friends told the driver that there were only three in the truck and he believed them. He asked them to get off the truck and they got off. He closed the truck door and locked it, leaving me alone inside.

I was so scared that the driver might reopen the door and find me. I was also wondering what the next step would bring me. I knew that once the truck reached the railway station, there would be scanners and watchdogs and that I would definitely be traced and caught. The truck suddenly started moving. The distance between that spot and the railway station was around three hours. I fell asleep. I had an iPad to tell the time, but I had to turn it off so as not to be detected. I woke up at 10:00 PM to realise that the truck had been five hours on that road.

I spent a great deal of time with refugees and immigrants and we were exchanging information. I was not courageous at all, as courage is about having lots of options. I was not left with many options. I had to take the risk. I couldn't go back to Syria, it was impossible. Returning to Lebanon was equally impossible as they had cancelled my entry visa when I left Lebanon for Turkey. And Turkey is hard to live in. When I was at the Calais camp, at the peak of my despair and entirely giving up trying to enter Britain, I managed to enter that truck. Could be fate or fortune!

So, five hours passed and I was still on that truck. I was not sure where the truck was heading. I was wondering where the watchdogs and the scanner that everybody mentioned were. I was also very thirsty and hungry as I had been eating only dry dates for three nights. It happened that I had a razor blade which I decided to use to make a tiny little hole in the cloth that covers the truck's roof, to see where the truck was. I realised that we were approaching the railway station to go on board a freight train on the way to Britain through the Channel Tunnel. By the way, the truck was carrying boxes of peanut butter cans and I was thirsty and starving. I took a can and started eating from the very salty peanut butter that made me even more thirsty. I also felt very guilty for eating without the driver's permission and I decided to pay the driver for the peanut butter if I arrived safely.

I suddenly noticed that the train was moving too fast which indicated that we were entering into Britain. Something that I could not believe. I was thrilled! I jumped, cried and shouted for joy. All that frustration, exhaustion, and hopelessness that overwhelmed me disappeared in a second. I kneeled and thanked God for saving me. I grabbed my pen and took the sealed label off the peanut butter can and wrote 'I am sorry, I was hungry' and I placed four euros at the side of the label which I sealed back. I realised later that the price of a peanut can is only two and a half euros! When I wrote about the details of my journey on Facebook, people thought it was something from a sci-fi movie, especially that part about me in a truck, the truck on a train and the train in a tunnel under the sea!

While still in the truck, I changed my clothes and combed my hair. The train stopped at around 8:30 pm and I was waiting for the driver to open the truck door which he didn't do. I couldn't wait anymore and had to knock at the doors and cried 'Help, help!'. The driver was shocked and bewildered when he saw me in his truck. I am sure he was scared that he might be charged with human trafficking and that would lead to jail. He called the railway police who helped me to get off the truck. I immediately told the police that the driver knew nothing about me and that I jumped and hid secretly in his truck. I told them in English, 'He doesn't know' and I pointed at where I was hiding saying: 'I was there'. When I told them I was from Syria, they were so polite and gentle with me. They welcomed me and took me to the office at Dover railway station. I was so pleased that I had made it to British territory. They offered me snacks and fruit.

Dona al Abdallah

Ali travelled three months after our wedding. We lived with his family in the village which I loved so much, and I also loved his family. Ali went to Lebanon and stayed there for a year. He was working and saving for his journey. Later, Ali called me to tell me that he was in Turkey and that his first attempt to travel via the sea had failed. Ali asked my advice for a possible second attempt. It was a very hard decision for me to take. I thought a lot about his second attempt and whether he would make it. My head swarmed with questions: What would happen if he failed? And what would happen if he made it? When would I be able to see him? I had no option but to agree with him that he should go for the sea journey.

I was so scared. Ali told me that he was ready to leave that decision behind and to join me in Manbij. At that point travelling from Turkey to Manbij, an ISIS controlled area, was a bit easier with the help of smugglers. I thought of all the risks, the expenses and the hassles of the journey from Turkey to Manbij. I thought of his future as well. What would he do in Manbij if he came back? ISIS's grip was getting tighter and tighter on people and especially on young men like Ali. If he returned, it would be a serious hardship. So, I encouraged him to take the sea journey. I left it to fate, destiny and to Allah to help us and to help Ali... *Alhamdulillah* Ali survived. He made it!

Ali used to contact me whenever he found a chance to do so. He called me when he reached land in Greece. In Serbia and other countries. But it took him a while to make it to the UK. When he arrived in the UK, he couldn't contact me. Later, I realised that he was so ill and had to be hospitalised. He was taken to the emergency service once he arrived in the UK. He called me once he was better.

"I packed my things and bade farewell to my family. I was aware that if things went well, I wouldn't be able to see them again. I cannot forget that moment."

Once Ali reached his destination, I was relieved. I waited around a year until Ali's mother was able to arrange for a smuggler to take us from Manbij, a heavily ISIS controlled area, to Asad's areas and then to Lebanon. It was a very risky journey. It was 10:00 AM. I packed my things and bade farewell to my family. I was aware that if things went well, I wouldn't be able to see them again. I cannot forget that moment when I was at my parents' house. My father has a disability and he couldn't accompany me downstairs to the outside door. My mother and younger sister accompanied me to the door. I also phoned my brothers in Turkey to let them know I was leaving. My mother was so scared. She was concerned that I might die on my way to Ali. She was uncomfortable with the fact that I would be smuggled to Lebanon.

Everybody knew how dangerous that route was. There were skirmishes on a daily basis between ISIS and the FSA. My mother was crying while praying for me and for my safety. I hugged her tight and felt suffocated. The car set off.

Ali's mother is such a brave woman. We were nine. Me, Ali's mother, three younger sisters and two younger brothers. One of Ali's sisters is married with two kids. And the plan was to smuggle her to her husband who was waiting in Lebanon. The car moved through a desert area. We were not allowed to take heavy luggage with us. I had no idea about that. I'd packed almost all my wedding stuff and was shocked when the smuggler asked me to leave my luggage in the car. He promised to return my stuff to Ali's home address in the village, but he didn't. My wedding photos and videos were on a hard disk. Sadly, all was lost. I didn't care much about clothes. But losing my dearest memories, my wedding memories, that was painful.

The car drove through deserted places, uninhabited houses. It was scary to see those scenes. It was sad too. ISIS forces, ISIS men were all around the place. Several barracks. They used to stop us every now and then and asked about our destination. Each time they stopped us we replied that we were visiting a relative. And with no heavy luggage, we didn't look suspicious. All I had with me was my handbag with my college credentials and related stuff. The car was heading to Izaz town which was a headquarter of the FSA. Therefore, it was a hotspot of constant bombarding and firing between the FSA and ISIS.

The smugglers led us out of the car to a very spacious flat that was full of smuggled people. I met a woman from Mosul with her daughter and husband. We were asked to keep our voices low and not to make a noise as that area was an ISIS ruled area.

At midnight we were asked to leave the flat and to walk or run, if we could, past the ISIS area towards an area ruled by the FSA. We began walking. It was a very hot summer night during harvest time. The road was full of thorns and weeds and we were very exhausted. In the middle of the journey, we heard firing and bombing. The smugglers couldn't operate cars in that spot for fear they might be spotted and targeted. We stopped. And my mother-in-law lit her cigarette in the middle of it all! She was so nervous and the cigarette calmed her down. I was escorted by Ali's sisters. Ali's brother held the kids and started running. Everybody was running for their lives. We were literally in the middle of the firing zone. We hid under olive trees in an olive grove. Then we heard an officer from the FSA using a loudspeaker asking people to lie face down for their safety. It was dawn when we arrived at another olive grove and rested there. That olive tree was a good omen. A few minutes later, we realised that we were in the safe zone of the FSA. Men from the FSA headed towards us and offered us water and food. They distributed food provisions to people around us. That was the end of the risky journey inside the Syrian borders.

The worst part was the ISIS-controlled areas. The rest were areas controlled by Kurdish forces, until we reached

Damascus. The plan was to stay for one day and then head towards Lebanon in a legal manner. We went to one of Ali's relatives and were so exhausted. After that we took a car and travelled to Lebanon legally. We arrived in Lebanon and I was so excited, so happy that we had made it safely. I was excited to meet with my brother in Lebanon. I hadn't seen him for over five years as he was working there. I was so relieved to be in Lebanon, safe and with my brother. I was excited about the future and about reuniting with Ali.

After ten days, I heard news of a severe air raid on the area where my family lived in Manbij. News was circulating that the building where my family lived was bombed. What made it worse was that I lost contact with them. No phone lines or WiFi and I almost lost hope of finding them alive again. After twenty days of angst and suffering, I heard that my family had escaped to a nearby village. Many of their neighbours died when their houses were bombed. Houses were levelled to the ground. My brother refused to leave my parents' house and was there rescuing many families from under the rubble.

I stayed for a year in Lebanon. Ali's family and I rented a house in Beirut. Ali couldn't apply for a family reunion directly. He worked and saved money for that. In the beginning, the application was rejected. Ali tried again and it worked. I waited in Lebanon for 364 days. A year minus one day. I was so pleased that I didn't stay there for over a year as I wasn't allowed to stay in Lebanon for a period longer than one year. Then I arrived here. I found myself in Heathrow airport.

Mohammad S

We were five. My mother, my eldest sister, my ten-year-old brother, my five-year-old sister Rayan and me. Rayan had a close girl friend who used to play with her every day in the neighbourhood. That girl died with her family in an air raid and Rayan was devastated. Can you imagine a five-year-old girl mourning such a loss?

We were guided by a smuggler. We arrived at the Syrian-Turkish borders and spent around five days waiting for a chance to enter to Turkey. They were long days and nights in the open air. We were covered by trees. When we ran out of water, we used to climb a nearby mountain to get water from a river. It was not pure water at all. By the end of the five days, we paid $500 to a smuggler who helped us cross to Turkey. No one was able to make it legally because most people had either lost their documents or were unable to apply for a visa through the Syrian government. So we paid almost all we had to that smuggler. We entered Turkey with very little cash left.

"It was the worst part of my life. I feel like my childhood and adolescence were taken away. I didn't choose it and I was forced to do it. But I learned a lot in the process. I wish I had learned all those things without the hardships I faced."

The Turkish standard of living was higher than that of Syria. We were completely ignorant of the Turkish language. We spent two days at a relative's house in Turkey and then we rented a flat. I found myself a casual job at a clothes factory. I didn't speak Turkish so I used sign language to communicate. The Turkish employer exploited me and made use of my situation. This was the case with almost all Syrian refugees working in Turkey. Because I couldn't read or write in Turkish, I had no idea about the standard wage or my rights as a worker. I was fourteen years old and I feel I was exploited. I was paid 800 Liras a month and I thought it was a great pay. I was paying for my family's rent and food. We used to shop for groceries from a cheap Bazar in the area where we lived. I was the sole breadwinner in the family. After a few months, I realised that I was paid less than the standard average wage. I used to work for twelve hours a day, six days a week. I had to accept that as I had no other choice. Slowly and gradually, I learned some Turkish and found a better paid job in a supermarket.

When my other brother recovered, he started working. He worked for around one and a half months and at the end, he wasn't paid a penny and eventually left that job. It was a sad situation when you know you are being exploited and can't do anything about it. The problem was that we were illegal workers. My brother and I had no passport or official documents. So we were exploited like hundreds of other refugees in Turkey. Language was the biggest difficulty. My mother and eldest sister stayed in Turkey for a while and then had to travel to Europe via the sea. They left my siblings in my care. One day my youngest sister had an

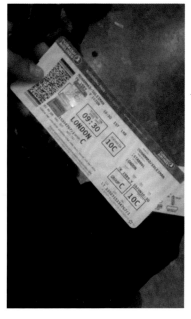

Mohammad's plane ticket to London.

accident. She had a minor burn in her arm and I had no idea who to call and what to do. I knocked at my neighbour's door and used sign language and he was so kind to call the ambulance.

After a while, when Syrian refugees' numbers soared in Turkey, some Turkish charities started doing charitable work to support and help people with language and other matters. Gradually I learned the language. I learned through communication with my fellow workers who were amazed at how fast I gained the language. I learned to speak it within a year and a half. It never occurred to me that I would learn Turkish. I was forced to learn it to survive.

It was the worst part of my life. I feel like my childhood

Photograph taken by Mohammad from the window of the plane taking him to the UK, to reunite with his family.

would be conscripted and taken to serve in the Syrian army and would die. Otherwise, I would be targeted by ISIS or the other forces on the ground in Syria now. I would have no future and no family.

Khalid al Saeed

I think any person responsible for a family, wife and children under very difficult war conditions would take that decision. I was not only concerned about my children and wife, but I was also afraid to stay. The war began with no end in sight. I was fully aware that my children were the first to be affected. Even if they stayed alive their education would be badly affected. After much thinking, I decided to take my family and leave the city. The plan was to take the family away from the conflict and to move to Jordan temporarily until the situation got better. Like many Syrians, I thought that the war would not last long.

We had three children and our fourth child was born in Jordan. My eldest son Mohammad was four years old, his sister was three and my other daughter was one. My eldest son Mohammad suffers from a severe disability. He was born with it. I have a minor neck disability as well.

It was in 2012. Jordan is the closest country. You know Dara'a is located on the border between Syria and Jordan. So the idea was to stay in Jordan for several weeks, a maximum of one month until we could go back home. It never occurred to us that the war would drag on and on and would get so complicated.

The closeness of Jordan to our city encouraged us to go there. You know Jordan is a poor country and the Syrian

and adolescence were taken away. I didn't choose it and I was forced to do it. But I learned a lot in the process. I wish I had learned all those things without the hardships I faced. My mother and sister went through many hardships and they almost lost hope before they made it here. My brother Sulaiman survived a big sea disaster. I was lucky to join my family via an aeroplane. If I'd had no choice but the sea, I would have gone for it, especially after all members of my family had reached the UK. Returning to Syria was not an option at all. In the current situation, it is a disaster. I exodus to Jordan was a big issue. I remember I read in the news about the huge numbers of Syrian refugees who crossed the border to Jordan – around 5,000 Syrian refugees a day! Life was very difficult in Jordan. When Syrian refugees fled to Jordan, the United Nations High Commissioner for Refugees (UNHCR) worked to register the Syrian children in Jordanian state schools. The UNHCR also offered some basic financial support to help people to survive. They offered the minimum help for a human being to stay alive. Even though what they offered was very basic, Syrian refugees were fine with that kind of support as they thought that their stay in Jordan was a temporary matter that would end soon. We were all planning for a short stay. We were all ready to sacrifice and endure whatever hardship we were facing for the sake of our families. For their safety. We were ready to return to our cities at any minute, once the war stopped.

We had lived very well in Dara'a. We had a big and a spacious house. Because Syria is an agricultural country, a country that depends on agriculture for its economy, the standard of living was not very high. House, life, financial aspect – all was good. But the biggest shock for us happened once we moved to Jordan. We found ourselves living in a place less than a quarter of the size of our home in Dara'a. It was very difficult for a family of five to manage without the basic infrastructure. Not only that, but the absence of social solidarity. Losing your home means losing the support of your neighbours, close friends and the social circle you used to have in your country of origin. These were harder to endure than the condition of the house

itself. We suffered a lot and the children suffered with us. Maybe they still hold some memories of our house in Syria. But they spent eight years in Jordan, and I think that they remember that stage and the hardships in Jordan better and clearer than Syria.

In 2017 – that was six years after applying – the UNHCR called me and suggested that I would be resettled in the UK with my family. This was because both my own health condition and that of my son had got worse without proper medical treatment over eight years. They also told me that they had selected me because I took great care of my children and tried hard to educate them despite the difficulties we were facing. So I accepted the UNHCR's offer and we were all so excited. We waited for a second call to inform us of the date of our travel. We had no idea that we would have to wait for almost two years before we could travel to the UK. The worst thing was the endless waiting. We were financially and psychologically devastated. Time was passing and even those people who applied weeks and months after we applied were resettled to the UK.

The UNHCR in Turkey used to update asylum seekers on their website about the progress of their applications and any decisions made. In Jordan there wasn't such a thing at all. I used to visit the UNHCR's office in Amman every now and then for updates. I explained to them that I was on the verge of financial and psychological ruin. At some stage, I even requested them to take my children ahead of me and my wife if that was possible. I really wished that my children would be admitted because I couldn't bear that huge responsibility and the despair I was feeling. No one

'The Weight of Waiting' by Alison Lochhead

gave me any update or feedback. The only response I used to get was: 'It is down to the UK to decide upon your situation and the date of your travel'. I wish that the UK or the UNHCR or any one responsible for refugees and asylum seekers overseas could create a link where refugees can get access to updates. I know a lot of Syrians who had mental breakdowns or committed suicide. I know others who returned to Syria and put themselves and their families under greater risk because they couldn't endure that endless wait in Jordan. They couldn't afford to pay their rent after eight or nine years of waiting. I heard stories of Syrians who were contacted by the UNHCR after returning to Syria. And in that case, they were considered ineligible because they didn't stay in Jordan. I went to the British embassy in Amman and asked for special treatment for my case and they responded negatively. I was on the verge of returning to Syria as that was the only option available. I was torn between taking that decision or staying and waiting. There was only a thin ray of hope which made me endure. I used to think that since we were accepted, we would certainly be resettled at some stage. Updates on our situation would have been a boost to our morale. A 'No' a 'Yes' or anything. If I had any update, I would be happy to wait further and endure more. After two years, I got that phone call and was told to be prepared to fly to Cardiff in June 2019.

Salih Hamza

At the beginning, we were divided into three groups. Some remained in Syria, some fled to Iraq and others to Turkey.

We were in contact with one another through our mobile phones. After two years, those who fled to Iraq managed to get to Turkey and stay there. My other children arrived in Germany leaving me and my wife in Syria until 2015. We then fled to Turkey. We stayed there for another five years during which we had to apply for new passports as our passports were lost during war. One of my sons who left for Germany was eighteen years old and we were eligible to apply for a family reunion by then. That first application didn't work. I had my first surgical operation and I was in a wheelchair when the UN's refugee office called me for an interview. I was deemed to be a priority case due to my health condition. They asked me to provide my sons' registration documents etc. The Office was in touch with my sons and daughters in Germany and they provided them with all the necessary evidence of their residency in Germany. After some time, the UN contacted me to tell me they accepted my family reunion application. There were two, three other interviews about this. They used to send a car and a supportive driver who helped me into the car and put my wheelchair in the car.

After being accepted, my wife and I had to wait for around a year and seven to eight months. Almost two years! After that period, I got a phone call from a UN officer who told me that we would receive our plane tickets that week and would travel on a Friday from Istanbul airport to Germany. That was great news, and we were so pleased that we would finally join the rest of our family. There was a small family celebration. My eldest son, his family, my eldest daughter and her family along with friends and relatives living in Turkey, they all came to say goodbye to us. Friday came. At 4:30 pm the same day, I received a phone call from the UN officer telling me that we had been rejected and wouldn't be allowed to travel to Germany! I was devastated and completely shocked. My whole body was paralysed at that unexpected news.

I was given no explanation. No one gave me a satisfactory answer. I was so confused and shocked. Not only the distress but also the fact that our financial situation in Turkey was so bad. I was unemployed and obviously couldn't work. I also couldn't financially depend on others for long. My son and relatives in Turkey were struggling to manage their own finances. Staying for almost five years in Turkey was a real disaster, a disaster, a disaster. I was physically, psychologically and financially ruined. My sons and daughters begged me to appeal and to reapply, but I didn't. I was so sad and I had lost hope applying and reapplying. The UN suggested to me that I should apply for a temporary visa to go to visit my children. I didn't do it as it wouldn't help.

After a while, I reapplied. I waited for two months to hear from them. After that I was accepted for resettlement in the UK! I was uncomfortable with this decision as I was planning to join my children in Germany. I wished that I could be admitted to a country closer to Germany but that's it. So I came here and got stuck in this country and it looks like it is even more difficult to join my sons and daughters from here. Everything looks difficult. There is also my disability and my health condition.

I am diabetic and I have lived with diabetes for a long time. But I believe that my physical condition deteriorated as a result of the ongoing distress I faced. Losing my children and not knowing where they were, when I was in Syria losing the house and fleeing. Shock after a shock until I lost my health and wellbeing. Not only me, but my wife also. We both were badly affected.

My sons and daughters took the sea journey to Germany. They first fled to Turkey and from there they were smuggled on a boat until they arrived in Germany. We Syrians have experienced death in many forms and shapes. People have lost their lives in that sea journey and some even lost their lives on a road journey. Only the lucky ones have made it. We witnessed all sorts of hardships, war, threats, loss, ISIS, the danger of the sea and many more risks and losses. I always think of how people flee death in Harb (War) to face death in Bahr (Sea).

Both my wife and I were like dead in life and had no clue about our sons and daughters. Now my eldest daughter is living in Turkey with her husband and children and my other son is married and has a kid. He has been trying to join us here in the UK, but it is very difficult. He cannot take the risk of the sea journey. It is too dangerous.

When the war broke my eldest son took his wife and child and fled to Kurdistan, Iraq. When my wife and I arrived in Turkey, I suggested that they join us there to take care of me and of his mother. So, my eldest son and his family were smuggled from Kurdistan to Turkey. But their journey was so risky. They spent twenty days between Iran and Turkey, in the desert area between Iran and Turkey under very cold conditions. Actually it was snowing heavily when they were making that journey. The story of my son is dramatic indeed. During his journey from Iran to Turkey my son and his family made it to a village area in Iran which was well known for being an earthquake zone. One day, at around 7:00 am my son was talking to his mum over the phone and he suddenly cried out saying *Yaba* [Dad] and we lost contact with him. After a few hours we realised that the area had been hit by an earthquake which was the second in a row. We were devastated by that news especially after losing contact with our son and his family. We were sleepless for over four days until we received the good news that they had survived the earthquake that had hit the area and destroyed nearly half of the houses where they were living. Later, they were smuggled to Turkey, but they were badly affected by what they witnessed throughout the journey to Turkey. They don't want to take any more risks. They are not ready to use illegal ways to reach Europe. They prefer to stay in Turkey and wait for a decision on their case than to undertake any dangerous journey.

Latifa Alnajjar

We travelled to Egypt because my brother was there. We hadn't seen him for a while and thought it would be a good opportunity for the family to visit him in Egypt. I was pregnant and the situation in Syria was so difficult. I was worried what would happen if I gave birth amid the chaos. The plan was to spend two months in Egypt to deliver my baby, to see my brother and to return to Syria afterwards. But we couldn't go back to Syria. Conditions had worsened back home, and we stayed in Egypt.

We lived in Egypt for three and a half years. It was good. In the beginning they welcomed us. Egyptians are very kind and nice people. But it was very difficult in terms of residency permits. It was too difficult for the Syrians to get residency permits in Egypt. In order to get one, we had to pay a large amount of money. My husband got a temporary job. You know, you can't stay in Egypt without work. We applied for asylum through the UNHCR. They helped us financially, but we couldn't depend on that. You had to work to pay the rent and living expenses. My husband worked as a taxi driver and he received several fines just because he was a Syrian.

Rama was two years old when I left Syria. It was her birthday when we left, and I was nine months into my second pregnancy. When I gave birth in Egypt, the UNHCR paid the expenses for my delivery. So my second daughter Masa was born in an Egyptian hospital and they were so kind and nice to me in that hospital, *Alhamdulillah*.

Once we arrived in Egypt, we registered with the UNHCR for legal reasons because we couldn't get our residency permit in Egypt. Once you get the UN's yellow card you will be protected in terms of residency. This same challenge was faced by Syrians who went to Jordan and elsewhere. The yellow card was the only legal option.

It took us nearly three years. During that time, we had to renew the yellow card every now and then. I was willing to be resettled in a place in Europe for my children's future. I was certain that my children would have no future in Egypt. I wouldn't be able to secure a good life for my children like my life back in Syria before the war. The UN contacted me and asked if I was willing to travel and I confirmed my intention to travel. It was a dream. I said 'OK' but I was accompanied by my *Mama* and *Baba* [parents] whom I couldn't leave behind. They were living with us in Egypt. We were interviewed over a year by the UNHCR. In the beginning they allocated us to the US and later they moved our files to the UK.

They gave us documents, but they didn't explain where in the UK. Our destination was Bristol. I did some research on Bristol and thought we would be living there. It turned out that it was Bristol airport and not Bristol city. Once we arrived in Bristol, I thought that that was it. It was a difficult journey. When we left Egypt – we left as one family – but no one accompanied us from the UNHCR. Usually a member of their staff accompanies refugees. Our language wasn't that good, and we were told to travel on board of a German aeroplane. No English language to help us. We were scattered all over the plane. My husband and I were seated in one place, my mother was in another seat, my father was seated somewhere else. My kids were seated separately from us. We were not treated as one unit. That moment, I was so scared, especially because I had to leave my sisters behind in Egypt. They were married and we couldn't apply for them to accompany us.

I was already burdened with the grief of being separated from my sisters. The confusion over our seats made it worse. The darkness of night – it was around 1:30 am – and the language. No one understood us. We couldn't speak to the stewards and I didn't know what to do. But then one passenger who spoke English offered to help us arrange our seats. The plane took off and we arrived in Germany around 6:00 am. We stayed at the airport from 6:00 am to 3:00 pm. It was a very tiring journey and it was so sad. I was scared because I didn't know where I was going. Especially when I was about to leave Egypt. Leaving my sisters behind was so hard. I was happy that I was heading towards a better life for my family and a future for my children. But I was distressed at the thought of leaving my sisters and wondering whether I would ever see them again. These thoughts were in my head. When we arrived in Germany, we were so tired. We sat on the chairs in the airport. We were introduced to a Syrian family who arrived from Jordan. They were accompanied by a UN officer who helped us a lot and directed us to the next steps.

The UN official accompanied us and the other family. He was with us when we took the second flight to Bristol airport. Once we arrived in Bristol, we thought that Bristol was the destination. We had no idea that there would be another stage. The UN officer then handed us to members of the British Red Cross holding placards with our family names on them. There were interpreters with them who introduced us to the others and took us to the coach. On board the coach, I had no idea where we were heading. I was so exhausted. Looking around, it was so dark – around 6:00 am, the 1st of November. It was winter. It was very cold. It was summer when we left Egypt and we came to cold weather.

Bristol Airport © Lewis Clarke, CC BY 2.0

Life in Wales

"Home is a sanctuary, safety, settlement. A place where you feel free and can express yourself freely. This is home. Syria is my first home, but the place that offers you all these elements is your real home."

Ronahi Hassan

It was 2009 when we arrived here. We left in 2008 and by the time we arrived it was just before the new year of 2009. We were on the road for many hours. I remember we arrived in Wales at around 1:30 or 2:00 am. We were taken to a hotel. As it was a very early hour in the day, the hotel staff were asleep. Someone came to hand towels and bedding to the people accompanying us. We were taken to a hostel next to the hotel. Our room was on the second floor. A room with four bunk beds. There was a small bathroom. They told me this is your room now, gave me the bedding and left. I woke up next morning and looked out of the window. The street and the houses looked too old.

Yes, it was Cardiff. When I saw that view, I had the feeling that I had been brought to another country, that this wasn't Britain. The old houses, the terrible condition of the accommodation. It was dirty and old. I couldn't understand anything of what they were saying. I thought I had some basics which would help me, but I discovered that my basics were nothing. I couldn't understand. Perhaps their accent was different. I had no idea about the system, the plan and what they were up to. I had no clue at all. Before taking the flight, I was told that I would be landing in Heathrow airport.

When we arrived, I didn't even know it was Heathrow. I was so frightened, stressed – looking at my children and thinking of their future. A future that was unknown to me. I had zero concentration on anything else. In a nutshell, I had no idea where I was and what would happen next. When I woke up in the morning and saw the houses around, the street, the condition of the room, I thought I was in an African country, another country. I was so scared. I cried out loud and was wondering what I had done to myself! I was suspicious that I had been taken to another country. I blamed myself for not being aware of what was happening.

I quickly changed my children's clothes. I planned to go to the hotel, where we had stopped by the night before. I wanted to ask someone, to find out which country I was in. To make sure it was Britain. My children and I walked around. I was looking around to find someone who might understand my language. I couldn't express myself. Suddenly, I heard voices of young men using Sorani Kurdish. I thought they were from Kurdistan, from Iraq. They were in the hotel, the same hotel we stopped by the night before. I think it was full of families and that's why I had been taken to an adjacent building. I tried my best to explain. But again, the Sorani dialect was very different from my dialect. Fortunately, one of the men spoke Badini Kurdish which is very close to my Kurmanji dialect. I asked him which country was this? He said, 'You are in Cardiff.' And I was like 'What! Cardiff?' He said: 'Wales.' And I became more confused: 'Wales!!' Then he explained. He said, 'This is in Britain.' That word. That moment. It changed my mood completely. I said: *Alhamdulillah*. He explained the map of the UK to me.

It was very difficult to contact family at that stage. I had no idea what was happening back home. My family had no clue about me or if I had made the journey. I remember when I was in the car at night, I was crying all the way from Heathrow to Wales. When the car stopped for a break, people approached me. They asked if I was hungry or thirsty. I couldn't stop crying and I think they were wondering why that was. Perhaps they were trying to comfort me. Sadly, the language barrier – I was so stressed and so frightened. It was a very difficult situation. The uncertainty. It was a mixture of fear, sadness, humiliation. I was thinking about the reasons behind leaving. Hozan, the eldest, was thirteen to fourteen years old. Rawan was younger, and my daughter Eman was nine years old. They were little children. They needed some comfort in that situation. They were shocked. I am sure they had many questions in their heads when I was crying constantly

throughout the journey. Perhaps they wanted to help me but they couldn't.

I was told that it was just a matter of a few days in that hostel, yet we spent about a month there. Afterwards, we were taken to Swansea. During that period, I was introduced to a young Syrian Kurdish man. He was newly married, and his wife couldn't speak English. She had no family or friends. We became friends and they used to visit me from time to time. I wanted to stay in Cardiff, and I told the Refugee Council that I was willing to stay in Cardiff. I made friends with that family and was pleased to meet them. We were from the same country, and we had the same background and spoke the same language. The Council refused. They told me that it was the Home Office's decision that I should move to Swansea. So, I moved to Swansea. Swansea is a lovely city. I made friends with people from Sudan, Jordan and Lebanon. It was a nice stage. I consider Swansea as the stage of action. Swansea was the beginning of a journey to improve myself.

Being in a foreign country, a different culture, a different language, you long to meet people who speak your language. This would certainly minimise feelings of isolation and alienation. In Swansea there was a caseworker who came to visit me on my first day there. She was accompanied by an interpreter. I asked if he could introduce me to a Kurdish family with whom I could build some contacts. He gave me details of a Turkish Kurd lady who was also new to Swansea. That was a good beginning for me. She didn't live too far away. We became good friends, and we are still friends to this day. We are close friends. She was just what I was looking for in a friend. An educated and open-minded person. And that minimised the feeling of exile. But my plan was to learn and to improve my life. I had arrived in this country, and I considered myself part of this country. I had a responsibility to learn about the country, to interact and integrate.

When I settled in Swansea, I thought that my life was going to be better. But it turned out to be very difficult. I was wearing the headscarf when I came to this country and there was a lot of racism again. The council offered me a house in a neighbourhood in Swansea, a place that doesn't suit a newcomer to the country. I was placed in an area that is well known for violence. It is a place for drugs. Believe me, every day, every single day there was an action film in front of my house. Every day police and emergency forces were present in front of my house. My children were bullied daily. My eldest Hozan was calmer and quieter. But my other son Rawan used to defend himself. One day he came back from school with his leg bleeding. When I asked him what had happened, I realised that my children had been beaten many times before, but they hadn't told me. Pupils used to form gangs. Maybe my children didn't realise that was bullying. Maybe they were scared. They never told me about it. I used to encourage them to go out and to play in the park. They didn't want to. I realised later that they were afraid of bullying. I had no idea. That day, my son Rawan had been hit by a metal maths compass. A boy had hit him on his leg with a metal compass. That incident made me realise that there was a group of schoolboys who

Swansea City Centre. Photo J WILLIAMS (CC-BY-SA/2.0)

would hit my children after school, every day. The children hadn't mentioned anything to me.

Once I learned about it, I was devastated. I was so hurt. I called my caseworker and the interpreter. Sadly, my caseworker couldn't do much about it. I had two appointments with the school, but the school couldn't stop it. That was so disappointing. One day I met a Lebanese person, to whom I am so grateful. He told me that my children's school was one of the worst in Swansea and he advised me to move my children to another school. It was hard for me to think that such things happened in the UK. I asked him to give me a list of schools where I could move my children. He drafted a letter for me to explain the situation to the new school. It took me a while to be able to find the right school. I suffered. I suffered alone. On top of that, there was the terrible condition of the house I was living in. Drunks and addicts used to knock at my door. They shouted, asking me to open the door. My children were so scared. Fearful moments. So sad. This made me realise that I had to depend on myself. I learned a lot from my experience with the children's school and my house.

I worked as a volunteer. In that role I used to travel from Swansea to Port Talbot. I used to travel daily. It was a charity to help children with disabilities. I was so glad to work there as a first step for me. I was pleased to be able to learn through that role. There was a big community in Swansea, and I worked with them as well. When the incidents of the drunks kicking my door was repeated, I called the police, but they didn't respond. It was terrible for my children and for me. I found some organisations to help me with that. It was a terrible environment in which to raise children. Not only the drunks, but I also experienced a racist incident. I was walking in the same area when a car stopped near me. There were two young men inside. One of them lowered his window and was swearing at me. I didn't understand. But it was obvious because he spat at me. I was wearing the headscarf in a modern way. It didn't look like the traditional scarf. But I think the colour of my skin could tell them I was different. That harassing incident bothered me a lot. But I decided to ignore it completely as a one-off incident. Sadly, two days later, the same car with the same people stopped by and did the same thing. This is the first time that I have spoken about this. At that stage I had no idea that I

should call the police. I had no idea that incidents like that are considered harassment! When you are new to the country, when you don't know the language, you don't have the key to things. You just don't know.

"I had arrived in this country, and I considered myself part of this country. I had a responsibility to learn about the country, to interact and integrate."

My number one priority was my children's school and my attempts to move them to a better one. I was also worried about the location of my house and was trying to move out. It took me a lot of time, energy and a lot of effort to be able to move out. It was very difficult. I was an asylum seeker, and the law doesn't allow asylum seekers to change their residence. But the police report and the checks on my house helped to convince the council to move me to another area. I also succeeded in moving my children to a different school. We were moved to a better area. It was so much better. I moved my children to another school. They got to a stage where they excelled in their school and their photos were placed in the school's hallway. Also, when we moved to Cardiff later, the teachers were very happy with them. In Swansea, the interpreter told me that the school was so proud of my children's achievement. In the beginning, I depended on the interpreter for almost everything. Later, I decided to depend on myself for translation.

My house was at the corner of the street. There was a distance between my house and the neighbours' houses. But my next-door neighbours were an old couple. They were nice and quiet. I cooked them some dishes, and they liked the food and were happy. To be honest, I had no time to interact with the neighbours. I was busy walking my children to and from school and volunteering. I was running around. Later I made friends and I also tried to make the most of my free time by attending some courses here and there. I signed up to a couple of courses at the university. Sometimes I couldn't understand half of what was in the course, but I was trying. Slowly, I made friends with English speakers and other nationalities. I became used to the system and was coping with life. Slowly and gradually my language improved through my volunteering roles in Swansea. The courses I joined helped to increase my knowledge of the culture and the language. Also, at home, I used to search for information online after I had put my children to bed.

All those steps took around a year and a half before my husband was able to join us. Then we had our residency status in the country. It was a very difficult stage for my husband, as he couldn't interact with people in Swansea. We didn't meet anyone from Syria in Swansea. My husband started looking for a job. He has a university degree in sciences. As you know, it is very difficult to use your degrees in this country. Back home, he worked as a teacher and then he opened a trade business. He had an office for exports and imports services. But here, he faced a great challenge in finding a job. Not getting the right

employment in Swansea, not knowing the language has increased his isolation. Because of these reasons, we decided to move to Cardiff. He believed that Cardiff would open better employment opportunities and would enable

The Hassans' Cardiff restaurant. © Ronahi Hassan

him to make friends and increase his social network. So we moved to Cardiff. I think it was in 2011.

Relocating to Cardiff wasn't an easy thing either. I had to do all that on my own again because my husband was new in the UK and had no idea of how things worked. By then, my English language had improved, and I was responsible for everything. For instance, searching for a good area to live, a good school. We finally found accommodation in the Roath area. My children were registered at a good school but that too was not easy. Gradually we settled well, and my husband opened a takeaway shop. My husband had no previous experience in the takeaway business. He was introduced to an experienced person in the field, and this was how it started. We became business partners with that man. In the meantime, I continued my volunteering in Cardiff and I joined many educational courses at the university. Then I decided to start a university course and it

The interior of the restaurant © Ronahi Hassan

took me a long time to fulfil the requirements. I did my IELTS, and I did all the levels of ESOL language learning requirements. I passed all the language tests for the ESOL *Alhamdulillah*. Then I was admitted to university and started my course! It was a three-year full-time course. The same year my husband opened a restaurant. It was the first Syrian restaurant to open in City Road. We had a special cuisine. We made a unique design for the restaurant. The walls were decorated with crystals. And there were portraits on the walls. It was called al Rayan restaurant. The style of our restaurant was new and creative compared to the existing restaurants in the area. It wasn't very common to have a restaurant with crystal decorations. Also, the food was brilliant. The first two months were a great hit. We were very successful in the beginning. It was so special because my husband and I planned every single piece in that restaurant. I used to study and help with the restaurant. Even when I had a late lecture at the university I had to go to the restaurant before going home. Every single stage we passed through involved an amount of effort, energy, and time. I am so proud of what we did.

My children grew up. They went to university, and my son and I graduated in the same year from university. My children and my husband were very proud. On the day when I went to receive my graduation gown, there was a young man to hand us the gowns. He thought that I was one of the parents because of the age gap. My colleagues were the age of my children! He told me: 'This is a students' room' and I said: 'I am a student.' We were queuing to get our certificates on the stage and the lady who was taking care of us and instructing us before mounting the stage focussed on me. She took longer with me than with the other students and I was wondering why. I heard my name, I went on the stage, shook hands with the professors. I heard them announcing: 'The University's Journalism Award goes to Ronahi Hassan.' It was a wonderful feeling. I had goosebumps. My husband and children were on the second floor watching me from above. It was indescribable. Under the gown I was wearing my traditional Kurdish costume. It was my statement about all the things I couldn't achieve in Syria. Perhaps it was my cry against oppression. I put on the Kurdish costume to say it loud that I have been nationally persecuted. The injustice and the persecution I experienced. After I was given the award and the certificate, I dashed out of the hall, and I cried hysterically. My colleagues were hugging me. I had made a vow to myself to get that degree whatever happened, and I made it.

Ronahi on her graduation day, courtesy of Ronahi Hassan

"Under the gown I was wearing my traditional Kurdish costume. It was my statement about all the things I couldn't achieve in Syria. Perhaps it was my cry against oppression."

It was a challenging situation. I am saying this for the first time. Women in Syria have experienced a lot of injustices. Our society works against women. Even though I grew up in an open-minded family, the community was so conservative. Because there were no universities in our region, it was very difficult for women to travel for their university education. There was a lot of gossip and a lot of judgements against women trying to travel to other cities for their university studies. We were victimised by that mentality. My graduation from the University of South Wales has brought to a conclusion all that experience of injustice and persecution. Getting that degree was a dream come true.

I am finding it very difficult to fulfil my dream and it is getting more difficult. Two years after getting my degree from the University of South Wales I was chosen as a winner of 2017 Wales Media Award. I wrote critical reports on the war in Syria, terrorism, and the politics of the country. I did my work experience at important media hubs like BBC Wales, BBC London, and ITV Wales. I also worked as a freelancer with Channel 4. I prepared a very important report for Channel 4 and I helped them, through my connections in Syria, to shoot in Syria. I helped to arrange the whole journey. I was supposed to accompany the crew, but it was too risky for me at that stage. In my work placement with Channel 4, I was acting as an informal advisor to the journalists here and in Syria. I wrote reports on Islam in Syria, I was interviewed by the BBC, and I talked a lot about the situation back home. I worked as a freelance analyst with the BBC at one stage. I wrote journalistic reports to the Western Mail Wales and to Wales Online. I thought that this career would enable me to get a job opportunity in the same field. I was so disappointed that colleagues of my children's age were employed.

[I have made] a documentary film. But no one has helped me to get this film out to the public. The film is about a very urgent situation regarding refugees and the international silence towards the Syrian regime. The world has become deaf and dumb towards the regime's policy. It is about a few Syrian refugees in Denmark who are about to be returned to Syria because 'it has become safe.' I can't see any logic behind considering Syria as a 'safe country'. I heard the news about those refugees, but I wasn't completely sure. So, I decided to make the journey to Denmark to film what was going on. I have commissioned everything from planning to travelling to everything else. I worked on the film, and I have just finished it, but no channel is willing to take it. The same scenario happened with my graduation project. It was about opening up opportunities for refugees

to thrive. The film was about an Iranian wrestler. I presented my film to the BBC and other channels. They liked it but they didn't give me the OK. I realised that the timing wasn't good, as it was during Brexit. The wrestler won many wrestling competitions and raised the Welsh flag in many places. His dream was to play in the Commonwealth games, but he wasn't allowed because of his refugee status. The man won several sport medals. He came to the UK with no English and no future and succeeded in sports and won medals. I worked hard on many projects and gathered very important information from Syria about sensitive topics, but no one helped me in this regard. I am still hoping that a chance will come my way at some point.

I am so proud of my children. My husband and I worked hard to support them, and it all paid off in the end. My two sons have graduated from university *Alhamdulillah*. My eldest one is still looking for the right job. His brother has got a job. And my daughter Eman is still studying. As to Syria – my children were deprived of their original home. They were deprived of the feeling of a big family. My husband and I tried our best to replace that big family, their uncles, aunts, cousins, which they miss back home. They speak very good Kurdish, and they speak Arabic as well. Even though my daughter Eman spent only one year in school back home, she understands Arabic, and she writes in Arabic too. My sons can speak and write in Arabic. They have good memories of back home and they love Syria. But they feel more at home here as they have been away from Syria for about 13 years now. It is quite a long time for a child to grow away from their own country. But I am struck by how they still maintain certain things from that culture. Of course, we tried to encourage them to integrate and interact with the British society and the British way of life. However, they didn't change completely. I am so pleased that my children are keeping most of the traditions and the customs which we grew up with. They love Syrian food a lot. When I compare my sons with boys their age back home, who gave up on so many traditions and customs. My children are still clinging to these customs, and they are proud of this.

So many things have changed. When I came here, I was wearing a headscarf which I took off later. But this didn't mean that I had changed. It didn't change my attitude. Now if one of my children wants to get married to a person from another nationality or ethnic group,I need to be prepared for that. As a woman from the Middle East, I used to have limited responsibility. Here in the UK, the responsibility has doubled. I think that we, the refugee generations who came recently, have been trying very hard to build a life to our children. I was telling my husband the other day that we are a generation who sacrificed ourselves. I wish we could just enjoy the new reality, but I don't think that we will enjoy it. We have suffered and will suffer, but I hope that our children will be fine later. There are so many things which I came to realise here. I think the democratic atmosphere has given me the chance to express myself better here. It had a big effect on the way I view things. I feel like I am more accepting of others. When I travelled to Denmark and made my documentary, almost all the Syrians affected by the Danish decision were Syrian Arabs. When I filmed them, I wasn't thinking of ethnicity. All that

mattered was to present an issue about the people of my country. It was also a surprise to them. They didn't expect a Syrian Kurd to come and talk about them. In Denmark, I reconciled with myself. I felt proud of myself, to be able to do that. And I felt sorry about the history of not accepting the other back home. Politics played a role and created enmity between the two ethnicities. I really felt like we just want our Syria back. A country for all. We are fed up of the empty slogans. We want our children to live in peace. We spent a lifetime with this situation and for how much longer? I know it is very difficult to have our country back, but we still have a glimmer of hope.

"Countries which have opened doors to refugees are not going to lose anything.We refugees are grateful for what you did for us, and you will benefit from us."

Earlier you asked me a question about the meaning of home. Home is a sanctuary, safety, settlement. A place where you feel free and can express yourself freely. This is home. Syria is my first home. But the place that offers you all these elements is your real home. I still have a small farm in Syria. Currently, it is under the Syrian regime's control. I wish that I could go for a visit with my husband and children and enjoy sitting in that farm. It is my identity, my past, my roots and I cannot eliminate that history. I moved between countries, but my history is there. I feel like that history and that farm is what makes me. I wish that Syria could become a country ruled by law and nothing but law. The country can accommodate us all.

And as to anyone who blames refugees for leaving their country, I tell them we left because of the amount of injustice and persecution we faced. We had good lives, houses etc. But our dirty, racist politicians stole everything. They stole happiness. And when we came here it wasn't a paradise at all. On the contrary, we suffered and are still suffering. We faced challenges to be able to cope with life here. We still need to do more and more to be able to build a life. I just want to tell everyone that these countries which have opened doors to refugees are not going to lose anything. We refugees are grateful for what you did for us, and you will benefit from us. Diversity and accepting diversity will benefit societies. Refugees are great people. They risk their lives, head to the unknown and do their best to build their lives. This country must be proud of any refugee who has succeeded in building a life from scratch.

M H

In the Middle East I worked as a dental surgeon. Currently I am trying to get my licence to practise as a dental surgeon here. It can be a very complicated process. It has been three to four years for me trying to resolve this. However, I have done different jobs. At the moment, I'm starting a business in a related field with a friend of mine and I do interpretation work for the NHS.

We have three girls now: one seven years old, a three-year-old and a one-month baby girl. When my wife and I

Dentistry students at Cardiff University. © Cardiff University

came to the UK, it was just the two of us. Then we created our family here in the UK as all my daughters were born here. We arrived on 13 October 2012. It was a student Tier 4 Visa for me, and my wife accompanied me on a dependant Visa. My wife did some academic English language courses when we arrived and once she was more confident with the academic aspect, she applied for a master's degree in Speech Therapy at Sheffield University. She is in her writing up stage and almost done. I did a master's degree in Dental Surgery and Dental Implants at Cardiff University based on a research project. I am happy to pursue this line and get involved in research as far as my specialism is concerned. I enrolled on an online course in November 2020 which will train us senior dentists to train junior dentists. I would love to get involved in something like this because that is what I studied. When we moved from Cardiff to the West Midlands last year in July 2019, I moved because I got an offer of a job with an Italian company that manufactures dental implants, which is my specialism. I was the deputy manager of the project until the Covid-19 crisis started. Sadly the company made newly appointed employees redundant and I was one of them, so I worked there for almost nine months and then was made redundant. But I always think that things happen for a reason and perhaps for the best. I try to be positive as much as I can and hopefully things will get better.

Even though I lost that job it opened up a new opportunity for me. I have started a new business with my friend in London. Maybe if I had remained in my comfort zone in the previous job, I would never have the chance of starting my own business, so I consider it a very good step forward rather than a step back. I always believe that once we try hard, windows open other windows and doors open other doors. We live in Solihull where Birmingham airport is located. I must say it was a big decision for us to take.

When we first arrived in 2012, we landed in London and we came straightaway to Cardiff because I needed to start my studies on the following Monday at Cardiff University. One thing led to another and we lived in Cardiff for seven years. We had our first two girls in Cardiff. They were both born in the hospital where I trained. We are very attached to Cardiff and to Wales generally. Our eldest daughter has already started speaking Welsh. When a friend of hers has a birthday party, she still sings it in Welsh, *penblwydd hapus* instead of happy birthday. Yes indeed, we all have a strong attachment to Wales and it was so hard for us to think of leaving it. But we had to weigh the pros and cons and eventually we decided to leave. Because when I was in Cardiff, I was working in academia and in student support, invigilating and supporting students etc. My wife was also doing some volunteering and casual jobs to gain a broader experience in her field and elsewhere. But that was not enough to support the family. So, after seven years of working here and there, I got that offer with a five-year contract, which was so attractive. We thought it was the right time for us to move because, if we waited until my daughters got older, it would become more difficult. Believe it or not, my daughter was five when we moved from Cardiff and she still feels very committed to her friends and to the place. We still visit Cardiff from time to time. We were there last night to attend a small wedding event for one of our friends. It was for just a few people. Before the lockdown, we used to visit our friends in Cardiff every fortnight. We have some close friends there who are like family to us.

I believe that big achievements happen outside one's comfort zone, even though people don't like change and resist it. The moment you move out of your comfort zone, you will be more creative and will consider a wider scope of options. And that's exactly what happened with us when we moved here. We came to this country on a student's visa, and not for a second did I imagine that I would remain here. The plan in 2012 was to come here, get my master's degree and probably just extend it for another year and go back. Our plan was to finish our studies and go back. We were thinking of risking going back to another country, Jordan, Saudi Arabia or Turkey and even Syria. To be honest, back in 2012 the Syrian situation wasn't as bad as it is now. There was a hope that things would change despite the escalation. It wasn't a burned land like now. The curse of being Syrians, just being a Syrian, was enough for us to be forced down this route that we have taken. And we are grateful, as it is the best thing that has happened to us and it is still better than any place we have been to. We don't feel that we don't belong here at all. My children don't see anywhere other than the UK to be their country. If you ask my eldest child 'Where are you from?' she would not say Syria. She would say 'I am from Cardiff'. Ask her again, she would say Wales or Britain. And the reason she says that is because no one has made her feel otherwise. In this country, no one can make you feel different and that's the beauty of a country that has values. Even though we are in the process of becoming citizens, we feel we belong here, a feeling that we didn't have for the countries we were born and brought up in.

We suffered a lot. The economic and political insecurity that Syria was suffering from in the 1970s and 1980s – that suffering is clearly seen now because of the social media that helped the whole world to see the brutal side of the situation. Hundreds of Syrian families were back and forth between Syria and their country of residence and that led to generations of offspring who are very confused and don't know where to go. They hold a Syrian citizenship that is a heavy burden on them. I raise my kids to be proud British as well as proud of their Syrian culture and where their parents came from. They must belong here, and they must also keep a sense of belonging to their motherland, otherwise they will be ignorant. If they ignore Syria, they will ignore the UK, the country where they were born, and the country of citizenship. After all, they are learning and getting their education here and will be contributing to this society. I sometimes think that things might change and my children will be able to contribute to rebuilding their parents' country.

This object hanging here, it is a handmade stitching of a Qur'anic verse made in Aleppo. We have something we call the box of treasure which contains the gifts I used to give to my wife which are very related to Syria. We show the children the contents and the stories behind them. And photos of what Syria was like and photos of family, relatives and friends back in Syria with descriptions of places. We speak English and we teach them Arabic at home and we take them to an Arabic school once a week. It is a bit of a struggle, I must say. But they will get there as we are raising them bilingual. When we were in Wales, my eldest daughter was raised trilingual as she was in a Welsh school. So, Welsh, English and Arabic. My children's English is better than their Arabic, especially with the little one. The eldest is putting more effort into learning her Arabic and is getting better. But the little one, she doesn't understand our slang and is struggling with the Arabic letters. Hopefully, we will keep them interested in it because if they lose interest in it, they will lose it. So, we are trying to keep teaching them and make it fun and simple. And one of the good things – it is a black comedy actually – when we go to meet the rest of the family in Turkey or in Germany, because my brother lives there with his family, the common language between all these kids will have to be Arabic. Because the ones in Turkey are coming from the Middle East and they speak Arabic and those in Germany do not use English. So, when we go there, my children practise Arabic a bit. And they started to realise that Arabic will enable them to play, communicate with the other kids and so on. Otherwise, it would be sign language! This is the case with many Syrian families: a brother in Canada and another in Spain etc. and they can't but use their original Arabic language as a medium of communication.

We intentionally let my daughter watch a programme on Netflix, released I think last year, and the lady behind it won a BAFTA award. I skipped the tough scenes and let her watch the struggle – how the woman in the film got from one house to another within less than a mile and had to pass through three security checkpoints. And how they lived for a month boiling old rice and clearing the insects from their rice before cooking. I told her this is how it is in Syria and it was never like this before, and it will be back to where it used to be. I explained to her why we can't go back. I deliberately showed her pictures of the family's summer house in Zabadani where I had my best memories of the time before the war, and what the place looks like after the war. Those photos were taken by friends and sent to me via their phones. You can see where a tank has passed by and caused damage, or a fence was hit by a bomb. A battlefield. My daughter became very emotional and sometimes she cries when we tell her these stories. She is a very sensitive girl and I think now she understands the importance of the values she has been taught in school here. The values of tolerance, freedom and respect. If it wasn't for these values, everywhere in the earth would be the same as Syria. She has become aware that because they messed with these values, it led to that destruction. So she cherishes these values more and more and has a great love and sympathy for Syria.

I was aware that unless there was a complete root change to the political system of Syria, things wouldn't change. I had to think of alternatives. I was already thinking of carrying out my postgraduate studies in my field. I was very interested in open dental surgery and in dental implants. I was in touch with several institutes in the USA, Canada, New Zealand and Australia and mainly English-speaking countries because my undergraduate curriculum was in English. Eventually, I settled on Cardiff University at the Dental Implants Programme.

Because of visa issues, we arrived in Cardiff one month later than expected. I had a reservation for student accommodation, and it was gone because of the delay we faced. So we stayed in a hotel and started looking for accommodation and it was a stressful time. We were looking for accommodation and worrying about the family in Syria, as the situation was deteriorating fast. My supervisor was very kind and was always checking on us. To be honest, I struggled a lot during my study because it coincided with the worsening of the political situation back home. I am grateful for the support I had from the university at that time. After one month at the hotel, we found a flat in north Cardiff close to the hospital where I was studying. My wife was trying to settle things in the new flat and it took her a couple of weeks. Once we settled, she signed up at an English language course to refine her academic English skills. She studied for her undergraduate degree in English and her language was fine. But we wanted her to be at a higher language level to prepare her for a degree which she did eventually. So, she signed up at a good English language institute in Cardiff and she spent three to

Match day at Cardiff – Boycezone by Jeremy Segrott (CC BY 2.0)

four months there, enjoyed it, learned a lot and made friends. Afterwards, she did her academic IELTS and had a score that allowed her to do a master's degree in speech difficulties at Sheffield university. It is a part-time study and now she is in the writing up stage for her dissertation.

I must admit that the first ten days or two weeks, it was a bit of a culture shock because I think we made a mistake. We made a reservation in a hotel in the city centre. It was at the Royal Hotel, very close to the Millennium Stadium. The other side of the road is Queen Street, I think, and it was during the rugby matches! It was just like going to an ongoing street circus outside. Then we realised that this is what it is like when there is a match. People have fun and go out and we got used to it. But when we first arrived, we were exhausted, worried, and very confused. Suddenly, we found ourselves amid a crazy atmosphere where people drink, dance, and throw their litter everywhere. In the beginning, we were thinking to ourselves that this is the norm perhaps. Later, we realised that things get crazy only during the matches. We ourselves went to rugby matches after that and we enjoyed it and loved it as we are both into sport.

The other issue was the difficulty of securing accommodation because you know how complicated it is in the UK. A guarantor, a reference and a history etc. Despite the complications, we managed to overcome them thanks to some nice people who helped us with that. We got around that issue by making an upfront payment of six months to secure a rent. Adjusting to the expensive life in the UK was not an easy thing at all because of the difference in the currency value, but we eventually adjusted to that. While waiting for our accommodation papers to finalise, we had to move from our expensive hotel to the Ibis budget hotel in the city centre. It was a difficult time when we were still at hotels, not settled, while exams were taking place. Luckily, my supervisor was so supportive and had a lot of sympathy for us and helped us a lot. I must admit that the situation had a bad effect on my performance and caused some delays in my submission. Later, I caught up with everything and the wheels turned again. I came to realise that everything happens for a reason, as the delay and the extension I got allowed me to work on more cases and get more clinical experience. We have been to many cities all over the UK – as far as Sheffield in the north, Brighton in the south and Tenby in west Wales. In most places we felt extremely welcomed and we had no issues at all in Cardiff. People in Cardiff, from different backgrounds, are very friendly. Our neighbours and colleagues, whether they were co-workers or students, were very nice and things went very smoothly.

I believe in Karma and what goes around comes around. When I first came here, I needed someone to guide me, show me what to do and what not to do, what to buy, where to go. I needed all that and it didn't come easy. I feel for the newcomers. My wife and I came across many families and couples who are now very successful academically and professionally and some of them even got their British citizenship before us! They were luckier than us in the process, in the documentation. I didn't come across other nationals other than Syrians who were looking for emotional support. I think the reason may be because they have a stronger community organisation that gives that support. So, you would rarely see a Sudanese looking for help, as his community would immediately take him in and provide help. Also, Yemenis or Iraqis. I helped a family find accommodation within twenty-four hours! Because when we met them, we had been living in Cardiff for four or five years and we had been able to build a network.

Unfortunately, we are not very organised on social media, at least not at that time. Maybe now we are better. You will find a few active groups on Facebook. You can post your problem and be contacted by someone about a solution. We are getting better and are heading slowly towards getting to a level of informal community support. In my time, five or six years ago, we would come across someone by complete coincidence: when you went to the

Friday prayer, on the way out or through someone you know. Sometimes at a Falafel restaurant when the one serving you is a new Syrian arrival and he introduces himself. We Syrians, we are usually proud, so we do it indirectly by giving a hidden message that I am reaching out to you. Maybe with me it was like that. To be honest, there is a very active charity that provided English language courses. My wife attended those courses for her preparation for her IELTS test. It's DPIA [Displaced People in Action]. It's run by a church and they are helping displaced people to get back into their professional life. They mainly focus on medical doctors. But they have a scheme to support doctors to have their exams in the English language and get the tests for the GMC [General Medical Council] done by covering the fees. They helped many people I know. My wife and I have met some Syrians through that charity during the courses. Most recently, there is a very strong organisation called RefuAid which helps you to practise your profession again in the UK. They helped connect me with some people. Sometimes it is word of mouth that connects you to people.

Before coming to the UK, I thought that my English was very good and strong in terms of vocabulary and grammar. But I was surprised that this wasn't the case as I did struggle with the local accent. But that got easier with time when you blend in with people. I even caught a little bit of the Welsh accent before leaving Cardiff. The language was practised daily, so we became better in English day by day and our confidence in communication became higher. And it is still getting better. Sometimes my daughter will correct me with the pronunciation of some words. She tells me 'Daddy, it is not this it is that.' Even though I got a master's degree from this country, I am aware that I would never be able to speak the correct accent as well as my kids. But my wife and I are proud of our English which enabled us to be friends with natives and work and study. For many others I met, it was a nightmare because Syria is not an English-speaking country. Most schools teach French and Arabic. English can be a confusing language and people didn't feel the need to speak or to practise it in Syria. The university curriculum is all in Arabic and unless you are specialising in English language, you don't use it. Syrians who come directly from Syria would struggle in English.

Once in a while, my wife and I tell each other that we have been in this country for eight years now, which is still less than one third of our life. We feel we belong here more than anywhere else. Not to our place of birth, nor to our country of origin. We feel it here. Why is that? No one made us feel we are different from them. When you apply for a driving licence you get it like everyone else; when you get a council tax bill, it is like everyone else; when you call the police, they respond to you like everyone else; when your children are accepted in schools, not for a second would you feel that you don't belong. Also, I would say, it is the decency and respect for common values that human beings should be getting. Here in the UK, you get that. So, that teaches you and shows you why and how you can feel that you belong to this country. We never suffered racism. Yes, it happened once when I was working, but that's a rare occasion and you get bad apples anywhere and

everywhere. That doesn't mean you don't belong to the place. There is no systematic method in this country that makes you feel that you don't belong to it, which you can find in other countries unfortunately.

"We feel we belong here more than anywhere else. Not to our place of birth, nor to our country of origin. We feel it here."

In this country, in my children's school, they encourage you to celebrate the spirit of your origins and your background. Being Asian, Arab, Jew, Muslim or a Hindu is cherished as an important value by the British community. We are very proud of showing that we are Muslims and we are encouraged to do so. This you cannot see in Saudi Arabia. When I was there, I was trying my best to show that I spoke their local accent and dressed like them to make them believe that I belonged. But I was never welcomed. Even in Syria, my country, I was sometimes trying to show that I knew high-ranking people and that I knew some of the privileged people, just to feel that I belonged. You don't need that here. You can keep your culture and you can keep your background, but all your values should not contradict British values. All these things together create a great feeling of belonging unlike many other cultures who force you to give up your own culture, which is never the case in the UK. I can understand that normal feeling of belonging in my kids, as they were born here, are still living here and will be living here. They are aware of the culture here more than anywhere else. But how do you explain the feeling of belonging in my wife and myself? We are two people who were deprived of that feeling in our countries of birth and the countries of our parents' origins.

I am the kind of a person that will always move on, try to make a change and work all available options. I don't like to sit and receive the government's financial help. I want to work and to earn. Yes, I get a little help with the kids and I got some help when I was in a transitional period. But apart from this, I am a very proud contributing member of the community in terms of taxation and the support work I do. I even went down on the career day at my children's school to talk about dentistry with the pupils. There was a great interest in it. We are a proud part of the community, and we always aim to rise with the community to achieve the best we are looking for. So, I am still working on my credentials and will never give up. At some point, hopefully, it will get sorted. These frustrations do not take the belonging feeling from me because it is an issue with the regulatory body. It has nothing to do with the community where we are and the country where we are.

To those in authority and power, I would say always think twice. These people are not your enemies and are not here to create trouble. They are simply here to live and be able to earn, to provide and to contribute. No matter how many refugees come in, the numbers will be nothing in comparison to the larger communities. So think about it as an enrichment and as something bringing new positives to the community rather than a burden or a problem. Yes,

there are bad apples and bad people among them. But that doesn't mean that the whole thing is to be treated in a different way. On the contrary, help them, not necessarily by money or by securing jobs. You will be surprised that most of these people are talented and skilful, and some of them are very knowledgeable and highly educated. Though some are not educated, they have the skills. So, use that and guide them towards what they can do best and keep them busy. They are already in enough stress, sorrow, sadness, and difficulty. Just don't make it gloomier and more difficult for them. They are already aware that they are in a foreign place and do not yet belong there. Just think about it like this – take a deep breath and count to ten before you pass a legislation to send people back or prevent people from settling in and making it difficult for them. That's what I want to say even to the far right and to those who are completely opposing this process by trying to manipulate the politics against innocent people. Anyone in their position would do the same. God forbid, I wouldn't wish this to happen to the British people. British people were in World War I and World War II and they came out victorious. But at one point, they were facing difficulties and they needed help. Some fled Britain and some fled from Europe to the UK. So, remember that it is all about the payback. And trust me, by helping them and making it less stressful for them, it will always pay back. Let's not judge by the actions of the very few and let's not just generalise it to everyone. Also, let's not generalise some racists by saying the whole area and the whole British community are like that. No, that's unfair. My wife, my children and I haven't experienced a single incident of racism for the duration of the eight years of our stay in the country as a family. Not even once.

My message to those fleeing and coming in, the refugees and the newcomers: trust me, the majority will welcome you and you are genuinely welcomed, and you will see that. Don't build walls between you and the community. These people are hosting you. Put yourself in their shoes. You are living nicely and peacefully and suddenly someone who doesn't look like you, doesn't eat like you and doesn't speak like you is living next door to you. You would feel strange and you would express that sometimes and maybe complain about it. Don't deal with that by being hostile towards them. Feel for them and think about what they think about it. To them it is a change, and it is something new. They don't know you have suffered and that you are fleeing war zones, bombs, crimes against you and your children, maybe you have lost a child or two, maybe you have lost loved ones. They don't know that, and they can't imagine this amount of suffering. They might be warm-hearted but can't take in this news and when they see you for themselves, they might understand it and accept you more and more.

N S

Neither of us have found the right opportunity or the right academic position yet. My husband works in a field that is close to his specialism and has been having trouble with getting his credentials accredited. I'm facing the problem of not being able to achieve the right score for my IELTS. I consider this to be the biggest hurdle. Because our undergraduate degrees are from the Middle East, I knew we would always face such problems here in the UK. I think that finding a job would have been easier if we both had our BA degrees from a UK university. I know about many people who re-took their bachelor's degree. Sometimes, I think about doing the same. But we both got our master's degrees from the UK and this should be a plus point.

I got in touch with the Royal College of Speech and Language Therapists (RCSLT) for guidance as to how to be qualified to work in the UK. The college sent me a list of regulations as to what is required for me to reach that end. One of the conditions they stated was that since my BA was not obtained from a UK university. This means I must score 8.0 in my IELTS for every single language skill and the overall score should be 8.5. This condition is a must and there is no exemption. I believe that it is all about my Middle Eastern undergraduate degree. And to be honest, I am not surprised because I will be working in the field of speech therapy! I did all I could to develop my language skills. When we were in Cardiff, I registered at Inlingua, a private language school in Cardiff. Later, when my first daughter was born, I was introduced to DPIA through some of our Syrian acquaintances. This is a Welsh organisation to support refugees with a medical background. DPIA provides support for IELTS preparation, exam fees and transportation fees. They focus on helping people in the field of medicine in particular. As I am not a pure medical doctor, they allowed me to enrol for free but they didn't pay for my transport expenses nor my exam fees. They covered one attempt at my IELTS exam only. It was a great experience which I found very useful because the IELTS instructor was so efficient and my colleagues were all medical doctors and mature people, which made me feel comfortable. A very comfortable atmosphere compared to other language centres where you need to mix with people aged 17-18+ or young rich people from the Gulf countries. Also, most of my colleagues were from Syria. Syrians are the majority, you know!

I was amazed by the number of people who enrolled on that course. There were people coming from Newport, from Bridgend and other places in Wales and the DPIA paid all their transport fees. We are all grateful to this Welsh organisation for organising such brilliant support. I did my IELTS and it was one attempt and unfortunately, I didn't score 8.5. It is frustrating. And it is a shock because we thought that the UK would appreciate skilled refugees and encourage them rather than putting more and more obstacles in the way of their developing and contributing. Every person is a different case. But by the end of the day this is the system, and we have to work accordingly.

I personally won't lose hope. If not a speech therapist, I will take a job as an assistant therapist when the opportunity comes. In the Middle East people are labelled according to their fields and they do that and nothing else. For example, this is an engineer, this is a professor, this is a GP etc. When we came to the UK, we learned that work won't shame you unless it is illegal. People respect you more when you have a job. Also, the system is more organised when it comes to earnings from work, such as the minimum wage for whatever job you do. People are

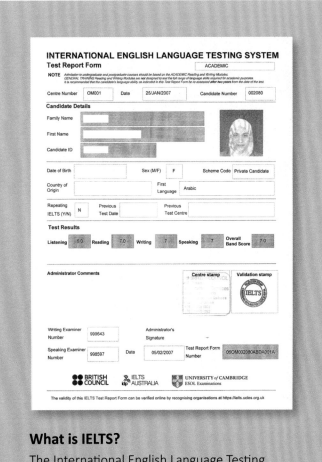

What is IELTS?

The International English Language Testing System (IELTS) is a test designed to assess your ability to listen, read, write and speak in English. IELTS is graded on a scale of 1-9. Each university, workplace or institution has specific IELTS score requirements.

encouraged to work and do whatever they can, be it temporarily or permanently. And this is what I have been doing. Even though some of the jobs I did were not in my specific field, I am satisfied that I did do some work. This experience has changed our mindset completely. Thanks to Allah for granting us resilience and a flexible approach to things. In our countries, the attitude is: you must act like me, behave like me or you will be judged and heavily criticised. Whereas here in the UK, I wear a headscarf and I haven't been bullied or treated differently because of my covering. This makes me respect people who respect my freedom. I don't like people with tattoos or piercings etc. But I must respect them because this is their choice and they will respect me for it. We have learned tolerance here in the UK. In our countries, we used to reject those who didn't look like us or behave like us. I am not saying there isn't racism here. There are exceptions but the majority here respect other people's freedom of choice and don't label others. One day, I was asking my 7-year-old daughter about one of her friends and I referred to her as an 'Egyptian'. She immediately responded: 'She is not an Egyptian, she is 'X', and she is British like me and the others.' Her father and I felt happy that she is thinking this way. For her, everybody is British as long as they live in Britain and that's it. And sometimes she asks us: 'How come me, my sisters and friends are British, and you are not?'

Mohammad and I are practising Muslims, but we are not strict, not radicals or anything. We only want our children to understand that we are Muslims and behave accordingly.

The challenge I am facing is with religious education. Here they teach children about freedom of faith. They tell children you are free to pray or not to pray and it is up to you. For us, it is not up to the child to pray or not. And here comes our challenge. It is a great challenge when it comes to teaching children what to take and what to leave. We want them to filter things, to take the good things and leave other things. We want to teach them to respect the things that don't match our faith and culture without hurting the feelings of others. And this is very difficult. To be honest we are facing this challenge daily. For instance when we explained that it is *haram* to have alcohol and eat pork or any stuff that includes these two substances. By the way, Mohammad and I are very flexible with *Halal* food as long as it is not pork. We can buy meat from any shop and say *Bismillah* before cooking or before eating a takeaway meal, for instance. When my eldest child was little, a boy at school gave her Haribo Sweets which contain pork gelatine. We explained to her that this is forbidden because it has pork in it, and we are Muslims and we can't take it. We were surprised that she was fine with the idea and it also didn't take her long to absorb it. We also explained to her that when we are free to buy an alternative, we would do it. We didn't want to give her the impression that we were ready to do that immediately. After this incident we realised that we, the parents, sometimes complicate matters for ourselves and that it takes some simple diplomacy to explain things to our children.

For example, in Wales, we lived in Rhiwbina, which is a white area compared to other places in Cardiff. My daughter was the only pupil with dark-brown hair. However, she was not made to feel different or 'other'. People were very friendly but had no clue about our culture and our religion. Here in Birmingham, my daughter is considered white compared to everyone else in her school. She is surrounded by pupils from different parts of the world and the majority are from a Muslim background. So, they are aware of these issues. We always tell her you are a Syrian Muslim, Welsh-British. She watched the film *For Sama* with us and she cried and was wondering why things are so bad in Syria. We try to make her feel grateful that she is living in a safe place.

When I see other nationalities, like people from Pakistan, for instance, I respect them because they have integrated without losing their language and their identity. They work here, and they made friends with the British society, and at the same time they put on their traditional costumes, use their native language and give their children Pakistani or Muslim names and are very proud of their culture, which is amazing. Sadly, I have come across some Syrians who have understood integration in a different way. When their child is born, they choose a name that suits the British culture like Alma, Ellen etc. I think this is unacceptable. I have to be proud of who I am. If I lose my identity, I will lose everything I am proud of. Britain is a multicultural country and people here respect us for all our differences. So why should we try to lose our own identity? I encourage people to contribute to society and be part of it and integrate and be productive and positive, but not to melt in with it and lose our identity.

I sometimes feel sorry for my daughters for not getting enough opportunity to use Arabic. I feel myself more privileged in this regard than them. Even though we try to use Arabic at home, I still feel it is a challenge. Most of the time we translate words from English to Arabic and use them. My second daughter has invented a strange combination of English words in a Syrian accent like *Ana Jumpeet* [I jumped] as an equivalent to the Syrian *Ana Nateet* [I jumped] so she finds this easier. What can we do?

We use some Arabic at home. And we deliberately use English with them when we are outside or when we are with people who don't understand Arabic because we don't want to offend anyone with our Arabic. In Cardiff, my eldest joined some after-school Arabic classes. Here in Birmingham, we didn't find a suitable Arabic school as most of the teachers are not native Arabic speakers and it was a bit confusing when it comes to certain sounds. So, I started teaching her Arabic at home, which has become an extra burden, to be honest. See here, I have made all these illustrations of letters, their shapes and how to pronounce them and then write them down. I am constantly thinking of new activities that attract my children's attention and keep them engaged. I usually watch videos online and try to invent my own coloured charts to suit my children's needs. I have created a class atmosphere here at home with a whiteboard! It is very important for us to teach them Arabic so that they can communicate with their relatives easily. I hope that my daughter will be able to send a message to her grandparents in Arabic one day. Also, to be able to read Qura'an and learn about our religion. As I told you before, Pakistani families are struggling with their Arabic, but they find it very important for their children to be able to read Qura'an. I hope we can succeed in teaching them the right things.

Everyone should understand that refugees are forced to leave their home. The newcomers need some time to understand how the system works. Not every person is aware that there is a government website where all the official announcements are found. My husband and I use this site and we are fine. But how many people are aware of this site? And how many are aware that what applies to their neighbour and colleague might not apply to them? So they must visit an official website or seek official advice. Everyone should be given a chance to work in their field of knowledge and expertise. Maybe because we come from oppressive regimes, we make comparisons and accept loss of opportunities in return for our safety or freedom, but this is not right. For instance, we studied hard and we paid money for our studies in the UK to get our degrees and we are still trying. But it is unfair when we don't get anything in return. The problem is that when we apply for other jobs, they look at us as overqualified. What do you want us to do, then? We are not given the right chance to work in our field and when we want to work somewhere else you treat us as overqualified! We sometimes think that maybe we shouldn't have done all that studying in the first place!

Don't think that you are coming to a paradise where fruit is all around you ready to pick. Some people think like that and I tell them this is a dream. Yes, refugees are entitled to certain benefits, but you have to prove that you are worth

it and that you have skills that will add to this society. I know many people from Syria who came to the UK and opened some simple food businesses, and they were very successful. This society accepts new ideas and celebrates them. So just think about adding your touches whenever you can. I met Syrian families who speak English and nothing but English at home with their children, as they think it is easier and better. This is unacceptable. In Wales, I used to take my children to an activity called Welsh Time where children, accompanied by their parents, attend and sing nursery rhymes in Welsh. I wanted them to get used to the language and to the culture but also use Arabic with them at home.

My advice is that when newcomers arrive, they must learn, educate themselves as the government provides loans and this is a great opportunity that they should make use of. They have to contribute and offer as much as they can. They are not tourists who arrive here for a short while and then leave. For instance, we have applied for our British citizenship and we feel we belong here, and everyone should think this way. Prophet Mohammad says that 'If doomsday is approaching while you are about to plant a tree, plant it'. A clear call for work and contribution and we have to follow this. I believe that we all should strive for our personal development. Otherwise, we would be drained. There are always doors to be opened, but we need to look for them.

I am keeping documents for my daughter's tree in Wales. The Welsh Tree Project is about planting a native Welsh broadleaf tree for every child born or adopted in Wales.

Every baby is given a certificate stating that a tree has been planted for them. This is one of the most wonderful projects that Wales has initiated. We feel grateful and it means so much to us.

Bashar at the Cardiff restaurant where he used to work. © Bashar Mousa

Bashar Mousa

I passed my Life in the UK test and will apply for the British Citizenship in a few days. I studied the online questions for ten hours. I spent ten to twelve days studying for the whole test and I made it! Also, my driving test. The theory one, I studied it for five days and passed. I love challenging myself and I studied for five continuous days using the app. I passed the practical test too and I am driving now! I always loved London and I love capital cities because they provide opportunities and as you know, London is one of those busy cities where there are lots of work and life opportunities. I feel that I have the right to be distinguished and do all I can. Why not?

In Wales, I lived in Newport and it is a very small town. And with my poor English, there wasn't a chance to even practise my English. I didn't like it at all and I felt depressed. I moved to Cardiff and had zero English. I made friends in Cardiff, I met with people and I started to do some casual work here and there. People in Cardiff were very nice, helpful, and supportive. When I moved to London, I felt that my life changed by 180 degrees. Life in London is not easy at all. If you can manage to live in London, you can live anywhere else easily. If you ask a question to anyone in London, they don't reply. They are very busy. They don't even give you a minute to speak to them. They don't have

time. I suffered a lot at the beginning but now I have settled well, and I am in a stage where I can support and offer advice to the ones who supported me. I can give guidance and advice on work, housing, etc. Now I feel that London has become my home. When I was in the process of relocating to London, everyone warned me against that decision and no one encouraged me. I always believe that things can be difficult, but nothing is impossible. It is you who creates difficulties and barriers. I am very comfortable in London and I would love to stay in London forever. I will visit my country when things become easier, but I prefer to live here. Britain has given me a lot. Arab countries made my life difficult. Once you feel settled and comfortable you will excel and achieve. Sadly, in Cardiff I didn't achieve a lot.

I have started a small media company, and I am running a small online sport business for sport suppliers, and I am working on developing the two businesses. I studied media for two years in Lebanon but couldn't resume my studies here in the UK. And sports are my passion. I couldn't resume my media studies in the UK because I had to do GCSEs and A levels etc. I couldn't do that because I was working. I had so many commitments and had to work to survive. Everything I earned and saved helped me to establish my current business. You know, in our countries you rarely find people who study and work at the same time. I am not used to working and studying at once. When I was in Cardiff, I used to work for fourteen to fifteen hours a day. When I first came, no one hired me. English employers look for those who speak English and with my poor English I couldn't find a job. So, I had to work at a restaurant to be able to survive.

I always loved sports and I was raised in a family whose members were sports fans. I have five brothers and one sister. One of my brothers was a sports instructor. I learned street-boxing techniques, judo and karate, and I loved kick-boxing and I trained in Cardiff for four months. I resumed this training in London, and I met with the award winner Riyadh al Azzawi and his brother. As you may know Riyadh is an Iraqi-British kickboxer. They helped me with guidance, training and advice and it was an amazing opportunity. I ran for 365 days and I didn't stop. I used to run for five to 15 kms a day. I was so committed to that. Commitment is behind my success. It wasn't an easy task at all. At times I was so exhausted. I cried at one stage. That daily routine was painful. Yet, I was so determined to do it. My message was mainly to young persons and children who survived wars. I wanted to pass on the message that they shouldn't lose hope and that there is a light somewhere in this life. I always wanted to tell people that if you want to reach to a certain goal you must walk to that goal everyday. You should work hard to achieve

Bashar after completing his 365-day run.
© Bashar Mousa

your dream. I ran for 365 consecutive days. I am considered the first to achieve that in the Arab World. This was documented in the Zaman Alwasl Journal.

> *"The first feeling I had when I arrived in the UK was that of freedom. The freedom that I hadn't experienced before in Syria."*

I was raised in a tribal environment where roots are appreciated and are highly valued. I always used to hear the saying, 'If you don't value your roots, you are considered disloyal.' I am a Syrian person and if I get my British citizenship, I would love to say Syrian-British. Citizenship would provide me with more rights, and I would feel freer. I love to travel. With my current Syrian passport and refugee status I have a travel document. Every time I travel, I get delayed and questioned. Because I am from Raqqa, I had to pay the price of the political situation back home. ISIS had a tight grip on my city Raqqa and because of that I was always stopped and interrogated. Once I get a British passport, I will have full freedom. Freedom of movement is so important. Also in employment and other matters and in voting. I will have better rights. I will be treated as a British citizen.

Living in a city is a pressure which I haven't been used to in my life before. However, I always think of it in terms of balance. I lost all the luxury of living in a rural primitive place and gained peace of mind. I have been trying my best to cope with the new life with all its challenges. It is a new chapter for me. I must adjust to the new stage and the new place. War rendered people poor and needy. They didn't choose that. They didn't choose to be poor. They didn't choose poverty at all. I am working hard to achieve a dream. I would love to do something for my people in Raqqa. I would love to make money to open a supermarket or even a mall for the people of Raqqa. I am thinking of providing employment for those people who couldn't leave the country or even to work inside the country. I have big dreams. I am looking forward to widening the activity of my company. One day in future you will interview me to ask about my production business and you will book an appointment to be able to meet me! My dreams and ambitions have no limits.

I had no idea about Wales before coming to it. The first feeling I had when I arrived in the UK was that of freedom. The freedom that I hadn't experienced before in Syria. Freedom of speech and of movement. Freedom of speech is what people miss in the Middle East and I found it here. When you approached me for this interview and when you sent me the consent forms to sign and told me that I have the right to have an anonymous name and to withdraw when I like, this gave me agency over what I am going to say. I felt free to discuss the topics you asked me to discuss. I have no fears or doubts that you might take my statements somewhere and hurt me. We lived an age of fear and oppression and we suspected everyone around. I feel free here. I am not afraid of people or secret agents. I am settled well, and I feel comfortable.

I came to the UK without a penny left. I didn't know anyone in the country. I was wearing a T-shirt and jeans, and that's all I owned at that time. I still keep those clothes with me as a memory. I also have a small diary notebook where I used to write down the details of my journey, dates, persons, places and so on. I still have the badge with the number given to me by the Italian navy crew who saved my life on the sea. These are dear objects of difficult memories and also a record of my survival.

The Refugee Council was my first point of contact through which I managed my life in Wales. They registered my name, personal details, and address. They asked if I needed any medical treatment. They instructed me as how to apply for housing or employment etc. While waiting for my refugee status to be issued, the Home Office provided shared accommodation and some pocket money. During that period, three to four months, I wasn't allowed to take any employment. I used to go to City Road in Cardiff and I met some Syrians and Arabs who directed me to services and places.

That was the worst part of it all. I had no English. I had some basics and that was it. That was so frustrating, but I did all I could to learn how to speak. I used to find excuses to use English with people. I had to break that barrier of fear. I felt that there was no time to waste in fear and embarrassment. I used to memorise vocabulary. But my grammar was rubbish. However, I pushed myself into speaking. I used to form funny sentences and my friends used to laugh at me. But I didn't care, and I tried and tried several times. I used my listening skills and tried to copy the

Bashar at BBC Wales studios for an interview. © Bashar Mousa

way people pronounced certain words. Language can push you forward or pull you backward. I realised that if I didn't speak English, I would be paralysed.

I spent two weeks on a course. I didn't find it useful at all and had to quit. They put us all in one level. There were people who were more confident and others who were less confident like myself. I was starting from scratch. And we were all in one class. So the good ones used to make fun of the others and it wasn't a healthy environment at all. Also all age groups were together!! There were older students, sixty or seventy years old sitting next to eighteen or nineteen-year-old students. During one of these classes, my mobile phone rang by mistake. I had forgotten to turn it off. The tone was a call to prayer and that was so provocative. A female student rebuked me saying: 'You are not in Syria.' I apologised, but I was hurt and embarrassed. I also registered for similar classes here in London and was late for one of the lessons when the instructor angrily told me: 'We are paying you to learn English, and this is unacceptable.' I found his statement hard. I felt bullied. It is so uncomfortable when someone gives you such a feeling. I could not continue. Yes, it was difficult. I am a young man, and I would like to approach girls and talk to young women and have a girlfriend or make friends with English-speaking people. I suffered for four years as a result of that language incompetency. Those four years were in Cardiff. I suffered a lot, especially with employment. No one wanted to employ a person with zero English. I worked at Arabic restaurants. I worked with Arabic-speaking people for some time. I worked in Deliveroo and was learning new words. It was also a problem as I couldn't apply to continue my studies at university. Universities asked for IELTS. They wanted me to score 5.5 in all skills for the IELTS and I couldn't. But I will do my best to do this IELTS at some point in future.

I like Cardiff and I liked the people. Before coming to the country, I heard a lot about racism and the bad attitude towards refugees. I haven't found this here in the UK. I lived in Wales and had only one incident – perhaps because of a conflict of interests or competition. I have been living in London for six years now and I haven't faced any racism. It was just one unpleasant incident when I was working in Cardiff city centre. I was working on a trolley. I made necklaces. They were all handmade and I thought it would be a great way of getting some cash. Unfortunately, there was another trolley for necklaces run by a young woman and her boyfriend a few steps from my trolley. They were very racist and they made fun of me in front of their friends and customers. It was tough. It was very painful. I had to leave the place to avoid trouble.

The worst thing any refugee would face is a lack of English. When refugees don't know the language, they are a burden. Language paves the way for employment and for life. Reading and writing skills are very important for any newcomer. This will provide a basis for communication. Language is the key to all the doors. Also, the Life in the UK test. This test or instructions on the test should be given to refugees in their native language to understand the rules, the new culture, their obligations, and their rights. All I dream of is to live in peace and to enjoy the freedom which is the right of every person. I am working towards expanding my own business so that I can help those who need me and those who helped me. I needed help many times and I know what it means to be desperate. I wish I could have the power to help as many persons as I can when they need me. Syrians are creative people, and they love to work and to contribute. When I opened my business, I hired eleven people. They have skills and are very practical. I wish all those wars would stop. We are from rich countries but sadly, our countries killed us.

"I had to break that barrier of fear. I felt that there was no time to waste in fear and embarrassment."

I wish I could reunite with my mother. She is in Greece now. I have been trying for three years to reunite with her, but I couldn't. My application was rejected twice. She is 65 years old. All my four brothers and their families are in the UK and she is there alone. It is very difficult when the family is scattered all over the world. I would say [to other refugees]: 'Chase your freedom wherever it is. Things are difficult, but nothing is impossible.' As to the sea journey, I believe this is a very personal choice. I don't encourage people to take great risks. I don't encourage them to do this and expose their lives to danger. But when there are no choices... Our life has turned into a long series of non-stop struggles. Stories of all sorts. I wish I could explain to people in the UK the struggle for survival, the stages we passed through and why did we did what we did to be here.

Sulaiman Sulaiman

I came to the UK in 2014. I applied for asylum when I first entered the UK and waited for five years, and I thankfully got my permanent leave to remain two weeks back. I didn't choose to come to Cardiff, but I was having clear directions from the Home Office to come to Cardiff, to start with the Jobcentre and take it from there. But once I arrived, I decided to improve my English and find a job. I found a job at a restaurant where I used to start early in the morning and close at around 2:00 a.m. Even though it was difficult to work long hours and study, I had to learn English. I joined a free English course at Cardiff & Vale and I was always late for my lessons as I could hardly find time to sleep from 3:00 a.m. to 8:00 a.m. Sometimes I used to fall asleep in the middle of the lesson. A colleague once took a video of me falling asleep in class and surprised me with the video afterwards. But day by day my English improved because of my interaction with restaurant customers.

I managed to bring my mother and brother here and then the other siblings. Later I brought my fiancée and got married in Cardiff. Now, I have a one-year-old baby. I feel that it is my responsibility to educate my siblings and provide a better future. A future that, at one stage, I couldn't pursue because of war and having to support my family. Most of my friends have managed to continue their studies and built a career here in the West. I am also determined to study and succeed and become an engineer.

We have never encountered any racist or unwelcoming attitude here. On the contrary, we managed to build very good relations with neighbours, and I have developed many friendships with Welsh and English people in Cardiff. When my family arrived, I took them to London to visit Big Ben and the London Eye and I took many photos next to these monuments. Last week, I was so excited to have my English language teacher at Cardiff & Vale pay a visit to the restaurant with a group of his students. He was so proud to find me owning a restaurant and he reminded me of the time when I used to fall asleep in his class!

I love Syria and I love my home city, and I follow and shed tears about what is happening on a daily basis. My heart and soul are there. But I can't do anything to change the situation rather than pray and hope for the best. Sadly, we are not the decision makers. We tried our best as revolutionaries, volunteers to help our nation but the conflict, the regime and its supporters are bigger than all of us – especially the Russian support.

I have settled well and I am so happy and grateful for having survived and succeeded. Even though I miss my friends and relatives, I keep in touch with them through Facebook and WhatsApp. I watch the news about Syria on my mobile on a daily basis. I wish to study civil engineering and I actually applied to many universities. I was recently accepted at Exeter University, and I am seriously considering studying. I am planning to go back one day,

Sulaiman Sulaiman working in his own restaurant in Cardiff, 2020. © Angham Abdullah

after the regime has changed and help rebuild my country. I admire the law and the way the system works here as there is no corruption, no bribes the way I knew in Syria. If you don't throw some money at a Syrian official, your documents and your life could be put on hold. I always feel that we, the Syrians, have participated in encouraging this corruption to thrive because this was how things worked back home. We didn't have many options. I hope that anyone who is considering the sea journey rethinks and plans for a safer route. It is better for someone to stay in any country out of Syria than to endanger their lives at the hands of merciless smugglers. People should also realise that the West is not a paradise and that they must work hard to be able to integrate and be accepted.

A M

I started my first year of architectural engineering at a private university in Damascus. Then, I studied for two years in Lebanon before coming to the UK. Now, I am in the second year of my postgraduate study, and I am supposed to graduate with a master's degree in architectural engineering. My submission is in two parts: the first part is a dissertation about Syrian Identity in Architecture; the second part is a project on an architectural design. It is all part of my dream to go back to Syria and rebuild the country using my architectural skills and expertise. God knows when the country will rise again. I do not think it will happen soon. Look at Iraq and see the destruction and the unstable political situation, years after occupation. If Iraq, the great country, is still witnessing chaos, Syria will be much worse. I cannot see a future for Syria with Bashar al Asad. Once he vanishes, we might see a glimpse of hope and think of developing the country.

I came to the UK for a two-week summer course at Cardiff University, arranged by the Arabian University in Lebanon. Before this course, I joined a five-week English language intensive course to prepare for my IELTS course. That intensive course was so hard. We used to start at 9:00 am and finish at 4:00 pm. And parts of the course were during Ramadan. You can imagine how hard it was. I entered the UK on the second day of Ramadan. I think I fasted for around 22 hours while travelling, because of the time difference between Lebanon and the UK.

While on the train to London for the first time in my life, I thought that I would be amazed by the designs of buildings, streets and houses. Coming from an architectural background, the first thing I noticed was the 'copy and paste' architectural designs. Without door numbers, people would definitely mistake their houses! How come that every house looks the same as the next house and the opposite house? Back home, we can distinguish each house's identity through differences in the designs, colours and door shapes. I think without house numbers and postcodes, we would all lose our way. I'm not joking about this as it really happened to one of the Syrian refugees I shared accommodation with. The man told me that when he first arrived in the UK, he was shown to his house and given his house keys. Next morning, he went to buy some groceries and, on his way back, he couldn't recognise the house! He told me he tried his keys in many doors before he found his house. It is a tragicomic situation. What made it worse was his zero level of English. It didn't occur to him to look at his house number as we don't have such a thing back home.

When I first lived at the Home Office accommodation, I was given a paper with all the details I needed: house number, full address, and many other details. My friends told me you are so lucky to get such a paper as not everyone gets it. I know the language very well and I had the basics. But it was the first time for me to use it in communication. My first English conversation ever was at the airport. Even though I understood all the questions, I replied 'no problem' to almost all the questions! I found it so hard to have a full, confident conversation. Gradually, my language usage developed as I volunteered as an interpreter to help refugees, and this helped me a lot.

I very much respect the way the system works and how everyone adheres to the laws. But I noticed, for instance, that most pedestrians don't follow the traffic lights. I've moved between three cities so far and in every city I found the same behaviour, which goes unnoticed. I've always heard that laws are so strict in Europe, but once here, I realised that there are loopholes. I love the diversity in London and in Cardiff and the way people from different ethnicities are free to practise religion. My mother didn't find any difficulty wearing her hijab and she didn't face any racist attitude when she was in London or Cardiff. Also, *halal* food and *halal* commodities are easily found and we have no issue with this at all.

My life in the UK started in London, I then moved to Leicester and after that to Cardiff. London was my first destination. I lived at my brother's house. Because my brother was too busy to accompany me to places, I had to download Google Maps and maps for London Transport, which helped me find my way easily. However, there were times when I missed my getting-off points on the underground or mixed up platforms. Life was much easier in Cardiff. My student accommodation was within walking distance of the university. There was a sense of stability in my life in Cardiff because I was part of a group of students guided and directed by the university, which provided us with a two-week schedule for our daily activities, destinations and people to contact. After two weeks in Cardiff, I returned to London and then settled in Leicester. So, I experienced two cities before I finally settled in Cardiff. Within the first year and six months of my being in the UK, I moved houses around eight times. I almost lost count.

I cannot wait to go back to Syria. It is interesting that while some families are struggling to leave Syria, I feel an urge to return to my memories, my place, my room, my bed and my house. I am studying architectural engineering to be able to go back and rebuild Syria. Sadly, everything has changed in Syria. A relative of mine went for a visit to Damascus recently and told us that the city's features have altered and people's attitudes have changed. They are tired, frightened and are suffering. It is not just about the newcomers, the new people who migrated internally between cities, but it is the old residents, the ones who were already there and haven't left Damascus. Their faces have changed, their characters have changed. She couldn't wait to leave Damascus as she couldn't cope with all that change. She couldn't stay any longer. I think the images of the place in my mind are about the good old days and if I return now those images will change as life has changed.

I think the more you increase your acquaintances, whether Syrian or British, the better. I believe a circle of friends around you will help you a lot. When I was in Leicester, I made many friends because I worked as a volunteering interpreter for over nine months. Everybody knew me. Eighty per cent of the people I knew were from Sudan as there was a big Sudanese community in Leicester. Also, when my mother came to live with me in Leicester, she built friendships with the people who knew me in the city. In Cardiff, I met friends in the mosque through the Friday prayer as I am busy almost all the week with my studies. I sometimes attend certain events organised by Syrians like restaurant openings and similar gatherings. For instance, I used to know the owners of the Royal Coast restaurant a long time ago when it was just a takeaway outlet. I know the staff very well because the restaurant is within reaching distance of the university. I used to visit them a lot when my mother was away. We usually discuss our present, plans for the future and perhaps the problems we are facing and memories of the past. It is about the sharing of feelings, suffering and happy moments. When I talk to them, I feel I am not alone in whatever suffering I am going through. I believe contact with people should increase, as there is no excuse now. But even with the closest friends, I get in touch perhaps once a year! I really hope I can increase my connection with relatives and close friends once I have more time to do it. I am too busy. Sometimes I feel exhausted from studying and wonder if there is a light at the end of the tunnel.

I am so proud that I finally graduated and got my undergraduate degree. I have moved between three countries to be able to get that degree. Even though an undergraduate degree in architectural engineering is not that great an achievement, I feel accomplished that I made it after all that I went through. Within a three-year period or perhaps more, I aim to become a professional qualified architect and return to build Syria. I hope by that time Syria will have become free. Within the three-year period, I would get my British Citizenship and British passport *inshallah*. My plan is to go back and take part in helping Syria rise again.

I think the journey to become a refugee has changed me significantly. I am a BME. I am simply part of a minority group. Imagine becoming a minority when you were a majority in your country. This makes you treat others differently because you are looked at as a minority. I must be honest, when I was back home in Syria, I used to look at some ethnicities and races from above. This inferior treatment of these nationalities was unfair. There are lots of cultural differences in the UK which we have to accept. We must accept and cope with them because this is how the country's culture is.

The Home Office announces that the average period for a decision on an application takes no more than six months. Yet, in some cases, the decision might take a year or more! Within this period, the applicant is neither eligible to work nor to learn English. I understand that employment is difficult without a legal status in the country. But why are they putting obstacles in the way of learning English for applicants? Therefore, NGOs like the Red Cross and other organisations interfere and give the applicant a maximum of four hours of English teaching a week. Can you imagine learning a language from scratch for four hours a week only?

In my master's project, I am trying to create a programme of workshops for refugees that would facilitate employment in crafts like carpentry or other crafts to engage refugees as soon as they arrive in the country. My focus is on using Syrian refugees' skills in mosaic-making which is well known in Syria. Mosaic is a rare skill that has already disappeared as a result of war and displacement. If refugees who master this craft are encouraged to use it in the UK, we will keep the craft going, employ refugees and

keep them engaged in a cultural activity that is so close to their hearts.

I discussed this matter with Wales Refugee Council and met with a staff member who told me that he has worked with refugees a lot. This person told me that when a Syrian refugee family is brought to the UK on a resettlement scheme, the authorities responsible for preparing housing, furniture etc for them has not enough information about them, apart from names and numbers. So, these authorities cannot make proper preparations for such a family to 'integrate'. It is not just about offering them keys for a fully furnished house and leaving them. What happens in reality is that charities recruit volunteers who do their best to arrange suitable living conditions for the refugees. It is all based on individual efforts. So community leaders, along with some volunteers and people from the neighbourhood, do their best to welcome refugees and organise activities so that the refugees are not left alone.

[Refugees] must bear in mind that language will be their number one difficulty in Europe. They must be aware that they are not coming to a paradise and that there will be many hardships and difficulties, like any other country in the world. I am not discouraging people, as I realise that no one would ever make the decision of leaving their country if they hadn't been in extremely horrible conditions. Yet, they should understand that they must do their best to survive. Also, refugees should not expect the new culture to cope with their culture, as they must accept the cultural differences. I think the young generation is more able to adapt to a new culture. I also believe that Welsh and

Scottish people are so welcoming, and they have proved to be nice and kind to refugees. My final note to refugees is to be flexible and get themselves into an employment that suits their abilities. They must work hard to prove themselves in this country and it is not an easy route at all.

Ali Zain

They took us to a detention centre where we were not allowed to leave. They searched my body and asked my permission to search my belongings and to take my iPad to check. They gave me clean pyjamas. When the officer was asking my permission to check my stuff I thought of the Syrian police back home and their abuse to people at the checkpoints. I couldn't help but make that comparison. I spent twenty-four hours in the detention centre where I had to give my fingerprints and went through an investigation. After that we were asked to go in a van and were taken to a nice hotel in Dover. Of course, it was a nice place for someone who had spent twenty-nine days of humiliation in the Calais camps! The next day we were taken to a hostel in Croydon. I was placed in a room with three Syrian refugees and stayed there for two months. We were supposed to sleep and spend time in that cold room and get down to the kitchen for lunch and dinner. We received no instructions as to how to go outside, where to go, how to talk to people etc. There was a TV in the kitchen. Internet was also there and I personally spent most of my time writing and getting in touch with my family and the online journals.

I wish there had been a language programme at that initial stage – an organised programme for English language teaching, particularly conversational English, as that is what each refugee needs at that stage. I realise a decision on our cases had yet to be made. However, I still believe that the English language was an essential part of my being in a foreign country. I wish I had been given one lesson a day while I was in Croydon. I wish I had been able to learn about British culture and given a chance to talk to English speakers. No one was talking to us at all. It was like we were there to eat, sleep and have our clothes cleaned. My roommates got their decision letters and were transferred to other cities two weeks before me. I had to stay in that isolation for two weeks until I got my letter. I'm surprised because this country is used to welcoming and receiving refugees. I expected things to be more organised.

"The only benefit I want from the government is to guide me… If you want me to contribute to this new society, you need to support me. I need your help to have an impact. I cannot do it alone."

Refugees must be prepared to integrate from day one. Integration would make them more effective in the society later. If the refugee learns the English language and is able to communicate effectively within the first six months while waiting for a decision on their case, they won't have to register at the Jobcentre. They could find a suitable job themselves and wouldn't need to get any [benefits]. The only benefit I want from the government is to guide me. Everyone should understand that refugees had a life that they were forced to abandon because of war and when they find an alternative life to parallel their former life, they would be effective members. If you want me to contribute to this new society, you need to support me. I need your help to have an impact. I cannot do it alone.

A refugee should not be left alone to explore a new life with no language. Refugees should be trained to reach a certain level of English that will qualify them to take on jobs. For instance, when an Arab refugee is introduced to Arabs from their community, the only mode of communication will be Arabic. My aunt goes to an English class in Cardiff and there is a lady from Somalia there who had been in Wales for the last twenty-six years. The lady has just started learning the English alphabets and cannot even use a single English word in communication. What kind of integration is this?

A greater focus should be placed on teaching English language to refugees. I would also tell the government that it is essential for a new refugee to learn about the country's rules, regulations and the whole system from the very beginning: traffic laws, recycling laws and lots of other daily issues which I came to learn about by chance or after I faced problems and asked someone. For instance, when I was living in Albany Road, I didn't know about the food recycling bin because my landlord was fine with mixing general waste with food waste. He simply didn't tell me about it. Only when I moved to live somewhere else did I

realise that there is a special food waste bin, a brown container for food recycling. Later, by chance, I watched a documentary from a Middle Eastern satellite channel on the biggest food recycling site in Bristol and how food recycling has been very useful in producing energy etc. How am I going to know about these matters if I wasn't told in the first place?

The government should understand that refugees come from different backgrounds and most of them have established careers back home. They have expertise in their field of knowledge, they have skills which they gained over time and were hoping to improve here in Europe. I had so many dreams that I was hoping to achieve. In addition to my skill in writing, I have hobbies in music, painting and other fields which no one knew about as I was unable to communicate it to others. I was placed on the waiting list for over a year to be able to get a place at one of the ESOL classes. Applying to a place for ESOL is a long process. Many emails, applications etc. You have to fight to get a place in an ESOL class.

The Home Office brought me to Cardiff because my cousin and my uncle were living in Cardiff. I was living in a 3-star bed & breakfast which was very good. But in that B&B we were asked to wear bracelets labelled with our names to be recognised as refugees so that we would be eligible for free meals. This was a humiliating practice that made us feel like we were being treated like cattle, really. The Guardian wrote about that practice and there was a hot debate on the topic which led the Home Office to change the procedure. I was then moved to Plymouth

ESOL is an acronym for English for Speakers of Other Languages

Oasis Cardiff, partnered with Adult Learning Wales and REACH Cardiff, runs Entry 1 classes. These classes are taught by a dedicated teacher and are adapted to the needs of students.

Oasis Cardiff also has an IELTS class which is taught on a voluntary basis. This IELTS preparation class is designed to help refugees and asylum seekers gain the IELTS qualification to enable them to enter further education, study for a master's or to re-train.

Photo © Oasis Cardiff.

where I stayed for three months. While I was waiting for the decision on my case, I spent long lonely days in my room there. As soon as I was recognised legally as a refugee, I was free to move and return to Cardiff where my relatives lived.

No one said anything about the ESOL classes. I knew about them from my cousin who used to attend these classes every morning. I struggled to find a house for me and my family. I contacted landlords and agencies to rent privately and all refused to rent a house to a refugee. In the beginning, the Jobcentre directed me to a school to learn English in Splott, Cardiff. I told them that I had the basics and that I could write, read and understand very well. All I

needed was conversational English and some advanced grammar. When I went to the English language school, I was placed in a pre-beginner course where they taught me the Alphabet (A Apple, B Bag, C Car etc). I registered my name at the ESOL classes in May 2016 and I heard from them in November 2016.

I was directed to Oasis to attend an English lesson where I found almost all levels – high, intermediate and low levels – gathered in one class. Oasis was good at introducing refugees to each other with the aim of creating a community. However, when people from the Middle East are introduced to each other, they will use Arabic, and this is not useful. I want to meet someone from Wales. I would like to be introduced to the Welsh culture, Welsh food, and Welsh history. Only when I joined ESOL did I learn something about the history of Wales through a tour to the museum. The Welsh Refugee Council supported me a lot in terms of documents, family reunion and related issues. I also attended some English language lessons there. I met an educational advisor for refugees at the Welsh Refugee Council who helped me to join a pathway course to University study. I applied to a pathway course in journalism which was so helpful, after which I applied to Cardiff University and was admitted.

Mosques organise events and gatherings. But there are some people who don't pray and don't go to mosques and there are people from different religious backgrounds. What is missing is a place that provides refugees with the essential knowledge on laws, regulations, lessons in language and in history. It was only by chance that I came to learn about the famous castle in Caerphilly in Wales. When I googled it, I realised that it is only so many minutes from my house to the castle by bus. I visited the place and was amazed by the scene. I always wonder why I have to discover these things by myself! I am sure there are several other wonders in this beautiful country.

I have not been through any racist situation. I love the freedom of expression and the freedom of practising one's religion. People are friendly but it is hard to build friendships easily. With my low level of English, I often find it very difficult to understand forms, applications, and lots of information. I am showered with paper forms, paperwork from the bank, the NHS, the Jobcentre etc. I sometimes don't differentiate between the most important and the least important post I am receiving. At one stage I ended up with a very big bag of unwanted paperwork from which I had to remove my details and put in the bin. I also learned something very important regarding correspondence. I learned that when I receive an email I must respond and not ignore it. Unfortunately, I don't respond to most emails as I think that I must respond with a similar level of language.

What surprised me are the questions on ethnicity, religion and colour which I frequently find on online and offline application forms. I look at this as organised racism or legal racism. I feel so disappointed when I find expressions like Black British, Black African, Asian and sometimes I don't even find 'Arab' on the list, so I choose 'other' etc. If you ask about my nationality, I will tell you 'Syrian', 'Iraqi' etc. I don't need to specify and describe the colour of my skin. I am not used to this at all. In the Middle East, we have every colour and skin tone. I believe this is the worst thing about application forms and I think the media is discussing this fact and that it will be changed soon, I hope.

My son is two and a half years old. I will tell him about the conditions which led us to leave Syria. I hope when he grows up, the whole regime will have been changed by then. I will tell my son that I didn't have many options when I left Syria. I had to choose between dying from Asad's bombings or dying by joining ISIS or other armed groups. I will tell him that I had a life. I used to study, teach, work and I was a productive person. I had to leave my house, my family and my land because I had no choice. When my son grows up and becomes a British citizen, I will always make sure that he maintains his Syrian identity, his language and culture. If Syria becomes safe, I will take him for a visit. My heart dreams of a free Syria to which I can return and initiate an educational project for children who were deprived of education because of the war. I hope I can do something for my village and its people. The other dream is to pursue a university study in journalism. I got the chance to study at Cardiff University, but I faced so many difficulties because of my language and because I had no idea how to deal with the whole situation. I hope I can fulfil my dream and get a degree in journalism, which is my passion. My biggest dream is to work for the *Guardian* or the BBC. I have started a podcast and I am working towards this end. I am thinking of writing a book about my experience.

I am in contact with my Syrian friends who are in Lebanon and who are struggling to survive and cope with the recent political developments. I support their decision to leave the country and to look for safety. Safety is a priority. If I were to pass a message on to them, it would be to explain the dangers I faced while on the sea journey. I do not encourage them to take that route at all. The best way to go is via the land journey. But they must decide what their objectives are. I will tell them about the successful experiences of friends and relatives who made it and have opened food businesses or cafes. Generally, Syrians do their best to get a job, as employment is very important to them. I will also stress

the importance of the English language in facilitating the lives of newcomers. I will direct them to the best options in terms of English language learning, of which I had no knowledge when I first came. Integration is not easy. There are people who can easily and quickly integrate, but there are others, like myself, who are willing to integrate but are confused.

"I will tell my son that I didn't have many options when I left Syria. I had to choose between dying from Asad's bombings or dying by joining ISIS or other armed groups. I will tell him that I had a life."

Whenever I feel desperate and helpless, I always remember that I am a father and a husband and that those people need me. My mother and sisters back home need me. My mother always sees me as a university graduate and she dreams of seeing me in Syria at some stage. This motivates me. Guidance and advice from others give me strength. I am always motivated by the people around me. Also, my writing – the recognition and the positive feedback I receive from editors and from the public motivate me to offer more of that.

Currently, I am planning to move to Bristol. If my life doesn't get better in Bristol, my next step will be Scotland. I have been here in Cardiff for four years and haven't managed to succeed in education and work. So, I prefer to move and relocate and try a new place and a new environment than to stay in a place that disappointed me. Yet, I love Cardiff and I consider it my home and I have become so familiar with its streets, corners, parks, and shops.

I have several digital photos of my home and the landscape which I am using as background for my phone and my laptop. My favourite one is an image of the four hectares of land in front of my family's house in Manbij. Every time I look at it, I feel like I am there immediately. I have a painting that I made myself. A big size 60 X 90 cm which I drew in Acrylic. I wrote Syria but I didn't finish it. I will attach a note which I will write next to the painting. They are lines from a poem for the exiled Iraqi poet Badr Shakir Al Sayyab. The lines say: 'The sun is more beautiful in my country than any other, and darkness – even darkness there, is more beautiful'.

When I feel nostalgic, I ask my family to take photos of certain corners in the house or the backyard and send them via WhatsApp. I have a specific image of the house which I am using as a desktop background image on my laptop as I spend much of my time on my laptop. I have another very special image of the landscape in front of my house which I am using as a cover photo for my current Facebook account. The images are so relaxing and so bright with the direct sun in them. I watch them all the time and especially when it is cloudy and dismal in Cardiff.

I literally have no friends here in the UK. I found communication with the people here very difficult as I don't know how to approach them and how to initiate a conversation especially with my bad English. I prefer to isolate myself from anyone around. I know this is not ideal, but it was safer to stay away than to put myself into

Photo taken by Ali Zain in 2014 of the view from his family home in Syria.

'The sun is more beautiful in my country than any other, and darkness — even darkness there, is more beautiful'.
Badr Shakir Al Sayyab

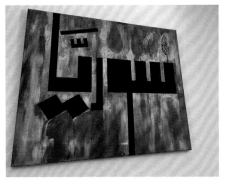

Ali's hand-painted calligraphy of the word 'Syria'

"I spend much of my time on my laptop. I have a very special image of the landscape in front of my [parents'] house which I am using as a cover photo for my current Facebook account."

Ali's laptop

embarrassing situations with broken English. When I started my university education at Cardiff university, I was hoping to make friendships with students. I was so excited about the multicultural environment in universities and was hoping to make as many friends as I could. Sadly, when I entered that large lecture room with three hundred other students, no one greeted me. No one even looked at me. I couldn't participate in the group presentations and I believe that it was because of my low English language level. When I was offered a chance to extend my first year of study, I was introduced to a Welsh colleague who sat next to me in the lecture room. She noticed that I was using an online English-English dictionary. And to my surprise, she told me that she uses the same dictionary. I asked her in shock, 'How come that you, the BRITISH student, uses an English-English dictionary?' She replied, 'Yes, I am Welsh and I find lots of English words difficult. Therefore, I have to use a

dictionary.' I was really pleased to know that I am not alone in this and that there are British people who are also finding English hard. When she started emailing me asking about myself and my family, I was replying with abrupt sentences. I couldn't continue with a meaningful conversation, and I avoided building a closer friendship with her or even introduce her to my family because I was afraid that I didn't have enough vocabulary for a meaningful conversation once I met with her. At the bus stop when a stranger tries to initiate a very basic conversation, say about weather, I immediately feel intimidated and lose focus on the words said to me. I feel confused as to what I should say and whether what I would say would make sense. I always reply either with a 'Yes' or a 'No'. I have worked all of my life and from a very young age. I am not used to being unemployed. I worked in the worst war conditions in Syria, and I worked from twelve to thirteen hours a day when I lived in Lebanon.

There was always something that I used to do between jobs. I have never been used to sitting and not doing anything. Being unemployed really hurts me.

My university education is becoming more complicated. I joined an ESOL course. They taught us English for two days a week from 9:00–1:00. I liked the speaking lessons and I loved using English all the time as I am good in grammar and writing. The instructor used to encourage me, and this built my self-confidence and I got A in the speaking skill. Then I had to move to the second level and enrol on a pathway course before my university course. I downloaded the meetup group app and subscribed for free to receive regular emails and invitations from the group. Last year, they sent me an invitation to meet them at Bute Park in Cardiff. I was excited to go and meet the group for the first time. But halfway I changed my mind and returned home. I played it safe and saved myself the embarrassment of failing to communicate. When by chance I meet my next-door neighbour, the only two things I say are 'Hi' and 'How are you?' I have many words and phrases in my head, but there is always the question of what if she asks me about something that I don't have an answer for? And what if I don't understand? So I try to avoid talking to English speakers. I signed in at a private English language institute CULT for three weeks and I spent around £705. It was an intensive course, but I couldn't continue as I couldn't afford it. So far, English language is my biggest problem. If I solve it, I will be able to resolve 75% of my hardships in this country.

Mohamad Karkoubi and his daughter waving the Welsh flag at a St David's Day event.

Mohamad Karkoubi

Mohamad ydw i. Dwi'n byw yn Aberystwyth. Dwi'n dod o Aleppo yn Syria. Mae gen i bedwar o blant. Dwi'n gweithio fel gof. Dwi'n hapus yn siarad Cymraeg.

[My name is Mohamad. I live in Aberystwyth. I come from Aleppo in Syria. I have four children. I work as a blacksmith. I'm happy speaking Welsh.]

Alhamdulillah we are happy here. But sometimes the feeling of alienation would be less disturbing if my father was here. My father is severely ill. I would love to see him around. We talk over WhatsApp from time to time, but it isn't the same. The death of my sister-in-law broke my heart. My sister-in-law was terminally ill. She suddenly developed cancer. We loved her a lot. We lived with her. We spent our childhood with her. I was looking forward to reuniting with her. We talked to the Red Cross about her. They did their best to issue the necessary documents, but we haven't heard from them since. It is such a misfortune. We had no response from anyone. She passed away. She left us while we were waiting to hear from them.

Now, I feel the same about my family. I am afraid I might lose them. I love this country and I am planning to stay here. But I wish I could be reunited with my family. My brothers are hard workers. Two of my brothers are master carpenters and woodworkers. The other two are blacksmiths. One of them is a widower. Sometimes he tells me I wish I could join you to work together for this country. If my brother comes here, believe me we would work. We would open our own blacksmith business. We can do doors, windows and all sorts of handcrafts and iron work. We gained this skill from an early age. We didn't continue our education, but we loved to work on metal and handcrafts. But *Inshallah,* I always say *Kheer* [goodness] will come *Inshallah*.

I respect the UN for offering me happiness, light and a new life. We lived in Lebanon, and I was working and things went well. But the most upsetting issue was that of the children. My wife and I were so upset and concerned about the children. Our biggest aim was to see our children flourishing and achieving. They had lost their home in the war. Education was so difficult in Lebanon. I was lucky. I was so busy earning a living with my work and people advised me to sign in with the UN to support me with the rent and the children's expenses. I was working all the time to be able to buy the family what they needed. Everything was so expensive. I will forever be grateful to the UN's support with the baby food and the essentials for the twins. After a while – I can't remember how long – I received a call from them asking if I was willing to travel. I said yes. They told me you will travel to a country in Europe, but they didn't specify which country. I love Europe and I respect all European countries. Europe is beautiful and I was thinking of working and improving myself and the children's future. Later I came to the UK through the UN.

I understood I was going to Britain but had no idea where in Britain. We were told on the plane when we flew from Lebanon. There were many Syrians on that plane. Some went to Scotland, others to Manchester and some were going to Wales. We understood that we were going to Wales. We arrived at Manchester airport. The Red Cross came. They checked our names, and they took us to Aberystwyth. Wales.

I had no English. But I loved Europe. And my family used to love Europe. We were always told that Europe was a beautiful place. *Inshallah* I was determined to learn. There was no fear. There was no fear at all. I came here and I learned the language. *Alhamdulillah* I am so satisfied.

"We were relieved. No noise of aeroplanes. It was safe."

They brought us from Manchester straight to this house to Aberystwyth. By bus. There was a group of other people with us. It was cold *Wallah* [by God]. It was windy. There was a storm. I remember we were in the airport and we were taken to the bus. I wrapped up my kids and I was wondering where we were going to. I felt safe. I knew I was in the UK via the UN. This is very important. If it wasn't via the UN, I wouldn't have left Lebanon. It is safe through the UN. I was overwhelmed. It was dark at night. But once we arrived, we felt relieved. We arrived at home, they opened the door and there was an interpreter. They showed us around the house, the rooms. *Haram* [Bless them] they were so generous. They had filled the fridge with food. We were relieved. No noise of aeroplanes. It was safe, that's the main thing for me.

The weather was weird – too windy. When we first arrived, we were so tired, but safe. We felt safe *Alhamdulillah*. When we arrived in Aberystwyth, I liked it. The team took care of us, and we were so relaxed. We woke up next morning and they took us for a tour. They showed us the small library. The only issue was that I couldn't understand them. I felt so embarrassed. I decided to study and learn this language *Inshallah*.

Wallah, honestly, I wished that I was surrounded by English-speaking persons only. This was very important to me. We already had some friends. They were with us on the same flight. They are our friends. Perhaps ten of them, maximum ten people. My wife and I believe that having a few of them is fine. But if we have more English-speaking people around us, it would be better for us in terms of

After a stormy day at Aberystwyth. © Marged Elin Thomas

learning. For instance, if everyone is an Arab, we wouldn't learn English for the next ten years and I wouldn't use English. It is important to gain it step by step.

When we first came here, we felt safe in this beautiful and lovely country which I will always love. I was so concerned about my son Mustafa not starting his primary education. But I remember how the Red Cross, bless them, were so kind and supportive, and they acted fast. Within the first two to three days, they placed us in the college and that encouraged me even more. They registered the children at a GP and made sure they were fine and not ill. My wife and I decided to learn the language. This was our priority. As everything else was secured – for instance the children were at school and we had the house – we were determined to learn the language and to work. We didn't come here to be idle. I really want to explain this. Health-wise, I am fine, and I am still young. I must work. I must show them I am here to work, and I am aware that I can't manage to work without the language. As to Arabic-speaking friends, we used to have a very close friend. He and his family were so close to us. They recently relocated to London. They used to live on the same street. We occasionally used to visit each other. I had my studies, and they had their own things. So there was a mutual respect for each other's time.

We enrolled in Ceredigion college and another place. There were two venues for our studies. I found it very useful. For instance, Wednesdays were for studying English and the rest of the week was independent learning. I used that time for volunteering. I chose to volunteer. They told me that I wouldn't get money for that work. I agreed to that because I wasn't after money. I was after speaking because I was so embarrassed when I didn't understand. My wife is better than me because she finished high school back home. I only finished primary school and then I started working. She was cleverer than me.

I wanted to volunteer to use the language, to talk to people. You must speak with others to avoid embarrassment with the English language. I advise newcomers to go out and to speak with people. Staying at home is never going to help at all. I volunteered at the Red Cross as a shop assistant. I used to iron the donated clothes. I did almost everything they asked me to do. I got a feeling when I started with the Red Cross. I began to know,

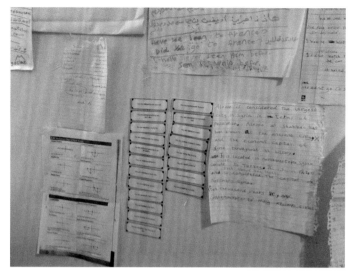

Notes stuck on the wall in Mohamad's home in Aberystwyth for learning English.

to understand what they were saying. But I couldn't speak with them. I told my teacher and he said: 'That is very good.' I understood. I respect this country. Aberystwyth. They were very friendly. They treated me in a friendly way. When I asked them, they used to explain to me. I realised I was benefiting from that experience. From an early stage of my life, I learned that free time must not be wasted. For instance, my lessons at Ceredigion college are from 10:00-12:00 and I had a break from 12:00-1:00 which I used in volunteering. From 1:00-3:00 I collected my children from school and spent some time with them. It's their right. I spend time with my wife. There is time for everything: time to study, to play and to work.

I also volunteered at Plascrug School. In the school I used

to paint the desks and clean. I had no issue with any type of work. I cut the grass. An environment of mutual respect. This has helped me a lot. The Red Cross encouraged me to join a group where I cut trees. I remember I worked at many places. In those places, I realised that there is a Welsh language. I noticed that some people use two languages. But some others use Welsh and most of my friends use two languages. In Aberystwyth they use two languages. I was determined to learn Welsh at the first opportunity!

I wasn't scared. On the contrary, I felt that Welsh is close to Arabic – for example the accent, the sound 'ch'. When I speak Welsh, I feel relaxed using Welsh. Some friends were scared. I wanted to learn the English letters, at least to pass level one and proceed, because learning two languages at once was a bit too much. But volunteering helped me a lot. A word in Welsh and another in English, Welsh grammar – I loved volunteering for this reason.

Honestly, people were so kind. I respect them. My neighbours are *Misk* [extremely kind]. I have been here in this house for six years now. The neighbours are so kind. Some Arabic-speaking families were very respectful as well. In terms of volunteering, the employers were very kind and helpful. But you must have the drive to learn the language. You must be independent. But they were very supportive. The ones I worked with later in my current job were also very supportive.

There is no big difficulty in each of these languages. It is just a matter of time. Learning a language requires time and focus. But the Welsh language – the accent is more flexible and a bit easier. For instance, when I say *Diolch, shwd wyt ti*. In English the grammar is more difficult. I push myself hard when I speak English. But I like the two languages. I believe that I must learn both languages if I am living in this country. I feel that once we are living in this beautiful country, we must speak its language.

"I advise newcomers to go out and to speak with people. Staying at home is never going to help at all."

I think ahead to the future. I am planning to start a business and to contribute to this country that helped me. I want to study, to go to places and to take my children around. All this cannot happen without language. The same with the Welsh language. We live in a place that uses English and Welsh and we have many friends. Many friends who are ready to exchange language and to communicate. I loved to learn Welsh when I started my volunteering role. I used to ask friends about words. I started with easy words. I heard them using Welsh words and I asked about the meaning of some words. They taught me some words about weather, greetings etc. I ended up memorising the words and I wanted to make progress. I learned how to introduce myself in Welsh and I became able to make a community. I made friends. Making friends is lovely. And I believe that learning a language is a must when a person comes to a foreign country. It facilitates integrating with the community.

I joined a Welsh course after developing my English. I joined it before Covid. A course at Aberystwyth University. And I thank the university for accepting me on the course. The instructor was so professional and so kind and polite. It was for two hours a week. After work. I was doing three things: learning English language on Fridays, working at a workshop in Tregaron, learning Welsh language on Wednesdays. And I was also studying for the driving theory test on the bus. It took me thirty minutes to get to Tregaron by bus. The bus was full of school students, and I was bored. I thought it was a good idea to spend that time revising for my driving test. *Alhamdulillah* Allah loves me, and I learned it. I used to revise every day for thirty minutes going to Tregaron. Yes, I was reading it in English using my phone. It was difficult, very difficult. I spent nearly two years studying. It was theory. It was full of academic language. This is difficult. I know words like should, must, when, where. As for driving, I used to drive in Syria and I have the driving knowledge. But this academic level, I had to translate. I used the Google Translate app. I don't advise anyone to use a translator. I just translated the academic expressions. I am sure you know them all. But to me they were all new words. I just needed the meaning of these words. Step by step, I made it *Alhamdulillah*.

In Tregaron they use Welsh. This fact encouraged me to learn through my work. And my advice to anyone who has come to this great country is to do their best to use the language and to volunteer. Work creates a community of friends, and this will help in gaining the new language fast. At work people used the Welsh language. Welsh was used more than English. This pushed me to learn. I asked them and they were so kind and so friendly. They helped me. For instance, how to ask about the weather. After work I used to take the bus, go home, take a shower and then head to university. I had the background knowledge from work. However, learning the language wasn't easy. I have a family etc. But it is a must. We are living between two languages, and we must understand.

The grammar is not that difficult. I would learn more and more if I had time. The difficulty in Welsh language to me is in writing. I find writing difficult. Reading is much better, but writing is… for instance, Cardiff is *Caerdydd* and school is *ysgol*. So, instead of the /s/ in school we have /y/. The words are different. My speaking and comprehension are good. I understand. But sometimes I can't communicate enough. Here, when they find me using Welsh, they help me. For instance, when I use the Welsh word for sunny, they help me to pronounce it properly.

My objective is to work, learn and take care of my children. I have all these learning levels to pass. So, I focussed on my family, work etc. I don't have many Arab friends. I greet them when we meet, but there are no visits, endless chats, or gossip etc. I have a few of them but there aren't close relations with them. I think I am the only Arabic-speaking person here to have this drive to learn Welsh. When I went to Cardiff – something that I won't forget, and I will be forever grateful to the government – they invited me to attend a ceremony. I do respect this country for this encouragement. The head of the Welsh language department at Aberystwyth University – I respect

Yr Amser Dyfodol / The Future Tense *Mohamad Karkoubi*

Bydda i'n talu / I will pay/be paying	Fydda i ddim yn talu / I won't pay/be paying
Byddi di'n talu / You will pay/be paying	Fyddi di ddim yn talu / You won't pay/be paying
Bydd e'n/hi'n talu / He/she will pay/be paying	Fydd e/hi ddim yn talu / He/she won't pay/be paying
Byddwn ni'n talu / We will pay/be paying	Fyddwn ni ddim yn talu / We won't pay/be paying
Byddwch chi'n talu / You will pay/be paying	Fyddwch chi ddim yn talu / You won't pay/be paying
Byddan nhw'n talu / They will pay/be paying	Fyddan nhw ddim yn talu / They won't pay/be paying

Fydda i'n talu? / Will I pay?/be paying?	Bydda / Yes I will	Na fydda / No I won't
Fyddi di'n talu? / Will you pay?/be paying?	Byddi / Yes you will	Na fyddi / No you won't
Fydd e'n/hi'n talu? / Will he/she pay?/be paying?	Bydd / Yes he/she will	Na fydd / No he/she won't
Fyddwn ni'n talu? / Will we pay?/be paying?	Byddwn / Yes we will	Na fyddwn / No we won't
Fyddwch chi'n talu? / Will you pay?/be paying?	Byddwch / Yes you will	Na fyddwch / No you won't
Fyddan nhw'n talu? / Will they pay?/be paying?	Byddan / Yes they will	Na fyddan / No they won't

Mae ffordd arall o siarad am y dyfodol hefyd – y tro yma trwy newid y ferf ei hun:

Tala i / I'll pay	Thala i ddim / I won't pay	Dala i? / Will I pay?	Gwnaf / Yes I will	Na wna... / No I w...
Tali di / You'll pay	Thali di ddim / You won't pay	Dali di? / Will you pay?	Gwnei / Yes you will	Na wn... / No yo...
Taliff e/hi / He/she will pay	Thaliff e/hi ddim / He/she won't pay	Daliff e/hi? / Will he/she pay?	Gwnaiff / Yes he/she will	Na w... / No h...
Talwn ni / We'll pay	Thalwn ni ddim / We won't pay	Dalwn ni? / Will we pay?	Gwnawn / Yes we will	Na w / No
Talwch chi / You'll pay	Thalwch chi ddim / You won't pay	Dalwch chi? / Will you pay?	Gwnewch / Yes you will	Na / No
Talan nhw / They'll pay	Thalan nhw ddim / They won't pay	Dalan nhw? / Will they pay?	Gwnân / Yes they will	Na / No

Ond gyda berfau sy ddim yn treiglo'n llaes – But with verbs that don't take the aspirate m...

Bwyta i / I'll eat	Fwyta i ddim / I won't eat	Fwyta i? / Will I eat?
Gwela i	Wela i ddim	Wela i? etc

Mohamad's Welsh lessons: learning the future tense

him so much. He is like a brother and a friend to me. I went to him and I told him I would love to learn Welsh. He signed me on the course and paid for my fees. I am so grateful. And they arranged trips for students. I took my kids and we enjoyed ourselves.

You know, it is not about receiving certificates, it is about the future. I want to learn more and educate my children. Suddenly someone called Siôn said to me: 'Mohamad you are invited to a ceremony in Cardiff.' He wasn't sure if it was me who would receive the award because there were many others. I thanked him and I thought it was great that the government had at least included my name. I decided to go and if someone else was awarded, good luck to them. To my surprise, my name was the second or the third on the award list. I understood the presentation. It was about me: 'Mohamad worked hard, he volunteered etc.' I was so pleased, and those words encouraged me even more.

It was somewhere near the train station. A grand hotel. They booked me a room. I heard my name and some friends made videos and took photos. I was so pleased. I've always felt that this country appreciates those who try hard. The more you succeed the better you are treated. It was a great feeling. I achieved some progress and they recognised it. Honestly, I wasn't after a show or to be seen by others. I appreciate that this country has taken my family in and taken care of us. And here we are trying to prove ourselves and work in a safe environment. That is all.

Once we had settled a bit and the children went to school, I began to go out and I was so embarrassed when people talked to me in English. There was an interpreter,

Mohamad's children with their new baby sister.
© Mohamad Karkoubi

but I cannot rely 100% on the interpreter. During our first or second night here, my son Mustafa got ill and I took him to the GP. The interpreter wrote to the GP that my son must go to the hospital. I prayed *Yarab* [My God] help me I must learn! They didn't understand me, and it took me a quarter of an hour trying to explain by sign language. Also, phone interpretation is sometimes unreliable as it can be inaccurate. Gradually I learned. My wife and I worked hard. We have organised a learning group with our children. I must not forget my children's role in teaching us.

What is amazing and surprising about my children, *Mashallah* they gained the language quickly. Mustafa speaks a bit of French, from friends, many nationalities at school. But the kids have learned better and quicker. I have been learning the alphabets. Suddenly I found them knowing about /she, he/ and the grammar. I wonder why I am struggling with /I had/! But my kids are so kind, and they are very supportive. They give me some homework, they help, they say to me: 'Daddy when you want to say this thing, use this word' and they correct me. They say to me: 'When you use "I would like" it is more polite'. They help me with many aspects. Even in Welsh they are cleverer. Sometimes they use some strange words in Welsh between themselves, new words to my ears. They help me with this too as their accent is better than mine. I believe that because kids have no responsibilities or worries, they learn things better.

I have made friends from many parts of the UK. From Scotland, some of them are from Ireland and from England. Yes, I found them here. And I can distinguish and tell from the accent. For instance, in north Wales, they speak Welsh in a different way compared to those in Aberystwyth. In Tregaron it is a different Welsh from here. In Tregaron it is easier. And also, in Aberystwyth. But north Wales I feel is a bit difficult. It is a bit heavier there. Here, I get the words quicker. Like Arabic. It is smoother. Sometimes I understand part of what they say but not the whole phrase. I usually ask where they are from. They tell me they are from north Wales and I have friends as well from this area. I wish I had more time. I need to focus on my work, and this affects the time I spend on language learning. I would like to improve these skills, not just to be able to communicate with the community, but I am thinking of the future of my business. I can work in the iron industry, and this requires languages.

I love my country, my homeland, the place where I was born and grew up. If we are talking about the time before the war and compare, it was a beautiful country. Aleppo is well known in history. It is an industrial area, and I learned a lot from that place. Aleppo is famous in many fields: industry, culture, and medicine. Study at university was free. Life was much better. It was cheap. No one would ever think of leaving. This was before war which led us to leave. We want to live, we want to be happy, to work.

We left for Lebanon and then to this country. We came here and we are planning to stay forever, if God wills. I always used to love Europe and my father used to tell us about Britain. And I've seen that Britain is a beautiful and a safe place. *Alhamdulillah* the children go to school, and I work and will hopefully be able to open a business. That's it. It is all about a safe living. Safe, this is the major point.

Mohamad and his family having a picnic on the beach at Aberystwyth. Mohamad is playing an oud. © Mohamad Karkoubi.

We have friends, and it is a dignified living. This is the most important thing, I believe.

I am happy here, but we have lost our families. They are far away, and this is a torture. We were happier back home before the conflict. We were together, eating with my brothers, the neighbours. It was a very friendly atmosphere surrounded by people we loved. Now we are exiled. My family is at one end and I am at the other, and we are not together anymore. This is the difficulty for us. I wish that my family could join us here. You know how unsafe it is back home.

Anyone who is planning to come here or to any place in Europe must be respectful to others. Not to be a problem maker and to be considerate of others. Make a community and speak to people. They should not seclude themselves. Not to gather around in useless talk and gossip over tea. Time is precious, and I personally don't waste it. My advice is to learn the language. Once a refugee comes here, they should appreciate it and contribute to a country that supports them.

My family and I are planning to stay here. We are fine here. Also, volunteering is so important. Don't sit at home. Volunteering is free, but it will lift your spirits. When I came here, I listened to people talking and I was wondering when I would be able to talk like them. I listened and I couldn't understand. But when I started learning, I understood the radio for instance. So, volunteering and working are essential for any refugee. If they are healthy and strong, they must work.

Latifa Alnajjar

They told us [at Bristol airport] we were going home and that it would take us four hours. We were so surprised when we learned that we still needed four hours on that coach. The children were asleep. My mother was tired and sad.

My father was asleep. I was wondering where we were going. Anyway, we arrived here. And bless them, they were so kind. On the bus, they tried hard to comfort us and reassure us. They offered us some fruit and took care of the

Latifa Alnajjar

kids and helped us. We arrived at this house and we met the landlord and people from the Red Cross. They asked my husband, myself and the children to leave the bus and get into the house. We carried the children to their beds as they were both asleep.

The moment I entered the house I was shocked. Ah! The smell – the smell of mould. Strange house. The house wasn't properly prepared. It was so dirty. I even found a black cat in the house and was wondering where this cat came from. I felt it was too much. I had a feeling that I had come to the wrong place. I started crying. I lost it.

Frightened, leaving my sisters and all of this. And the house! I was wondering how I would clean all this mess! I was so tired. How could I even sleep? I couldn't even manage to sleep. I didn't see any Syrians around. I was hoping to find a Syrian. I wasn't expecting a Syrian to receive me and to make me food, not at all. I was just looking for a Syrian to reassure me.

Yes, I wished I could find a Syrian or an Arab. I only saw English speakers. They were kind and nice. But I felt – honestly, I was scared. The group explained how to handle things around the house. I was totally absent-minded when they were talking to us. They left. I went to the bedroom and didn't even change my clothes. I sat on the bed and contemplated the new situation. My husband was lying in bed, the children were asleep. I wondered what we had done to ourselves! I wanted to go back to Egypt. Those were my thoughts and feelings.

I didn't know anything about Wales, England. No details. They told us that this was Aberystwyth, but I had no idea where it was. When I received the documents in the first place, I was notified that I was going to Bristol. I googled Bristol and searched online to get more information about Bristol. This is why I was surprised when I was told that we would be taken to another place.

All I knew was that I was going to the UK, and it is one country. I knew there was England but no idea about other places. So, it was a difficult night. Next morning, I found my mother knocking on my door. My parents had been taken to a different house. When we first arrived, I had no idea where that house was. No internet, no phone connection and I had no idea who to contact. I had my phone, but I didn't have a UK number or an internet connection. When my parents were taken to a different house, it broke my heart even more. My mother was also so sad to be separated from me. It was just a five-minute walk from my house to her house, but we had no idea! We didn't know! It was dark on the first night. My Mum and Dad went for an early-morning walk. My kids woke up and they were so excited: 'Mum, we love the staircase to our bedroom. Mum, we like this two-floor house!' These comments made me laugh amid my distress. I laughed at how the kids were so excited about the house and the stairs. It is different from the design of our houses back home. The kids stood outside the house and they suddenly saw my Mum who was walking around the area trying to find our house. It was so emotional when I saw her. We hugged and wept.

My Mum was so worried. She saw me crying the night before and then left to go to a different house. And neither of us knew how to reconnect. She came very early. We had a morning visit from a member of the Red Cross and a translator to check on us. When they asked how things were, I told them 'I don't want live here. I don't want to stay here. I want to go back to Egypt.' I cried and cried saying 'I want to go back to Egypt. I don't want this anymore.'

The house shocked me, and I felt I was in a remote place. I had no idea where this place was. When I entered the house, I felt like a stranger. The lady from the Red Cross, bless her – I was trembling out of stress not of cold – she offered me her winter shawl. I won't forget that and I want to mention it. She was so kind to wrap me with her shawl. Slowly and gradually things became better. That first day was the most difficult.

After three days they took us to the town's library and

High St, Aberystwyth. Photo © Bill Boaden (cc-by-sa/2.0)

through WhatsApp and I used to send them voice texts full of tears and angst. It took me six months to recover from that distress and it was the same for my mother. Gradually, I was introduced to some women and families in the area. There was a lovely lady, Jumana, who supported me a lot in the initial stages. She never left me alone and was always with me. Jumana is Syrian.

"I didn't know anything about Wales, England. No details. They told us that this was Aberystwyth, but I had no idea where it was."

introduced us to two Syrian families in the library. We were also introduced to the Mayor of Aberystwyth! The translator informed us that she wouldn't stay with us for more than three days and that if we needed something we had to ask her on that day. I asked if they could help me with cleaning the house. The Red Cross supported us a lot. We signed the contract for the house and did many other things in the Jobcentre. They also helped us signing in at a college for our English classes.

The landlord replaced the old carpet. He brought us new ones and helped in fixing some issues here and there. The house suffocated me. Before I came to the UK, I had subscribed to some social media group of friends and relatives who ended up in the UK. They used to post photos of their houses which were so different from the house I found myself in. We exchanged texts and voice messages

I met Jumana in the library. She is a person who is willing to help. Not everybody is like this. Not every person is willing to stand by you. She supported me, accompanied me to malls, shopping. I didn't know the language and she helped with translation. It was impossible to communicate with anyone without her. When the Red Cross translator left, I was so scared. Myself, my children – not a word of English. But when I visited my children's school, I was reassured. It was such a relief when I found two Arabic-speaking female teachers. One was from Yemen and the other was from Egypt. I was comfortable that my daughters wouldn't feel like strangers. Someone would be able to understand them. I was so pleased, so pleased with the school's arrangement. To be fair, the school was very good in this regard. This made me feel safe. I felt that my daughters were safe and in safe hands *Alhamdulillah*. It was such a mental relief. The two teachers, Wafaa and Nuha, were very supportive. They helped the kids a lot in school, with translation.

Rama, my eldest daughter, used to cry every morning. Masa, my little one, was fine. Rama was upset because she missed her aunts to whom she was so attached. Masa was only three and a half years old and wasn't aware of the situation. She was a little kid when we left. But Rama knew that we had left my sisters behind.

Rama was five years old. But she is so sensitive. In two weeks she told me: 'Mama I don't like the staircase any more. All I want is to go back to my aunties.' These words added oil to the fire. They affected me and made me cry. But, *Alhamdulillah*, now I feel... After I went to the college and met with people, I found them so kind. I realised that the people of Aberystwyth are so sweet, so kind and friendly. They are very respectful. Step by step they've become a family to me. I was introduced to Eryl, a lovely lady who comes to my house weekly. She helps with language and with so many other things. She helped with the kids. Eryl is a volunteer who works with the Red Cross. She helped with the English language. A very respectful lady whom I feel close to. I sometimes wonder what I would do without her if I had to move somewhere else! She takes the children for walks. She has played a major role in my life.

This is our fifth year. We are in the process of applying for a permanent leave to remain. I do worry. Yes, I worry that we might not get leave to remain or citizenship. I need it a lot. I need to get it to be able to travel and see my

Latifa's two daughters, in their school uniform © Latifa Alnajjar

sisters. With our current Syrian passport it is very difficult to travel. All doors are closed to us with our passport. I need this permanent status to have free movement. Now I feel like I am imprisoned within this status. Getting citizenship will enable me to reunite with the family I left.

Within the last five years in this house, I haven't been introduced to neighbours. There are people around but maybe they are students. I usually say 'Hi', but they don't try to come and talk to me or get closer. A year ago a neighbour from China came to live next door to me and our children play together. She looks like a lovely lady and I am happy to have her next door.

We used to have lessons twice a week, Mondays, and Tuesdays. On Wednesdays we usually have a coffee morning. The coffee morning is a two-hour lesson where we communicate with people. I was introduced to many people. I personally found it very useful because they ask pairs of students to have a conversation. The class was led by Miss Sarah who was a brilliant instructor. It was a very important conversation class. The major problem we faced with the ordinary classes was that they used to mix up all levels in one class. For instance, I was sitting next to someone who was one year ahead. They put all levels in the same class.

All Syrian families here in Aberystwyth feel like they are not achieving any progress with the English language. Since I started, it has been always the same. I feel like this year is a bit better. We have a good teacher now. She divided us into two levels: one and two. However, they haven't mixed us with foreign students. When we find non-Arabic speaking students we are forced to use English. When my colleague is an Arab, we will use Arabic most of the time. And many problems took place because of this. There are students who want to chat and have fun, others want to learn etc. I wish they would give us a chance to use English with English speakers to gain the language like our children. Our children spend almost all day from 9:00 to 3:00 with English-speaking kids and they learned fast. I have friends in other parts of the UK who achieved a lot more progress than us here. They even got certificates and moved further. This year I was looking forward to moving to another level. I signed in for a course in hospitality and catering but couldn't do it because I was too busy.

My instructor gave me a test to assess my language performance to see if I could move forward to a specialised course. I did well *alhamdulillah*. As you know, I already have the foundation of the English. I am good in grammar, reading and writing. But I don't understand everything and I am sure if I had had a good start, I would have done better. In Syria there wasn't a great focus on communication. It was only one English lesson a week. I am happy with what I have achieved so far. I don't know, sometimes I feel like my brain is regaining the basics I studied back home. Perhaps the best thing that improved my English language was my work with the dinner project!

In the beginning my daughters didn't like to eat the food offered in school. They just found it different. Gradually they got used to the English food, but they still love my Syrian dishes. Yes, they do ask me to cook foreign recipes and I have to google recipes or watch YouTube videos to learn how to make them. Honestly, my children got used to the English food. They got used to it. I personally must cook a Syrian dish daily. I can do with a mixture of dishes but a Syrian dish is a must.

I am trying my best to use Arabic and encourage them to use Arabic language at home. I also tried hard to find an Arabic teacher. I have been trying for the last five years. I found an online Arabic instructor which was a big relief. I wasn't happy that they were not learning Arabic on a regular basis. Luckily now they are learning Arabic online every Saturday from 9:00-12:00. And they also study Arabic twice a week for two hours. And this is what I am doing with my little son. I know that he will learn English anyway. I

Latifa and her friend Eryl, a volunteer at the Red Cross © Latifa Alnajjar

always think ahead about their future. We might go back to Syria, who knows! So, Arabic is very important.

Before lockdown all Syrian families used to go to a centre to learn Welsh every Friday, thanks to Aber Aid society. They helped us a lot in this regard. They organised this course for families and their children. In school my daughters learned some Welsh songs, words. I do feel there is some similarity between some Welsh sounds and

Arabic sounds like the 'ch'. I also feel like the Welsh traditions are close to our own traditions. They have the family spirit. They visit one another and they visit us. When I settled well and learned some language, I feel like I am with my family here. Honestly, they visit me, take care of me, check on me if I am ill. Eryl, the friend I talked about earlier, is so kind. I was unwell at one stage. When she knew it, she came over, took my children for a walk, took them to the swimming pool and to a pizza restaurant after. She is a very kind and nice person.

I was so upset when I first came here and found no Syrians around. Later on, I realised that it is my duty to support the newcomers the way I wished to be supported. My friend Najla'a came here a month later and I couldn't wait to introduce myself to her. Same with Rula and the other families. I really didn't want them to feel isolated the way I felt. I never want to see anyone feeling depressed as I felt. We all left against our will. We didn't choose to leave. I think we all love to travel as tourists but to find yourself living in a foreign country that is totally different from yours in culture, traditions – in everything – this is frightening. And we are all in this together and must support each other. We've had enough distress in Syria and we don't want to relive that experience here.

A friend of mine whose name is Rose used to help my parents with their English language and later worked with the Red Cross. She tried our food. She is my age and she put heart and soul to support refugees and to support us. She wanted to do something for the Syrian community. Something which enables Syrians to show their abilities and

Latifa's friend Eryl with Latifa's two daughters. © Latifa Alnajjar

skills. She liked our food and suggested that we share this food with the Welsh community. We were encouraged by her words. And for the first time all the Syrian families took part. Each lady cooked a dish, we went there, and people loved our food. We were around seven families. Yes, seven families each prepared a dish and it wasn't for business at all. It was meant to connect with the community through food. We were offered a basic fund to buy the essential ingredients. So, we made it and it was a lovely day!

The event took place at a community centre called the Castle Rooms sponsored by the church. This is where we started. Rose arranged it. She sent email invitations and advertised for the event. Many people came including the Red Cross, Aber Aid, the charities here and people I know here. My friends and others. We handed them paper notes

for reviews, and we received very positive feedback on our coffee, dishes, and everything. It was a well-organised event. Rose was there all the time, and she was the one explaining about the food and the ingredients to people. Rose was very helpful in this regard. She is behind the whole idea and the whole project.

After one month we arranged a second event in the same place. At this stage, some families who started didn't want to continue with us. Some didn't like the idea. They have other commitments and special circumstances. Gradually things developed. When I first came to Aberystwyth, I visited Medina restaurant. We began our activities in Medina. I was first introduced to Medina by a friend who invited me to the place. I liked it. I liked the Arabic vibes of the restaurant. I had a green Moroccan tea there and I was comfortable. I loved the restaurant. The quiet atmosphere. It was lovely. When we started thinking of the project, it started as a Syrian community. It had no specific name. Later we chose the Syrian Dinner Project. Rose and I used to tour around restaurants. We asked restaurants if they were happy to allow us to rent their places to present our food etc. We visited Medina's restaurant and they welcomed the idea. She was so pleased. She sympathised with us. Medina is the female manager of the restaurant, and it was named after her. So, she welcomed us in her restaurant and that's how we started.

It was a very big step for us. To make food and to present it at Medina! Medina, the biggest restaurant in Aberystwyth. It was such an overwhelming experience and feeling. To make food and to present for the first time at a restaurant. Such a beautiful place. It was a great feeling. Medina helped us with that. She advertised for the event through her restaurant's Facebook page. She invited people to the Syrian food with details of date and time etc. We had to get food certificates to be able to cook and to present food in a restaurant. The certificates were essential. Rose organised a one-day course for all the Syrians involved. And we got that certificate. It was a one-day course in Arabic. The course is offered in English and Arabic. But we had it in Arabic which helped us a lot. So, with this licence we all became eligible to work at any restaurant. We presented the licence to Medina and started organising things. Medina was with us every step of the way. She helped with the washing, the tidying. Medina is a wonderful lady.

Some dishes were prepared the day before, like *Halawt al Jibn* [cheese desserts], and maybe we made *Qatayef* as well. We prepared those dishes the day before and we refrigerated them using the restaurant's fridge. Rose helped us with the food preparation too. We cooked *Shish Barak* and Rose learned how to make it with us. It was such a lovely spirit. And, *Alhamdulillah*, we started and it was a success! People loved it. We set up a Facebook page and began communicating with people. At this stage Rose had to leave us to begin a course in London. Thus, the project developed.

The biggest hurdle we faced was with Covid-19. Before Covid we used to organise food events only. We hadn't done takeaways. With Covid we began our takeaways to be able to continue with our work. And people loved it. When customers purchase their takeaway, they always ask us about our next round immediately! This attitude inspired

Rose, who came up with the idea of the Syrian Dinner Project, with Latifa and her friend Rula. © Latifa Alnajjar

us and encouraged us to make more food and to work. We learned about the vegan, the vegetarian, the gluten-free food and about food allergy. These are very important, as well as the paperwork and the labels. How to freeze food, how to cool it. What's the right temperature for food etc. We learned about all those things from the one-day course we had. Issues around cleaning before and after and many related topics. We usually fill in three forms: one for cleanliness, the other for allergy, and the third one on the food temperature.

Latifa in the kitchen. Photo courtesy of the Syrian Dinner Project

The majority of our customers are English and Welsh. Even now I rarely find an Arab customer. The majority are Welsh. They write me very good Facebook reviews and they sometimes send me emails. I don't think they were complimenting or flattering me. Because they often text me saying the food was lovely and we kept some for the next day and we were pleased to have it and so on. But the majority of our customers are from Aberystwyth.

The year before Covid started, we celebrated the Syrian Dinner Project's birthday on the 15th of March. We made cake. There was a student who was also celebrating his birthday on the same day. It was a lovely day and we sang for both of us! Rose's birthday was also on the same day. Next time we will have a big party!

Slowly and gradually, we learned many expressions related to our dishes. Our writing and reading skills developed. We can read the stickers about the nut allergy or eggs allergy and we can differentiate and recognise them easily now. We have the stickers saved in folders that Rose already prepared for us. All I do is to print them out. I have a printer at home, and it is easier this way. Rose did all the basic work for us. She typed everything and showed us which is which among the files and this is how we learned about the different files.

Oh! Sorry I forgot to mention the Wales for Business service. It was through Rose that we came to know about them. And they provided us with the necessary documents on how to start with the community. Yes, they were so supportive. Catherine and Cliff who work there, I am still in contact with them for inquiries or issues. They are responsible for the legal side of the business. We have no idea and they take charge of the legal side and they help with any other detail around business.

This contact has improved my English language a lot. People also had a role in this. They helped me. Sometimes when they feel that I am unsure of what they say, they slow down and repeat what they said. They speak to us all the time and that's how they helped us. I always ask them to correct me, and I don't feel embarrassed to make language mistakes because I am willing to learn the right usage of language.

Even Medina and Cletwr – you met the manager of Cletwr, a very respectable and kind lady. She gave us limitless support. She advertised for us, helped us, opened her restaurant to us. We can't thank her enough for what she has been doing with us. Also Aber Food Surplus. They open their shop to us. For instance on a Saturday we go there and make Falafel and Shawarma sandwiches. We did takeaways at markets like the Christmas market and Lampeter's. All this paved the way for us in terms of language.

We usually pre-make food at home and we also pack things and label them at home. But if we have our own restaurant, space and facilities, it would give us more freedom in choosing what to cook. Also, when you prepare food daily in a restaurant, it is different from when you make food once a month. You find us very busy preparing everything from scratch and everything is freshly made. Syrian dishes must be cooked fresh. I also learned from the food course that rice must not be served cold. Once rice becomes cold it will host bacteria. So, rice shouldn't be served cold or served next day. This is the nature of our food in Syria, but I love to learn more food facts. I try to make healthy food. Not too spicy or hot. I personally don't use loads of spices because I want people to get the flavour without too many spices. When I make falafel or vines, I love people to feel the vines themselves without too many additions. Same with *Kibbeh* etc. If I keep using and adding the same spices, there won't be much difference between one dish and the other.

This project is not 100% about profit. I believe that what we are doing is driven by our love of food and communicating with people. My husband encourages us. But sometimes he worries that I am overloading myself. He worries about my health and the children. He is so supportive. He drives us to and from markets and events

Latifa's husband and their two daughters in Aberystwyth.
© Latifa Alnajjar

and helps with groceries and with the shopping. My husband is pleased with what I have achieved, and he is so proud of that. But he has concerns. He worries that I might get too exhausted in a way that affects the children. He worries about the children. He doesn't want them to be on their own. He encourages me but is concerned about me as well.

He works as a deliveryman at a Pizza shop. He didn't wait long before getting a job. He got his job really soon after we came here. We came here as refugees, but it is very important for us to work and be independent. Back home we've never been unemployed. We love to work. Life is difficult without work. He used to work for a detergent company. They find working in delivery is better in terms of the English language. It is easier than working in a field that requires the use of computers because of their low level of English. So, working in delivery is far better in communicating with people. Their English has improved a lot.

Work gives power. I am not used to sit and do nothing. I know that I have a big role to play in the upbringing of my children and in taking care of the house. But I believe that it is very important for any woman to achieve something. Especially in our case. We are in a foreign land and it is necessary to prove ourselves. We are not just refugees. We love to work, we have skills, we are open to options and to new ideas.

My mother works hand in hand with us. I feel safe and reassured when my mother cooks by my side. It is not just about her immense help with the work, but the feeling her presence gives me. Her great experience in cooking and her skills are so important. We sometimes argue over recipes! She has her own opinion and I have mine. But in the end, it all goes well.

I feel that the name is behind our success. The name – Syrian Dinner Project – I love it. And it means a lot to me. It's our beginning. I also aspire to make a book of recipes. I will call the book *Syrian Dinner Project*. It will be on Syrian food and in three languages: English, Welsh and Arabic. I hope Allah will help us achieve this.

I hope this dream comes true. I hope a restaurant would also help the community. The community helped us and supported us a lot in our food journey. It would be an opportunity to return the community's favour and kindness.

There is a proverb that says: 'You can't clap with one hand only.' In this project we help each other. I believe we love what we are doing, and we love to support one another. I can start a business on my own. But the beauty of this business is about working as a group. I help my mother, when I am tired, she helps me. And it goes on like this. There is this spirit of cooperation. We were gathered around something we all love to do in this place. I don't like to work on my own. It is such a lovely feeling when you work with your friends. When we finish after a long day, we sometimes dance, sing, and have fun. We celebrate our achievement. We achieved. If I am doing it alone, it won't feel the same. I loved the idea of food-making when I realised how people loved our food. This inspired me to do more because they were happy with it. It was such a nice feeling when you find people who like your work. In this way, I don't look at it as a financial gain only. Honestly, we cook with love.

I have two daughters: Rama 10 years old, Masa 8 years old, and my little boy was made in Wales. He has recently turned two. My second girl was born in Egypt and my son in Wales. An international family! When my first child Rama was born in Syria, it was the beginning of the crisis in Syria, the beginning of the troubles. I gave birth to her in the middle of that chaos and I can't remember how I felt at that time. All I know is that we were all having a very difficult time there. When I travelled to Egypt, I was also under the psychological pressure of leaving my country. In this country there was a different feeling. I think it's because I gave birth to my son after I settled here. So, I was more comfortable and more relaxed. When I decided to

Latifa with her mother, her friend Rula and Rula's daughter selling their produce at a farmer's market in Lampeter.

have my third child, I was relatively comfortable. It was an easy delivery. I got a lot of support from the people around me. I consider it the best of my three deliveries! In my first two deliveries I had a general anaesthetic. With this child, I had a partial anaesthetic. When Maher my son came, they handed him to me and I took him in my arms and it was a wonderful feeling. The nurses were very helpful. They were all around like family. Mum was by my side, my friends, Rula, Lamya from Sudan and Aunt Om Ali from Iraq. I was surrounded by kind people. I felt great!

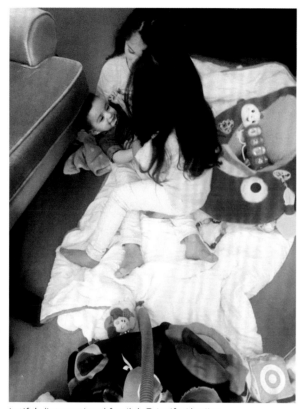

Latifa's 'international family'. © Latifa Alnajjar

I grew up in a family that encouraged learning. As I said before, I got a diploma and joined a course in nursing, I also worked in a gym and nursing centre. I am not used to being idle and inactive. I learned many skills before coming here. I joined a computer course. I loved to join as many courses as I could. I even learned how to play piano during my childhood. So, I was very active. I had never said no to activities. Same here. I still love to learn. But it is a big responsibility when you manage a business, being in contact with people, communicating with others in a foreign language. I consider language to be the main obstacle. I am always very wary of using the wrong words. I don't mean spelling mistakes etc, but it is more about the meaning and the message I want to pass to people. I have some friends who help me in this regard. My friend Hala, from Tunisia, has helped a lot with translation – for instance, when I want to post an advertisement. She helps me by choosing a different word. She corrects grammatical mistakes. Bless her. Also, Miss Nuha from school is very helpful. I am grateful to all those people around.

It is very difficult to manage time fully. Sometimes I don't even find time to drink my coffee in a relaxed mood, especially with my little son. I really don't know how people do it. But at least I feel satisfied, and I am happy. I wish that the government could support refugees in a way that enables them to achieve their goals and to do something for this country. If they could just help refugees offer something to the country. This support has inspired us to continue with this project so far. My advice to refugees is to just do it. Don't hesitate or be scared. We started from scratch, with no language. This shouldn't be a barrier at all. Even when there is support around us, we also have to depend on ourselves and try to improve our language.

Thank you so much for this lovely interview which I enjoyed. Thanks to anyone who listens to people's stories and listen to their problems. I am so pleased that I was given this chance to talk and to express my opinion and wish you all the best of good luck.

"When we finish after a long day, we sometimes dance, sing, and have fun. We celebrate our achievement."

Najla'a Hadle

My name is Najla'a Jamal Hadle. I was born on the 7th of April 1987 in Aleppo. I have been here in Aberystwyth for five years. I moved from Lebanon to here. I had two children before coming to the UK. My third child, Amal, was born here. Now she is three years old. I left Syria for Lebanon in 2012. When I left Syria, I was three months into my pregnancy with my second daughter, Sakena. We stayed in Lebanon around four and a half years. We worked and lived there *Alhamdulillah*. We were able to survive.

We applied to the UN because I was due to give birth to my second daughter, Sakena. To be admitted to a hospital there, I had to be formally registered through the UN. The UN sponsored me. They gave us a call to inform us about the opportunity to travel. In the beginning we were surprised. We didn't want to travel. We were planning to return to Syria. We thought the war would end soon. We were looking forward to returning home and to settle well. After some thinking, we realised that travelling would be better for our children. Living in Lebanon wasn't sustainable. School would cost thousands of dollars. We couldn't afford to take our children to such schools. They blamed Syrians for taking their houses and so on, and we didn't want this. We applied as a one family.

Before taking the flight, we were told it was Wales. But where in Wales? No more than that. We had a map, and we asked some passengers about Wales. We realised that Wales is *mashallah* big. We arrived at Bristol airport. From Lebanon to Germany and then to Bristol. In the German airport we met many Syrians. They were coming from different places – Turkey and Jordan – and we were all gathered inside that German airport. We were then taken on board a special plane. All Syrians were taken to Bristol airport. We had no idea who would come to collect us. We were told that some people would be receiving us in the airport. We found a person from the Red Cross waiting for us.

There was a female Arabic interpreter and a bus driver. Huda, the interpreter, stayed a long time with us. And Graham from the Red Cross was responsible for us. They told us that they would take us to our houses. An indescribable road journey. It was a long and tiring journey. It took us five hours on that road. The kids were exhausted and we were so tired. At some stage my husband said: 'What have I done to myself! Why did I come to this hell?' We had no idea where we were heading, and they were trying to calm us down. They were so kind to us. They gave food to the children, tissue papers, wipes and bags for those who might get sick. They were so kind.

We left Lebanon at 10:00 pm and arrived here next day. I still remember it was 7:00 pm – even later than 7:00 pm. It was night time. We arrived here on 8/12/2016. There was someone from the Red Cross waiting for us in the house. The landlord came to greet us. To reassure us. Then some

Syrian ladies visited us. I didn't know anyone. We were in shock in the beginning. Couldn't speak, very tired. It is a shock when life completely changes. Our lives changed when we left Aleppo for Lebanon. Living in Syria is different from living in Lebanon. Later, things changed differently because of the English language. You also don't know the laws. After a year, we realised that there was a Welsh language. We had no idea that there was a Welsh language. When we arrived on the first day, we were introduced to those people [from the Red Cross]. Then they left us to rest.

> *"When we rested our heads on the pillows, we had no idea about the life to come... We were thinking about the weather. It is not our country. Are we going to be accepted?"*

On the next day they visited us. They offered us some money for essentials. They told us that the currency here is the pound. They had already filled the fridge with *Halal* chicken, food, and bread. Toys for children – all that we needed was there. They gave the children the feeling of home. The first night was very difficult. When we rested our heads on the pillows, we had no idea about the life to come, what was waiting for us. It was a difficult night and we couldn't sleep. We were looking out of the window. We were thinking about the weather. It is not our country. Are we going to be accepted?

It was December. We were lucky that it was sunny. People told us that December is the best – Christmas time, preparations. The people from the Red Cross handed us documents to sign, for the house, the Jobcentre etc. They took us to the GP for registration. We were checked for diseases. We told them that my mother-in-law had been receiving cancer treatment. They introduced us to Aberystwyth, took us around. We had a tour to the sea and the shops. They showed us the way to our house and back. On the first day, they showed us everything. There was an interpreter. The second day they drove us back home. Then we were left on our own. It was as if you were waking up from sleep.

The first thing that attracted my attention and the children's was the sea. We love the sea! Back home we don't have a sea. We used to travel to other cities for seaside scenery. I haven't found door numbers strange or weird. I found the system around bin collection a bit strange. I thought all the waste would be collected same day. Things like drinking water – in Lebanon we never used tap water as they have a salty water. We used to buy bottled water. Here, my children found it a bit weird to drink water straight from the tap. The other thing is the bread. It is different from our Syrian bread. Many things like the prices – everything is priced differently from our country. No bargaining. We also found the medical system different. Registration. Back home we don't register at a clinic. Here, they took us to the GP. They took the children to the ophthalmologist.

They took my daughter and showed her the school that she would go to. It was a dream come true for her. In

Lebanon she wasn't allowed. She used to watch the schoolchildren and she always felt sad for not being able to join them. She cried out of joy. At the end of her first day in school, she cried. She wasn't missing me. She just didn't want to leave school! She loved the school. They made life easier for us. You know we had zero English. There were two female teachers: one is from Egypt and the other is from Yemen. They were a great help to our children. They are still helping us. The council appointed them to help our children in school.

Language wasn't an issue for the children. They got the language faster because they were younger. They just loved it. The Arabic-speaking teachers were always there for translation. And they helped them with the pronunciation. My daughter had no idea of any education system as she hadn't been to school before. Gradually, she got used to this system. She learned how to keep quiet and not to get too excited when she saw me inside the school. My children were so pleased. However, after two to three weeks, my daughter became depressed. She used to cry a lot. She used to look out of the window and she began asking questions like 'Why have you brought me here?'

Masa made friends, but the difficulty was that she had lived in Lebanon. She used Arabic on the street. Things like going to a corner shop for small errands. I used to stand on the balcony to watch her. The grocery man used to lead her back to our house. For her, here, people are different from the ones in Lebanon. In Lebanon we had friends and relatives whom we visited. She accompanied us. She had friends. She missed all this. The poor child was like that for

Najla'a's little daughter on the beach at Aberystwyth. ©Najla'a Hadle

two months. Skeena was three years and a half. She was little. She was psychologically affected. She got frequently ill. She cried a lot. She wanted to go back to Lebanon. All of us were psychologically affected. We were down. My husband was down. At one point we lost our appetites. We only had a small meal once a day. We were looking forward to making friends.

We were introduced to some Arabs, but there were no close friendships. No visits. We were so emotionally exhausted that we couldn't make friends. Later, we did. When we came here, Christmas holidays started a week

Najla'a's daughter on the footbridge at Trefechan, Aberystwyth.

college for English lessons. This was by the beginning of 2017. I remember it was on the 8th of January 2017 when we started our first English lesson at the college. We started from zero, as we couldn't even write our names in English. I couldn't write. My husband is better at writing as he studied English during his secondary school education. So, he was fine with writing.

He used to be a painter and a bird breeder. He was so down. He became bad-tempered and nervous. He was so nervous. In Lebanon he had many friends. Even though he worked long hours from 6:00 am to 5:00 pm, he used to play with the kids for an hour after work. He used to meet up with his friends over *Argeileh* [Hookah]. He used to come back by 9:00 pm. Those two hours – sometimes he used to visit *Khaltu* [his aunt from the mother's side] or *Amtu* [his aunt from the father's side]. We came here and we missed all that life. We came to a new life, a new language, and a new house. Everything was new for us.

When we first came to Wales and to this place, I saw people smiling at us saying: 'From Syria?' We didn't know what 'from Syria' meant. We smiled back at them. Later, I realised that it means 'Are you the Syrian newcomers to this area?' They had an idea that some Syrian families would arrive in the area. I felt that they were smiling people. And that their smile always precedes their communication. Later we used to go to the Art Centre for the Wednesday coffee morning sessions where we met English speakers for language exchange. Those people used to bring gifts for the children. In the beginning we were hesitant, and we didn't understand the language. Then we

after we arrived. During those holidays, those responsible for us left us on our own. We were totally deserted. Going to the supermarket was a big hassle for us. It was difficult. We had no idea. We were here for just one week when the holidays started. We struggled a lot. No one was around to instruct us. During the Christmas holiday, we felt isolated and were psychologically down. After the holidays, those responsible for us came back. They asked us to join the worked with them. We asked the interpreter to write down some of the difficult words, new words in both languages, so that we could use the words during the exchange sessions. We memorised 'hello' and 'thank you'. We were introduced to Arabic-speaking Syrian families and the children found some friends their age to play with. Gradually life began to improve.

> *"They told me 'You are a sister to us' and I still remember their tears. They were so emotional. I felt I had real siblings. I will never forget that."*

I became pregnant when we came here. It was a different healthcare routine here. A completely different GP system. To visit the hospital for a pregnancy appointment, I had to be accompanied by someone. I had a friend who knows English and Arabic. Also, the Red Cross didn't leave us on our own and there was always an interpreter. But for urgent appointments my friend use to accompany me. I had a difficult pregnancy with some complications. I had to travel to Cardiff. We were in shock because of the new way of life, followed by a complicated pregnancy. When I had those issues, my husband was away because of his mother. I was all alone with my kids here in this place. It was so shocking when I received the news that I was pregnant with a baby with no limbs. I was on my own when the doctor informed me of this. It was a severe shock. I wished

that my mothers, my sisters were there. When you have these people around you, you can vent your feelings, cry. I wished that my husband was there, but he was away. He had to accompany his mother for her cancer treatment at another place. But, thankfully, the hospital arranged for an Arabic-speaking doctor. He calmed me down and told me: 'This is God's will.' Of course, I believe in God's will and the first word I uttered was: *Alhamdulillah*. Allah will always choose goodness for us, and we believe in this. The Red Cross and those responsible for me, the doctor contacted them to facilitate my travel to Cardiff. He didn't want me to travel to Cardiff without an English-speaker to accompany me. The doctor contacted the Red Cross. I was alone when two people from the Red Cross visited me. They reassured me. They told me 'We are here for you, and we are praying for your safety and that of your baby.' I was so emotional at that moment. I felt that I had my siblings with me. Honestly, the attitude of the young man and the young woman! They told me 'You are a sister to us' and I still remember their tears. They were so emotional. I felt I had real siblings. I will never forget that.

I made friends with English speakers. When I greet them, they greet me back and when I smile at them, they smile back at me. Step by step. I used to ask the interpreter to write down certain conversational phrases like 'How are you doing?' Gradually, I went out with some of these people. They supported me and corrected my mispronounced words. I understood them but couldn't speak fast like them. Random people on the street, in the shops, during my shopping trips – I meet them, they smile at me and sometimes they ask where I am from. I realised they were willing to know about me and I liked that.

I gained more confidence in going out and talking to people. This happened a year after we arrived. After a year, we regained our strength and self-confidence. We had the basics in language and we realised that we were building the foundation of our life in this country. We became stronger. At that stage I started going out on my own. I wanted to buy small coffee cups from a second-hand shop. There was a young woman working in the shop, and she noticed me buying such cups many times. She wondered why I was buying those cups. I told her I use them to drink Turkish coffee. We don't use mugs for our coffee. We'd rather use the small coffee cups. She was curious to know about Turkish or Syrian coffee. I explained to her that our coffee has no milk and no sugar. I asked her if she was willing to try it and she agreed.

Next day I made coffee and took it to the shop, and she said 'Wow, such a strong coffee!' She liked it and she asked me for the coffee's packaging. And we have been friends since then. Also, her daughter is in the same class as my daughter and this strengthened our friendship. I was introduced to other friends. Mums of kids in my daughter's school. I met a Polish mum. In the beginning, we didn't talk to each other. One day I was having coffee with my friend Latifa, and she passed by. I said to her: *Tafadhaly* [come over]. I offered her coffee, and she drank it. Then we became friends because of the coffee. The magic of coffee! She, Latifa and I are still friends and we go out together. She loved our coffee and learned how to

make it. She tells me that she drinks it whenever she feels stressed. It is calming!

When we first came, we couldn't make traditional Syrian food because some elements necessary in Syrian dishes were not found. In the beginning *Halal* meat was not available. We struggled with that. Also some ingredients were missing for instance: *Mulukhiyya*, *Waraq al Enab*, *Burgul* for *Kibbeh*, vegetables for *Mahashi*. For a while all of this was missing. So, we cooked Syrian food but depending on the available vegetables alone. We used to cook what was called the summer dishes which are oil-based dishes. Syrian food has no alternatives. *Waraq al Enab, Mulukhiyya* – we didn't have them here in these parts. And the small vegetable pieces for *Mahashi*. We had to cook other things. After seven months, my husband travelled to Swansea to accompany his mother. He wanted to get Syrian bread and Arabic food like meat, for instance. We were craving those things – Syrian cheese, *Mushallalieh* and the fatty stuff like *Samen*. We never found them. This is our tradition – *Kibbeh*, *Waraq al enab* and *Mahashi* are essentials. We had to cook at least one of them each week. Also, *Freekeh*. No one knows what *freekeh* is here. But these are the ordinary Syrian dishes. We Syrians love our bellies!

In the first stages I suffered a lot from the absence of spices. Several spices which are essential in our food were not to be found. I used to cook the same dish without them, but the dish wasn't as good as before. After six months, when my husband travelled to Swansea, he visited the oriental shops and brought us all kinds of spices, *Mulukhiyya* and *Falafel*. Everything that we needed at home. We spent a lot but managed to get Syrian bread. Every four months my husband used to go to Swansea. Every three to four months we were preparing *Mooneh* [laughs] because it was difficult to find such shops here. It was two years before a shop called Bookers opened here. They sell *Halal* chicken and meat. I was also introduced to some English friends here in the area. When they plan to travel to Cardiff, Swansea or London, they always ask if I need something from these cities. They suggested that I gave them a photo of the ingredient or write down the name in Arabic so that they can buy some or ask the shopkeeper to contact me.

They are friends from the Aber Aid organisation. They supported us all these years. They used to visit their families in Cardiff and other places every month or two to three weeks. They used to bring these things with them. Then they got used to the food! Once a lady brought me *Makdous*. Syrians love *Makdous*. She was curious about *Makdous* and wondered how we serve it. We laughed and we invited her to have some with us. Later we made them Syrian breakfast and she tried it. She said to us 'If I ate all of this, I wouldn't be able to move!' She asked me to pack some pieces of *Makdous* for her husband to try it. Later, she started asking her husband to buy Syrian food like Syrian coffee, Syrian bread. Those people helped Syrians a lot. For instance, they used to provide Syrian groceries and distribute them. Aber Aid placed groceries in bags and distributed them as gifts to us. Spices, rose water. They told us: 'We know you miss all this stuff, and we are giving you this as a small gift to you from us.'

Syrian coffee

To return their kindness and to thank them, we used to get together every Thursday or Monday to cook some Syrian dishes for their lunch. They were so pleased that we were sharing food with them. During our two Eid events – *Eid al Fitr* and *Eid al Adha* – they gave us practical and emotional support. They organised parties for our kids. They offered gifts to the children. They told us, 'You share Christmas with us, and we must share your celebrations too.'

They used to say: 'Wow!' and they took photos of the food. They said: 'The smell is good. What did you add?' Most of the dishes we made were vegetarian dishes because most of them were vegetarians. Even if the dish was meat-based, we tried to turn it to a vegetarian dish. We became creative in this! Some of them didn't mind the meat-based dishes and we cooked that as well. They liked it and they told us our food was tastier. Some asked us to write down recipes. Now there is a book with the names of some of the Syrian ladies. I was ill when they wrote it and couldn't take part. They have included many Syrian dishes in it.

People suggested to us the idea of food selling. Here, the Red Cross, Rose from the Red Cross provided the Syrian ladies with all the necessary ingredients to make the dish. She suggested the idea of making food and presenting it in a church. We were to choose a dish and make it the Syrian way. She ordered everything that we needed to include in the dish to save us spending on the dish. All we did was cook and join the other ladies in the event. We were amazed by the huge numbers of people who attended the event. The idea was a charity initiative. It was to fund a tour around Wales for Syrian children. It was difficult for families to afford a trip around Wales for their children.

That food event took place at the beginning of the summer season. It was sometime in July as far as I remember. Many people attended. English speakers and our friends. The young lady advertised the event and spread the word among her friends. And everyone came. She works at the Red Cross. It was her idea. She told us that she knew about many groups in Aberystwyth who were working on food. Instead of providing food and sharing it for free, how about selling the food, introducing people to your food, and making some profit as well? This is how the idea of the project started.

During the first event we made a big sum of money for the children's trips. The Red Cross and the Council worked on managing the budget and funded the trips. They took the children on so many trips. They made the children's summer! Before the Christmas holidays, an English person wanted us to cook some Syrian dishes for a party he was organising. He respected us for being Muslims. He was responsible for the cost of the food. The money we got from selling the food was allocated to the Syrian children's activities. He didn't want to introduce himself to us. He donated the money to the Red Cross. There was a second food event during summer where the Syrian ladies took part. That was how the Syrian project started. From a young woman's idea to a bigger thing. From a small dish to a big project.

People here smell our food, and they like it. We are trying to make vegetarian food and they are finding it healthy. They make food but they feel that ours is tastier and healthier. For instance, the desserts in our culture. It is not just biscuits and cakes. We are very creative in making our desserts like *Haresah, Basboosah, Muhalabiyyah* and *Baklava*. This is all handmade. And we all cook the same dish in different ways.

Some Syrian ladies here are planning for a food business. I personally believe that we must dream big. Not just about food. I cook food daily and I am used to doing it. I have an English friend who comes to visit us. She doesn't have children and she loves my kids and she plays with them. After having lunch with us, I always give her a sample for her husband to try it. Her husband ended up telling her 'I am going to marry a Syrian woman. They are good at food. You aren't!'

Kibbeh consists of a dough made of meat, bulgur (cracked wheat), onions and mint leaves, formed into football shaped croquettes, and filled with more meat, onions, pine nuts and Middle Eastern spices. They are then deep fried, so they are crisp on the outside and soft inside!

Waraq al Enab are vine leaves. In Syria, grape leaves are used in two dishes:
Yalanji, which is vine leaves stuffed with rice and vegetables, and Yabraq, where the leaves are stuffed with rice and meat, cooked in lemon juice.

Fattoush is basically a Mediterranean fried bread salad that typically includes lettuce, tomatoes, cucumbers, radishes and fried pieces of pita.

Esh Al-Bulbul means "Bulbul's nest" (Nightingale's Nest), the dessert's shape is similar to the nest of the Nightingale. Baklava: made with layers of honey-soaked crispy phyllo pastry and a delicious nut mixture

© Najla'a Hadle

I am planning to learn English and to improve my language further. Later, I am planning to work in the care field. For instance, I would love to work in a hospital, to take care of the elderly or to work with children in a nursery, as I feel I can deal with children. Yes, I like to do this sort of thing. I love to cook, and I sometimes come up with new ideas on food. I like to copy new recipes and make them. I watched some English cooks on the net. They make nice dishes which I am not familiar with. I copied them and started making these recipes and they were nice ones. My children are used to Syrian food. When they started school,

they were offered English food. In school my son asked them for Syrian food. He said: 'I want my Mum's food.' The teacher told him: 'You will have it when you are back home.'

"I would never take my children to hell again… I sacrificed everything for their sake, and I will do it forever."

Yes, I would very much like to improve my English and then work in a field where I can benefit others and benefit from it myself. I might use my cooking skills in a care home where they need it. I have a cooking certificate which entitles me to cook from home. I cook for my English friends for free! I make lots of free food for guests.

[British citizenship] will be useful to my children, for their future and for their studies. If for any reason we return home, they will be able to come back to the UK and continue their studies in a safe place. Whatever they will choose to study in the UK will have a value and a significance. My daughter loves to draw. She wants to be an artist in future. My son wants to be a pilot. So, *Inshallah* if they have these dreams, they will be able to achieve them here. It is about them, and it is because of them that I left home and left my family and my whole world. I want them to be well educated and to achieve something in future. We, the parents, didn't have good education, so let them be better than us.

We feel safe, settled and we feel like it is a new life. We

miss our country and we long for it. But the children don't miss the country because they were too little when we left it. I might go for a visit to see my relatives and friends and come back. But it is impossible to think of a final return to Lebanon or to Syria. Those two countries are unsafe. I cannot take my children back to either of these countries. My children feel safe here. They go to schools, and they get checked by a doctor. Drinking water straight from the tap is a blessing. In Lebanon and Syria these things don't exist. I would never take my children to hell again. If I take them back to any of these countries my children would be mentally affected, and I don't want this to happen to them. I sacrificed everything for their sake, and I will do it forever.

People have been so kind and nice with us. I must thank everyone who helped us here in Wales. They supported us. The elderly stood by us like a family and the youth have been so helpful and caring. They never hesitated to help. They are aware of our language difficulties. And they have been very supportive in this regard. They do their best to understand us. They are very respectable and I must thank them all – the council and everyone in Wales. It is a beautiful place. I hope that the coming days will be better for everyone – for us, our children and thank you so much.

"When I placed my head on the pillow during my first night in the country, I was so reassured, calm and had an inner peace that drove me to sleep immediately."

Noor

We stayed for six months in Manchester until we got our residence ID. Later, we moved to Cardiff. As my brother was already living in Cardiff, he recommended the city as he had faced no troubles settling in. Sulaiman thought that Cardiff was a quiet and a beautiful city. He believed that the diverse nature of the city with its multiculturalism, ethnic and religious groups would certainly make it a very suitable place to live.

My first impression of the UK in general was that it is a peaceful country. When I placed my head on the pillow during my first night in the country, I was so reassured, calm and had an inner peace that drove me to sleep immediately. I felt safe, respected and treated as a human here. Throughout the course of our journey from Turkey to Europe, my mother and I had witnessed several episodes of racism and inhuman behaviour, especially in France and Denmark. Luckily, we have never experienced such attitudes here in the UK. When we lived in Manchester, we rarely left our accommodation as we were still new to the area and were afraid of losing our way. Once we moved to Cardiff, we had more confidence walking around, going to parks and to the city centre, and we got used to using public transport. We lived with Sulaiman for two weeks as he was living on his own and the neighbours were so nice and kind to us. We then rented a separate house for us.

Nowadays, social media is playing a big role in introducing newcomers to the community. There is a Facebook group for Syrians in the UK. Two days back, someone in the group notified us that a single mum with

"Catching the bus" by Jeremy Segrott (CC BY 2.0)

two little daughters from Syria had just arrived in Cardiff and that she needed help. So, we contacted her and arranged to meet her and introduced her to the city centre and the *halal* shops etc.

When my mother and I came to Cardiff, Sulaiman facilitated things for us and we settled in the city in no time. However, Sulaiman was so busy with his study and work and had no spare time for us. So we relied on ourselves to discover Cardiff and started using public transport easily. What I liked about transport in Cardiff and other places in the UK is that buses would always take you back to the first bus stop you were picked up from. This means you will never lose your way. When we were first in the city centre, we took a bus from a certain point and we were sure that it would bring us back to the same spot upon our return.

At the beginning we used to visit Oasis. Oasis offered English lessons for total beginners. I used to accompany my mother for her English lessons in Oasis. My mother couldn't go on her own as she wasn't confident of using public transport and new streets. My mother could easily lose her way especially with the old buildings and old streets. I wish that the government could work on modernising the old buildings which look very similar to one another. We also used to visit mosques, especially during Eid and religious events. Al Baraa' mosque organised several events for children and families which helped bringing people together.

We left my siblings in Turkey in August 2016. We arrived in the UK in January 2017 and were reunited with them in November 2017. It was almost a year until we were reunited.

I tried my best to self-learn English. When we were in Huddersfield, I used to visit YouTube channels for learners of a second language. In Huddersfield we shared a house with a lady from a foreign country whose English was far better than mine. I was embarrassed to talk to her for fear that I might commit a mistake. She encouraged me to use English with her to improve my communicative skills. I would say that she motivated me to self-learn through YouTube. I worked hard on those speaking lessons and I used to take notes and practise memorising vocabulary. I focussed on the words that I needed for my daily use in shopping, on the bus and at the railway station. When I came to Cardiff, Sulaiman introduced me to a lady who helped him with his ESOL. She encouraged me to sign in at a language school. I registered myself at Fitzalan High School for the entry 1 ESOL, which was a beginner's course. Next year, I did entry 2, but the teachers upgraded me to entry 3 as they thought my English level was higher as I had some basic knowledge in English from Syria. I was so excited to be in that higher level. As it is a high school, I had to study for a full day from 8:30-3:00 pm Monday to Friday. I did a GCSE in Arabic language and then I did my two A levels in Arabic language and I got an A*.

I have encountered some situations which made me feel uncomfortable and different. On a rainy day in Cardiff, my mother and I were waiting at the bus stop when we saw our bus coming. At that moment, I started waving the bus down, but the driver didn't stop. We were both very annoyed as we were the only persons at the bus stop, and we were sure that he saw us signalling at the bus to stop. I tried to file a complaint, but my mother didn't encourage me to do so. Even though I haven't encountered any verbal bullying I sometimes sense nonverbal facial or physical gestures, menacing or contemptuous looks towards me or my mother, especially on public transport.

I am from a Sunni sect and my best friend is an Iraqi Shia Muslim and we hadn't experienced any difficulties in accepting each other at all. My friend's mother is a friend of my mother as well and we visit one another, and we never discuss our differences or care about them. We are both refugees and this is the thing that unites us. You know, both countries have suffered from sectarian conflicts and we don't want to bring those conflicts here.

I love the space given to women to explore their potential and develop their skills. I love how the law protects women and supports them, but I think women should understand how to use these rights. I've heard several stories about women from the Middle East in the UK whose marriages were ruined because they misunderstood these rights. In the Middle East, there is nothing like child custody or social care homes where children are kept when troubles erupt between parents. So most of the time women or even men don't realise the consequences of their behaviour towards their children once police or social services are involved. I am aware that arguments and issues might take place in every marriage and all these issues can be resolved in one way or another. I heard about a woman who called the police and raised a

ESOL class at Oasis Cardiff © Oasis Cardiff

complaint against her husband for a silly argument. The issue was resolved but their relationship was ruined forever. I know another couple who were recently divorced after many arguments because the husband didn't buy his wife fast food!

I think integration is a two-way process. For instance, when we first lived in the UK, neighbours greeted us with a 'hi' or a 'how are you?' and that was it. Next morning, they might greet you with a 'good morning' or might not see you at all. We were left to find our way on our own. We got the impression that most people here don't know or don't even bother to know who lives next door to them. My mother recently moved to Ely in Cardiff. Her next-door neighbour is a lovely lady whom I invited for coffee and she came and enjoyed the Syrian coffee a lot. But she didn't invite us back. So, I think they must do some effort to get to know us better. Otherwise, we will both take a long time to get to know one another. We are trying our best to learn about the culture of Wales. But they must make some effort to know about our culture as well. I think such a mutual effort would minimise isolation to a great extent.

Once I was granted residence status, I was informed that I was eligible to apply for British Citizenship right after the expiry of my residency. I did my Life in the UK test and succeeded at the first attempt. I still need to pass an English-speaking test that qualifies me to apply for British Citizenship later. I feel confident about my English language and I am sure I will pass that as well. I don't think there is a reason why the Home Office wouldn't offer me citizenship.

I am grateful to be in a country that offers equal rights to its citizens. I am looking forward to seeing my children have a better future in terms of education and learning. Of course, Syria is our first home, but in the current situation, the UK offers a brighter future for me and for my baby. I will tell my children about Syria and why we left. But I am not going to talk about the pain and the humiliation I faced. Perhaps when my children grow and become mature, I will tell them about the details of the journey. I think by that time they will be able to understand better.

I have a mixture of feelings. The war and ISIS put an end to a beautiful dream that I wanted to achieve. There were only few steps towards achieving my dream of entering a university, which I couldn't complete because we had to flee. I did my ESOL and I studied for other courses but there are lots of steps which I need to follow for a university degree. However, I feel happy that I made it to the UK and I am sure there will be several educational opportunities for me in future.

Anyone wishing to have indefinite leave to remain in the UK or naturalisation as a British citizen must pass the Life in the UK test.

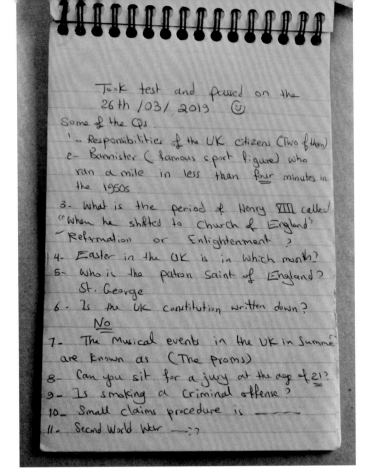

Notes taken of her own Life in the UK test by Angham Abdullah

I left Syria at the age of 16. I can't remember anything but fear, uncertainty and darkness inside Syria. I don't want my children to go through that. The only place where I felt at peace is the UK and I will do my best to stay in this peaceful country. I will do all I can to protect my children and to provide them with a decent life where they can continue their education and have a future. I feel sorry for the relatives and friends I left behind but there is nothing that we can do except pray for their safety.

I have two uncles with their families here in Cardiff. Both uncles were living in other areas in the UK, but they moved to Cardiff to be close to us. I have a sister who also lives in Cardiff with her husband and her little son. My eldest brother Sulaiman lives in Cardiff with his wife and son. My two youngest brothers and little sister live with my mother. At Eid time and other social events, all the relatives gather at my mother's house as she is the eldest in the family.

I hope I can get a chance to continue my studies in the health sector or in a field that enables me to help people and improve their health conditions. When I got injured in Syria and was taken to hospital, I realised the shortage in medical staff. On that day, I wished that I could have the knowledge or the skill to help as many of those injured people as I could. I am determined to get a degree in a medical-related field.

> "I left Syria at the age of 16. I can't remember anything but fear, uncertainty and darkness inside Syria. I don't want my children to go through that."

Life is going from bad to worse in Syria and if people can get out safely for a better future for their children and themselves, they should not hesitate. I also want to tell them not to feel embarrassed about their low level of English. I used to feel very embarrassed. They should always ask others and be confident and not be scared or ashamed of making mistakes in language. I made many language mistakes, but I learned a lot and I am still learning. This is a country that respects people, and newcomers should understand how to respect the rules of a country that opened its doors to them.

I am so pleased that you have asked me all those questions and given me the chance to share my thoughts and feelings with you. It is so comforting to talk about dreams, suffering, insecurities. I think it is important that people know about how we suffered and what we have been through until we reached here. Thank you for giving me the chance to talk about all those worries, concerns and happy thoughts.

Dona al Abdallah

I did a diploma in dental implants at the Institute for Dentistry in Aleppo University. I worked for about a year in a lab for dental implants. Dental implant is an art. If someone has drawing, carving, and moulding skills, they will excel. I very much enjoyed working in making teeth from porcelain and metal. I used to go to a place for English language classes, but it was outside Cardiff. It was a bit difficult especially when I got pregnant and had my first child, Hassan. I do have my documents with me. But now I am pregnant with my second child and I don't feel I am excited or encouraged to work anymore. I don't know why. I am so discouraged here. Even though my husband encourages me to try and get training. In Syria I was so excited about my job and about learning everything around it and on developing my skills. But here ... I think the main

reason is English language. I feel I am isolated and I miss my life back home. I miss my friends and my family.

Most of [my friends] are living in Hamah and Homs and at one point, there was no connection with them. I think some changed their phone numbers. I searched on Facebook but I couldn't find them. My mother, sisters and brothers are all there. I have three brothers and three sisters. I am the eldest and I have a twin sister. My sister did a degree in business administration and is doing a casual job. My eldest brother works as a builder in Syria and my middle brother is a barber. My family is depending on him financially. They are relatively safer. Kurds are in control. People work and live normally, but financially it is very difficult. They are just surviving. Surviving day by day. Struggling to make ends meet.

How do people return? Their families back home are starving. People are barely able to support their own children. And everyone knows this fact. There are no incentives. Life is getting worse and worse there. The conditions of life and of living are deteriorating. How does he [Asad] expect people to exchange safety for danger and suffering? No one would do it.

I arrived at Heathrow and I didn't have enough time to see the city. I immediately took the train to Cardiff. It was a totally different world to me. I was overwhelmed. I realised that now I was on another planet. My mind was full of the faces of my family members – parents, sisters, and brothers, my friends. I was thinking of them all the time. I was wondering if I would see them again. But the fact that I would be reunited with Ali made it easier and calmed me down. I didn't like the way houses were built. All the houses looked similar. The first days in Cardiff were very difficult for me. I could hardly recognise our house. Streets looked similar, and houses were painted and designed in the same way. I was bewildered. Without Ali I would have lost my way. When we were living in Albany Road, I went to visit a relative three streets from our house. I lost my way. On my way back I couldn't recognise our house. I phoned Ali and he directed me. I was always scared of losing my way. I depended on Ali 100%.

Even though it was difficult, I was able to adjust more easily because Ali's relatives were living close to us. When we moved to this new area here in Roath Park, I felt like I had been estranged. I don't meet with those relatives as frequently as I used to. I don't mix with people at all. I don't have many Arab friends. I was introduced to a lady from Jordan, and we became friends but sadly she travelled back to Jordan when her husband finished his studies here. When I became pregnant with my first child, I volunteered to teach Arabic at a private school that teaches Arabic and religious education in Cardiff. I enjoyed that and I met with many nice families. I left that volunteering post when I was nine months into my pregnancy as I was exhausted and couldn't stand up for too long. I didn't resume that work because I became a full-time mother.

I didn't make friends with any English speakers. I am not confident in my English and this is one of the things that prevents me from getting to communicate with people. In Syria, English language was not taken seriously. We studied English grammar and the focus was on grammar not on

A Cardiff terraced street

speaking and communication. When I joined the ESOL English language lessons here I was very good with grammar, but my speaking was poor. I also found it very hard to follow everything that the teacher was saying. I found it too hard. I spent seven months in those ESOL lessons, but I couldn't continue. I made no progress and was so disappointed and had to quit. Also I was in my maternity period and that made it even more difficult to cope with lessons outside of Cardiff.

Throughout the first days or even the first weeks in Cardiff, I was so sleepy. I felt like I needed to sleep forever. From the day I left Syria and landed in Lebanon, I couldn't have a proper sleep. Even before leaving Syria. I was scared that Ali might not make it. Life under ISIS, me moving between my family's house and Ali's house, the journey to Lebanon, living in Lebanon for a year, the uncertainty about

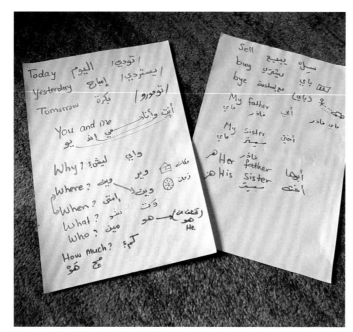

Notes on English words in Arabic.

the rejection of my application and reapplying… Lots of concerns about my future and that of Ali. On top of all of that, the devastating news about my family back home and the air raid on their house. I was so stressed. When I came here, I felt that I was safe at last. I was still worried about my family in Syria, though. But it also felt as if a big burden had fallen off my shoulders and I needed to sleep. I was mentally and physically exhausted and I needed that sleep. I felt that this was my home. Ali took me to places in Cardiff and we were always together. As I said before, I didn't dare to go out on my own for fear of getting lost. For the first couple of months, I was fully dependent on Ali.

I can read in English very well and understand most of the words, but I was just afraid of trying to go out alone. I know many people who haven't mastered any English words and have managed to go out on their own. Ali was working as a volunteer at a charity in Albany Road close to our previous house, but I didn't try. The ESOL lessons were not very helpful. It was all about 'do', 'does' and 'did' and the grammar. We learned the basic vocabulary. It was very basic. I had four hours of study a week. I was faster than others in writing and understanding what was written, but I had great difficulty in understanding the speaking. I am used to the BBC English which I can understand very well. But I can't cope with local English. I struggle a lot when people use a dialect.

I finished two language entries and when I was seven to eight months into my pregnancy, I couldn't continue with the lessons. I was very heavy and couldn't walk normally. I was at home and Ali was with me. He took me to the hospital. I spent a whole day in pain. I really struggled. I was surrounded by Ali and his relatives. I wished that my mum was around. I thought that if my mum were there it would be much easier. Once I saw Hassan, I felt better. I thought life would be pleasant with him. I felt that my life would be changed now and I was excited about that new change. Even though I had no idea how to deal with that child [laughs]. I didn't know how to bathe him, to soothe him etc. Thankfully, there was Ali's relative. She is a very kind woman. She used to bathe Hassan. Bathing was the most difficult part of it. In twenty days, we learned how to bathe Hassan. Ali and I started doing that job on our own [laughs].

I am planning to take my children to visit Syria from time to time once I get my passport. They must meet with their relatives, my family, visit my family's house, Ali's house. I would love my children to keep the Arabic traditions. I use Arabic with Hassan all the time. I know he will learn English in the nursery and at the school later. I want Hassan to mix with other kids his age and become sociable. Once Hassan feels OK about going to the nursery and settles well there, I will be relaxed. I will focus on my second baby. I hope that Ali can get a good job opportunity and that we educate our children and provide them with a decent living.

I wish I could work as before. When I was in Syria, I was independent. I wish I could get into work and socialise with people and make new friends. I used to do a lot of things back home. I had my job, colleagues, friends. All that was gone here. I long for those days. Despite the war and the hardships, I had friends. We used to meet up every now and then. I made friends in my workplace. We used to enjoy ourselves despite the bombings and the chaos. I feel like that independent life was taken away from me. I was an outgoing person. Work gave me a lot of self-esteem and confidence. I was very close to death on a couple of occasions.

My workplace and the nearby hospitals were always targeted. But I survived. I even long for those days. I was alive. With that life I was alive because I was working, thinking, and moving. Working was a great achievement. It always offered me a sense of achievement. Look at me now, a housewife spending almost all my time at home. I go out when it is necessary. The weather doesn't always help. Not very confident about my English and no close friends

to meet or to visit. Always at home. And this is not the life I am used to at all. I feel like I am living this life against my will. I know many women from Syria who came to the UK and are doing really well. I know that I have new responsibilities as a wife and a mother. But I wish I could achieve something of what I was doing before. I really suffer because of this.

Improving my English would help me to communicate and to socialise. My next-door English neighbour is a nice and kind old lady. She is very friendly. She brought Hassan gifts during Christmas and at other times. She surprised us with gifts at the doorsteps. She always offers to help with taking our bins out for the bin collection. She frequently volunteered to take the bins out and brings them in the alleyway on her own when we were busy. She lives on her own and her son visits her from time to time. Sadly I don't communicate with her a lot because I am lacking confidence in my English. She is friendly and I could see she wanted to have a conversation with us, but I was embarrassed about making mistakes or not knowing what to say.

Many people came here without any background knowledge and they learned faster. It is a beautiful country and I always remember the Arabic proverb : 'A paradise without its people is not a paradise.' I became so lonely here. I use social media with my family and friends and that's it. And Covid made it worse. With my pregnancy and Covid I became even more cautious of meeting others. Even with social distance, it is very difficult for me. I minimised my walks to shopping centres or to grocers. I have not been to the city centre for ages now. My outings have been limited and restricted to Roath Park only. I take Hassan to the playground when weather allows and that's it.

Mohammad S

When I came to Wales, I learned English quicker than my sister who had come to the UK before me. You know, I came via family reunion. My mother and sister came to the UK first and then my siblings. I was the last to join. In the beginning my application was rejected because my passport had expired. I had to work hard to pay for a renewed Syrian passport. The applications of my two younger siblings were accepted while mine was rejected. My mother reapplied and this time the British embassy asked for my DNA as a proof of my ID. I waited for one and a half months for that application to be approved. In the meantime, my younger siblings had already arrived in the UK and were admitted to schools in Cardiff.

I didn't have great difficulty in developing my English in the UK. When I was in Syria my father used to take me to an English training course during my summer holidays. It was an American summer school which opened before the war. I had the foundations of the English language. When I was in Turkey I thought that the hardships I faced had erased my English language. But then I realised that the basics were still there in my head. When I came to Cardiff, I joined Fitzalan High School. The ESOL course. There are usually three language entries. Each entry requires a year to pass to the next level. I passed entry level 1 and 2 in one year. In the second year I did my entry level 3 with a GCSE

in maths. I was so excited. I felt that the language I learned during my childhood was there in my head. And I was comfortable. I was totally concentrating on my studies and had no other concerns. I had no pressure. The pressure of earning, of work and of family responsibility all gone and I felt I was a student again. I was so pleased to be able to regain that feeling of being a student with a family who takes care of me instead of me taking care of them. It was more difficult for my younger siblings to start from zero in the UK as they had no foundation. They stopped going to primary school in Syria when the war began. Sadly, they

Mohammad S after being interviewed

had to go through the experience of being a refugee before experiencing school or education.

I was shocked by the weather. I found it hard to understand why it rains while other countries are enjoying the sun or complaining about hot weather. I found that strange. I loved the diversity in my school. I met students from many nationalities and backgrounds. In Syria, I had never experienced such a diverse environment. I was introduced to many different nationalities and I learned a lot about their countries, traditions, and food. In my English language class, there were students from Pakistan, India, Bangladesh, and Morocco. A female student from Vietnam took us to a Vietnamese restaurant in Cardiff and I was amazed at the variety of flavours and colours. I took the students to our restaurant and introduced them to Shawarma and they liked it a lot.

I was stressed at the beginning. I was embarrassed to take part in class discussions or to talk to students. But gradually, I regained my confidence and I realised that there is a lot stored in memory. Also I was relaxed here. I felt safe and happy that I was finally in the UK. No fears, no threats, no worries, and I am not the sole provider for my family. I felt that I was more prepared to focus on lessons and studies. I finally started doing something I really liked, and I found myself getting into the study mood and beginning to participate in discussions and presentations.

I made many friends at the language school. When I moved to study in the college in the Welsh countryside, I made friends with Welsh students. I learned many words in Welsh. My Welsh friends introduced me to many things in

Fitzalan High School certificate photo, courtesy of Mohammad S.

Wales – to places and things about their culture. I also introduced them to the Arabic language and explained a lot about our culture.

I prefer to be British and to get the nationality as soon as I can and to integrate into this society. But Syria is my homeland and I love the country and will always love it, be it war or peace. I am proud of my Syrian identity as it is very important to acknowledge those roots. I would love to go to Syria for a visit at some point to reconnect with my relatives who could not manage to get out of the country. It's been ten years now since the war began and many of my relatives and friends died.

I consider myself lucky that I lived through a stage of peace before the war. I was a child, but I can still remember the good days and know what it means to be at war. My sister Rayan was born a few years before the war and opened her eyes on war. She was five when the war began, and you can imagine how her memory of Syria has been completely shaped by war. Children her age would definitely think that life is war and that suffering is just a part of life. My mother told me that when she went to collect my siblings from Heathrow airport, Rayan covered her head with her arms and ran towards my Mum with tears in her eyes. She was frightened by the loud noise of the aeroplanes. She was used to hiding from air raids in Syria. Rayan and the children her age would never be able to believe or even imagine that there was a peaceful Syria or that people were having a normal life. It is difficult for them to imagine a life they did not live.

When I was in school here in Wales, a word or a picture or a name could easily trigger a series of memories which would stay with me for the whole day or possibly for days. One day there was a class discussion on our favourite toys during our primary school stage, and one of my Welsh colleagues was describing how Lego was the best toy he had in school. Later, I was asked about my favourite game in my primary school in Syria. The class was amazed when I told them about the various activities we had at that stage – how we were encouraged to play sports and about the beautiful school environment before war. They don't think we had a life. I was very good in maths and geography. I was very good in drawing the maps of most Arab countries bordering Syria.

"The children… would never be able to believe or even imagine that there was a peaceful Syria or that people were having a normal life. It is difficult for them to imagine a life they did not live."

I still remember a phrase about the weather in Europe: 'Europe's weather is mostly cloudy and cold.' At that time, I couldn't imagine how a country's weather can be mostly cloudy and cold until I came here! And I would add: 'Rainy and stormy'. We memorised the names of the capital cities of almost all the countries of the world. But nothing about Wales. I learned about Wales when I was in Turkey waiting for my family reunion with my family in Wales. I read about Wales and I loved the Welsh flag which is different from the Scottish and the English. I knew where Turkey is and I studied about Turkey. I had always dreamt of visiting Turkey as a tourist not as a refugee.

I faced lots of difficulties and I was desperate in Turkey, but I also learned a lot. I feel that hardships helped me grow and take responsibility and become an independent person. Currently, I work in the restaurant with my brother Sulaiman, and sometimes I work long hours and I study at the same time. I am so pleased to be able to work and to study at the same time. I am still young and I feel I can achieve a lot. I have great ambitions to continue my study and get a degree. Despite the difficulties I faced I feel I am luckier than men my age back home.

People in Syria are suffering not just from the aftermath

of war and lack of the necessities, they suffer from being unsafe. When parents send their children to school, they want to see them coming back whole, not as corpses. When young men and women walk in the streets, they want to feel safe and not afraid of being kidnapped or abducted.

When we move from one city to the other, we don't want to queue for long hours at checkpoints. We don't want to bribe officers for easy entrance. People are tired. They are exhausted from all of this. Parents want to feel that their children are learning and that there is real education. Young men aged over eighteen who are not in education can be easily forced to serve in the military.

Even places under the control of the Syrian regime are not considered 100% safe. For instance, if you face a problem – a theft or a missing person – the police won't help you. It is a corrupt and chaotic apparatus. People queue for hours and hours to buy bread because not all bakeries are operating. Priority is given to regime officers or high-rank military positions. Bread has become very expensive recently. And with extended families, getting enough bread has become a struggle. Exploitation and corruption is rife. When the regime is corrupt, everything else is chaotic and people can simply be exploited. Recently Bashar al Asad invited Syrians to return to Syria! How does he expect people to go back to an unsafe, life-threatening and corrupt place?

There are families whose houses were bombed by the regime, and they lost loved ones. There are people whose belongings were looted by the regime's forces after bombings. How would all those people forgive the regime and go back? How would anyone like to live in an unsafe environment? Where would people live? Under the rubble of their ruined houses? Nothing was done to reconstruct or rebuild a safe life or even a decent life. The other funny thing is that each returnee must pay $100 as an entrance fee! Imagine a family of five persons living in the camps in Jordan or Lebanon – if they have $500, they will rent a flat, so how would they pay this much when they don't have the money?

I learned a lot. Living in a war zone with a single mother and younger siblings forced me to grow. When I was in Turkey, I was only 15 years old and was the youngest among my co-workers to work full-time in that clothes factory. Everybody else had either finished their education or were working part-time and studying. I was the only one who could not pursue my studies and had to work instead. On my way to the factory in Ankara, I used to pass by a secondary school every day. It was so painful to me. It was very painful to see young boys my age in education when I was deprived of that chance. I couldn't join secondary school in Turkey not just because I had no legal documents or valid IDs, but also because I was earning a living and was responsible for my family and then my siblings.

Before lockdown I used to go to a football centre in Cardiff. A diverse football team where you find Syrians, Iraqis and several other nationalities playing next to Welsh men. I also used to go swimming in a swimming pool in Cardiff. I love the gym. I have an indefinite leave to remain. And I recently passed my Life in the UK test and my language test. I also had my driving licence. It wasn't easy to get back to study after almost five years of being away. Also, it wasn't easy to adjust to a new study system. It took me some time to be able to digest the education system and the requirements here. I am planning to study Civil Engineering. Firstly, I finished my three English language entries and I am preparing and revising for the IELTS. This would prepare me to take a pathway course or a foundation course in Civil Engineering before I get admitted to university. I hope to become a civil engineer. And once Syria is back to normal life, I would go for a visit. By the way, my brother Sulaiman had also finished his English language entries and passed his IELTS and now is doing an online foundation course in engineering.

"I learned a lot. Living in a war zone with a single mother and younger siblings forced me to grow. When I was in Turkey, I was only 15 years old and was the youngest among my co-workers to work full-time in that clothes factory."

I love diversity a lot. Intermarriage is a great opportunity to learn a different language, accent, another culture and other traditions. Even though I am not considering marriage or relationships at this stage, I believe that nationality should not be a problem. Not even religion. It doesn't matter. If two people are happy together, religion shouldn't affect their relationship. If I am going to get married to a Muslim woman, I wouldn't care about the headscarf at all as I think that a head cover is not a measure of faith.

I think each person has the right to choose what they believe to be right for them. As long as they are happy and are not doing any harm to anyone else. It is a free society and each person must practise their rights freely. For instance, at the Eid festival I love to go to the Eid prayer in the mosque and visit my relatives and enjoy the religious celebration freely. No one should prevent me from practising it. The same thing goes for other religions, ethnicities, and minorities. I don't interfere with people's choices and I don't see any harm in being a gay or a lesbian as long as it is a personal choice.

There is no organised Syrian community. There are Facebook groups. There is one for Syrians all over the UK which is very helpful, especially with Covid-19. People use this platform to support each other and to guide one another to services and regulations. There is an Arabic translation of new government announcements. They sometimes provide English lessons in a simplified manner, for instance twenty-five words each week. Before Covid the mosque used to arrange activities for children and for women. Also, some Arabic lessons for children. But under the lockdown all these stopped.

I wish that the government could facilitate jobs for young men and women. I appreciate there are Covid-19 restrictions, but this will not last much longer, I hope. Lots of young men and women among the newcomers, the new refugees, would love to get a job – say a casual or part-time job where they can improve their English language. Could be a job in Costa, for instance, or other places which do not require qualifications to start with. The government should make use of those people and offer a job with a minimum wage. It is not ideal for young persons to stay at home, get benefits and learn English. It would be great if job opportunities could be offered to people from day one. Instead of giving weekly or monthly benefits, why not recruit people and make use of whatever skill they have so that they contribute to society, communicate, improve their English and integrate.

I personally get a student's loan from student's finance and I don't have to sign up at the Jobcentre. My friend who is nearly my age is registered with the Jobcentre and he sometimes consults me regarding letters and emails he receives from them, because his English language isn't that good. I find that they send him links for websites where he might find a job, but they don't help with finding or matching skills to certain employers. He must create a CV, a covering letter and apply on his own. You know, there are several forms to fill and lots of details to send. People with a low language level wouldn't be able to do all this on their own. With low English levels those people would either forget about the emails sent to them, ignore them, or refer them to a private interpreter who mostly wouldn't be very helpful. Paperwork and bureaucracies can exhaust people especially with a low level of English. Many forms and many long questionnaires or loads of information are tiring.

At the end of the day, employers look at professional CVs

Mohammad walking in West Wales. © Mohamad S

and well-written covering letters and exclude the less professional ones. Those refugees might be more skilful and more committed to work, but they are less privileged in terms of language level and this is unfair. So, they end up losing many job opportunities.

I think maintaining our Arabic language is essential. If I have children in future, I would insist on teaching them Arabic. Many of my friends consider me lucky because I speak Arabic and English. I love how Welsh people are using Welsh and are very proud of speaking Welsh and speaking about their Welsh culture and Welsh food. And we love to have Syrian food. I don't have preferences. I love Syrian dishes. My mother is trying to learn to cook international recipes. Recently, she cooked lasagne for the first time, and it was excellent. It was delicious. She is mastering pizza these days as well! And I love to try international food all the time.

The food business is not very complicated. Most of the Syrian food projects are done by women from home as they master cooking, and they find it a great opportunity to make profit. And also to introduce this food to the British society. Syrian food does not have a lot of competitors in

the form of other nationalities. Recently, a new Syrian pastry business was opened in City Road. It is called Manaqeesh and is doing really well. A small restaurant where the owner is supporting himself, recruiting some Syrians and introducing this new dish to the UK. We serve a combination of Syrian and Turkish food because these are the types that are missing. It's the food that we do well and we find people, Syrian refugees, who are willing to work for us. During the very first lockdown we were only depending on the dining-in service. You know, the indoor restaurant service. And that had a bad impact on us, so we had to close. Later on, when restrictions were slightly eased, we shifted to providing delivery service. During the firebreak we shifted to delivery and takeaway. So, we adjusted to every kind of restriction. In this case we had to lay off our waitresses. But, we are managing well now.

I am looking forward to becoming a civil engineer. Yet, if I get an opportunity to open a food business to increase my financial status I would do it. But I would be a manager at that stage. I wouldn't work in the restaurant as I am doing now. If I become a manager, I would like to hire as many refugees as I can because most of them have all the skills needed for a successful food business.

When people's lives are in danger and when they are living under inhuman and horrible conditions, they have to leave. In Syria the future is dark. The financial situation is deteriorating, life's necessities are not there, and education and employment are getting worse with corruption. Young men in rural areas are getting married at a very young age, supported by their families. I think it is a reaction to the frustration around them. In two years' time or so they find themselves with at least two kids. In that case, they will be totally engaged with their responsibilities. Providing for the family and that's it. No dreams and no ambitions. Their life would be a cycle of work, pay for family, work and pay. I would love to tell those young men that there is a life to explore. Life is not just about marriage and kids. There are so many opportunities which need to be explored outside that limited zone. I know it isn't easy and the route to what I am talking about is not without its price. If they choose to take to the sea, they have to be very careful. Smugglers and human traffickers don't care about people's lives, so they need to be extra careful. Recently, the Greek authorities have tightened rules regarding refugees on boats from Turkey. We heard many stories of refugees who were placed in dinghies and sent out to sea on their own. When they reached the Greek shores, they were immediately forced by the Greek authorities to return to Turkey. In a case like this, they lose their money, their chance to travel further and they will be destitute in Turkey.

I would love to explore the world. But with my travel document it is very difficult because we require an entry visa and bank statement even for Turkey. A British passport is easier to use and provides free movement. My sister and her family live in Turkey. My other brother is also in Turkey and he has recently got married. The rest of my family is in Cardiff. Family members are all around. If I were alone and single it would be very difficult to settle. Currently, I am living with my family. We are living in temporary accommodation for two years and are planning to move to a council estate where the rent would be affordable. We can live in a council estate for a long time with no contract but at an affordable rent.

I am proud of taking responsibility for my siblings when my mother travelled. I worked hard to keep them safe and to keep an eye on them at that early age in their lives. I used to pay for them to learn Turkish. In 2015, Syrian refugees were not permitted to join Turkish state schools. Now they are permitting people to register their children at schools, and they are offering residency status to them.

Natali Hadad

The Home Office had been in contact with me for a long time before I left Turkey. 'What facilities do you require in your new house? What about your husband's medical situation? Does he need any special equipment for the entrance or inside the house? The toilet? The shower?' They required specific details about myself and my husband's needs. I had already explained that I wanted to join my daughter in Cardiff, and they were fine with that as they understood my situation, and at my age being close to my daughter would make my life easier. So, I came directly to Cardiff.

The council was always in contact and they used to send staff to introduce me to the city, the neighbourhood and the main facilities, routes and transportation etc. And of course I have always been made welcome. Now, after one year of living in the city, I don't feel like a stranger. I find people here very friendly. If I suddenly look someone in the eye, they smile at me and I like this attitude which is similar to saying 'Hello' in Islam. We have the famous Hadith that says 'Your smile in the face of your brother is a form of charity' but we don't really practise this in the Middle East. We have only found it being practised here in the West.

Paperwork is important here. I have accumulated so many papers and I never throw a single sheet away. I have ended up with a bulky file! I haven't faced serious difficulties because my daughter has always been able to help and support me and currently I am living with her so no real difficulties so far, *alhamdulillah*.

While we were in Turkey preparing to travel to the UK, my husband passed away and that was a tragic incident in the life of the family and in my life in particular. So, when I arrived in Cardiff, I was overwhelmed with a grief that stayed with me for a long time. It almost felt like I was obsessed with the memory of my husband. I struggled to try to forget and cope with my new life. I am still trying. Everything else around me is fine and I feel comfortable in my daughter's house.

English was one of my favourite subjects in school. English and maths. *Subhan Allah* (glory be to Allah) I knew the basics like forming questions and some grammar. During my residency in Turkey, I studied English and Turkish. I studied English to prepare myself to live in Britain, but my Turkish improved faster as a result of communication. When I came here, I was a bit hesitant to use any of the words I had learned and was scared that I might not pronounce my words correctly. Later, I became braver in using English and I am so proud that it didn't take me too long to be able to communicate.

As I am living with my daughter and her children with whom I share a bedroom, I suggested to my six-year-old granddaughter that she try and use English with me as much as she can – and to assess my language as a teacher! My granddaughter loved the idea and was so excited to play the teacher's role with me. For instance, she frequently asks me to 'read this word' and 'that word'. She uses her own books, bedtime stories and colouring books to teach me English.

I don't miss Syria. I don't think I will go back to Syria as everybody has left. My parents passed away, my husband died, my friends and my relatives left the country. If I went back, I would be all alone. I have my daughter and grandchildren with me here and I am looking forward to meeting my sons in Europe and I feel happy and well settled in the UK. I wish I could go back to work but because I am 65, I think it is impossible. I really wish I could do that work here, Laboratory Diagnosis.

If [refugees] can cope with the new culture, it would be great. However, if they want to impose their own traditions on the host country it would be impossible to survive and cope. They will always be annoyed and will annoy others.

Friends are a source of strength. Once I feel that I am comfortable with the company of a person or a group and I relate to them, I decide to continue seeing them. Community and people. I am so sociable and I love meeting new people. I have made many friends through the college where I study English. I feel so happy and excited when I am with them. It makes me happy, and happiness is better than strength. We try not to mention Syria or the traumatic past. We engage with the present and plan for the immediate future. Just a normal chat. We arrange visits, we gather for coffee or lunch. By the way, I am the oldest in the group. They are all much younger than me, but we get along very well and we are so happy when we meet.

> *"We try not to mention Syria or the traumatic past. We engage with the present and plan for the immediate future."*

Alhamdulillah, I achieved what I wanted to do and dreamt of. For instance, I studied medicine not to be a medical doctor but to work in a lab, which was what I really did do. I feel like I have run out of dreams. This period is retirement for me. I have worked all my life and did my best to bring up my children. I am enjoying being with my daughter and grandchildren. I have lovely friends at college and I have also made additional friends through my daughter's connections. Recently, I joined a neighbourhood social group of different nationalities and backgrounds where we meet in the library every Thursday. We discuss many topics. My English has improved immensely because of this group. I use WhatsApp a lot. I have many WhatsApp groups: the first one is for my childhood friends from Syria, the second is for my friends from Turkey, the third is for my friends in the UK and the fourth is for my sons. I also have a Facebook account, but I am not very active on Facebook.

[Refugees] must realise that things are not easy. Asylum

is not an easy thing and they might end up in a country that they were not planning to enter. For Syrians they must think many times before taking the decision to come to the West. They must think whether they can cope with the new culture, new society and new life or not. They have to bear in mind that the journey is not easy and that if they want to make it by the sea, they have to think of the dangers and the deadly risks. They might face unexpected situations in a different culture and a different system and they should be able to cope with these difficulties. They must be ready to face difficulties.

Salih Hamza

I was accepted for a resettlement in the UK. I was uncomfortable with this decision as I was planning to join my children in Germany. I wish I could have been admitted to a country closer to Germany but that's it. So I came here and it looks like it is even more difficult to join my sons and daughters from here.

We arrived in November 2019. Doctors have confirmed that I am in a critical situation. I had surgery in my right leg in Turkey. This leg has tubes installed and the left foot is completely paralysed because of diabetes. I can barely see with my right eye. Also, my hands are not very well. As you've seen, I couldn't even sign your papers. Eating is a disaster. I find it too hard to hold the spoon and it is such a mess when it comes to eating. Luckily a close friend comes to check on us with his wife from time to time. He gives me a shower and helps me with almost all my daily needs. I can't shower without a chair which the landlord provided. I

wish that at least one of my sons was around to take care of me. I often feel so embarrassed when that friend accompanies me to the bathroom. He is so kind, but he is a stranger to me. He does everything. He takes me to the barber's and helps me with shaving. I feel happy when he is around. Not just because of the care but having someone to talk to.

I feel I am in a cell, in a prison. It really feels like a prison. I sometimes feel that I am punished for a crime that I haven't committed. I have six children. I have sons and daughters who can take care of me. But none of them are with me when I am in need of them.

I spend my time here in this room. I am surrounded with several cushions to support my back and my legs. We have this living room plus a very small bedroom. We spend all our time here in this room. We have this small window. The window overlooks the main street, and we cannot leave it open all the time for safety reasons.

And Covid-19 made things worse for us. Before Covid-19, our caseworker used to visit us once a week, but after that we haven't seen him much. Everything is being done over the phone. Since the beginning of the lockdown, a caseworker has been to us twice. He talked to us through this window.

Maybe we are unlucky to come to this country in November and to face this pandemic shortly after our arrival. But once again, I hope the authorities could understand my situation and try to help me get to Germany as a refugee or facilitate my son's entrance to the UK to stay with us. It is too much. I have witnessed enough shocks, shocks, shocks. I am mentally exhausted. Our misery started in 2011 and is still ongoing. When ISIS took over, our life turned into endless nightmares. We fled to face other nightmares. Then what? Not being able to unite with my children. This is another nightmare. When a loved one dies – say someone loses a loved one, it will take them two to three months to get used to the loss and perhaps forget about it. They will finally accept their fate as long as it is from Allah. But when you have children who are alive and are far away, when you can't be with them when you most need them, it is so difficult.

> *"I lost everything in life. And I lost the most important thing anyone needs which is my health. All that is left to me are those children with whom I want to reunite before I completely wither away."*

My wife was born in 1963 and she is over 55 years old. She cannot speak Arabic. As you can see, she sometimes understands most of what you are saying but cannot communicate in Arabic. She has a problem in her spine. She had spine surgery in Turkey and had another surgery for blocked arteries and she suffers from constant backpain and body pain. I believe our mental health is worse than our physical condition. She spends most of her time talking to our children over the phone.

My children didn't see me like this when we were living in Syria. I wish that I could have stayed there. If I died there, at least I would die in my birthplace. I would be surrounded by people. There are many acquaintances who are still there. But the living conditions are so bad, so bad. They are surrounded by uncertainty. They don't know what is waiting for them. Death is lurking at every single corner. Threats from explosions, explosive barrels thrown from the air, ISIS, Turkish forces, Iran. The main curse is Hezbollah, Iran and Turkey plus Russia and the list goes on. We have paid a big price for wars and violence. But loneliness is so bad. I haven't committed a crime. I haven't stolen money from anyone, and I haven't been involved in politics either. Why do I have to pay the price?

When I came here, I thought that my problems, my suffering and all I faced would come to an end. I don't care about benefits, house, food or anything else. I just want them to consider my situation and reunite me with my sons and daughters. I lost everything in life. And I lost the most important thing anyone needs which is my health. All that is left to me are those children with whom I want to reunite before I completely wither away.

I am a sociable person, and I have spent my whole life making friends and meeting with people. I lived in a village and you can imagine people coming and going to our house all the time. Here, it is very difficult. If I were in a real prison – say there are fifty prisoners in one room, you would at least make friends with five of them. But here, look at my situation. There is no one around. Sometimes, I go for a short trip from my house to the main road in my wheelchair and I quickly change my mind and return home.

I don't know anyone around, and nobody knows me. *Wallah* I am distressed, distressed, distressed. In Syria, in my hometown I had my hairdressers for twenty-nine years. For twenty-nine years I came to know lots of people and have made hundreds of friends. Suddenly, I find myself in this situation. Completely alone.

I am used to socialising with others. I would love to have face-to-face meetings. I wish that I could meet real and not virtual persons. I have already joined several groups on social media. Groups of old friends on WhatsApp. Friends and relatives from Syria who were scattered in different parts of the world. Friends from Germany, Turkey, Sweden, Denmark, and Kurdistan. We chat and discuss matters. We talk at different times of the day, evening and night depending on the time differences of these countries. As I am sleepless, I spend most of the night talking to those friends and sleeping during the day. Socialising is part of my nature.

Halah al Shami

Not only had my three sons left, but my daughter and her husband also travelled to Canada. So I stayed in Beirut by myself. Things were unstable in Lebanon and with my Syrian nationality it was difficult to settle and build a future there. By that time, my daughter was due to deliver, and I decided to join and stay with her and her husband, as this was her first experience of motherhood. I was granted a multi-entry visa to Canada that ends when my Syrian pass-port expires. I stayed with her for over a month and was due to return to Lebanon after that. While I was in Canada,

I was thinking a lot about whether to go back to Lebanon or to Syria. Because once I went to any of these countries, I wouldn't be able to see my sons again as it would be impossible for them to come to visit me in the current political chaos. As for me, it would be equally impossible to get a visa to the UK to see my sons, with my Syrian passport. After deep thinking, I decided to cancel my ticket to Lebanon and book a new ticket to Turkey with a transit in the UK. And this is how I arrived here. I was left with no other option than this risky decision which I had to make.

Things were not so easy at the beginning. When I applied for asylum at the airport, the British authorities were very respectful and treated me with dignity. However, I felt I was being detained. I was put in a closed waiting hall and was not allowed outside without permission. I had to knock at the window if I needed something. They took my passport and my details and the details and addresses of my sons and relatives. There was an Arabic interpreter who helped with telling my story and why I was applying for asylum. Then, I was asked to fill a form and was given a date. I stayed like that for around eight hours. After that, they asked me if I need accommodation and I told them I preferred to join my sons who were living in London at that time. They called my eldest son and he came to pick me up. After filling the form and finishing the legal procedures, I was allowed outside to meet with my sons.

At this stage, my middle son was still living in a shared accommodation provided by the Home Office while still waiting to hear about his asylum status. I had to stay with my eldest son and his wife in London. My eldest son was doing his PhD and his wife was pregnant for the first time and was so stressed as she was unwell due to the pregnancy. They were living in a one-bedroom flat and I used to sleep in the living room. I wasn't used to that at all. I had spent my whole life in big houses of my own. Even when I left my house in Syria and moved to Lebanon, we lived in a nice flat where I was the boss. Suddenly, I found myself living in a tiny little space shared with others.

A memento of Syria and the fountain in the courtyard of Halah's home in Syria.

I have the basics of English and I understand most of the words and sentences. When they interviewed me at the airport, I understood almost everything, but I found it very difficult to communicate. We had hardly any chance to use our English back home in Syria. I can read and write in English, but it is so difficult to communicate.

When I lived with my son in London, I was introduced to an Arabic-speaking community who used to attend English language classes every Saturday, which was so great. It helped me a lot and boosted my self-confidence. Then, I

was introduced to a lady who was arranging an English language course for Syrians willing to improve their English which helped as well. To go to that course, I had to use the underground. And this was my first dilemma. My first experience with the underground was a mess. I was so confused! I took the wrong train, going in the opposite direction. I found two people who were so helpful and gave me directions as to which train to take and which platform to use. This was my first hurdle and I had many hurdles like that. But as soon as I got used to platforms and routes, I was so relieved and so confident and felt that I could be independent and go to places without too much worrying.

I am not used to sitting at home and not doing anything. I was a full-time employee all my life. Working long hours daily was my usual routine. The evenings would be spent with my sons. My sister used to visit me for a cup of coffee every afternoon when her husband went to work. I miss those days a lot. Staying at home in London was so painful. But that English course made life easier for me, as I was introduced to new people and spent quality time for around six months. Then, I moved to Leicester and found myself a room near my son's accommodation, which made it easy for us to meet and spend time together. In Leicester, I was introduced to the Sudanese community with which my son was working as a volunteer interpreter and social worker. Because of that type of work, my son was so well known in Leicester! I was introduced to new people and was able to make friends with a lady with whom I exchanged visits and conversations. My trips to the Jobcentre were also very useful and improved my English a lot. I also attended some English classes organised by the Jobcentre. But I had to stop taking them when my daughter in-law had her first baby. I had to go and take care of her and the newly born baby in London.

While moving to the UK and waiting for his asylum decision, my son lost the chance to commence his university course because he couldn't do his IELTS without his passport. Also, universities asked him to start from year one when he had already spent two years studying in Syria and Lebanon. The only two universities which offered him a place in year two were Cardiff and Leicester. So, he chose Cardiff University as it ranks higher. We both moved to Cardiff in 2016. Initially, we rented for six months a house which was in an awful condition. Then we moved to this flat which is much better.

The time in Lebanon was so stressful. When I lived in Chtaura, I had no relatives or friends. My sons had to travel to Turkey for applications and interviews leaving me with my daughter who was busy preparing for her wedding. So, that was a very difficult time in my life. It was scattered between my work in Syria and my house in Lebanon. Travelling, worrying, TV news, online news reports and the bitter reality of the situation back home resulted in a severe depression. But, the situation got better when I moved to Beirut as I was introduced to new friends and I also have relatives there which made it easier to integrate and accept the new reality.

In the initial stage [in the UK], I relied on my eldest son's English competency as he has an excellent command of English which enabled him to get a full scholarship for his PhD. He was also teaching a few hours while doing his PhD research. When I moved to live with my other son, I had to rely on his English. He is also very good in English and he was responsible for the paperwork and the follow ups. He is doing his master's and living with me now. So, I am lucky.

I am very frustrated because I am unemployed. I spent my whole career working in senior positions back home. I have to pass an Occupational English Test (OET) first. The first stage was an ESOL class where I passed two levels in the first year. I did another year, and currently I am attending similar OET classes. But I am not happy with all these processes. I am not young anymore and it is not easy for someone my age to go through all these classes. It is not easy to experience the pressure of tests all over again. Even if I sit for an exam and pass, there will be a series of other tests.

And what next? I will then be treated as a new graduate with no experience and have to start in the system from scratch. It would be a great disappointment to find myself working with or supervised by new graduates of my children's age. The British system is a difficult one indeed. I am aware that when I reach the level of employability, I'll be at retirement age.

I left my job in Syria in 2013 which is almost seven years ago, which makes it hard to start any kind of work now. I worked as a volunteer several times in the UK, but what is next? I was wondering if any of these voluntary roles would become a part-time or a full-time job.

I can't understand how this system works and I feel that these tests are a real hurdle. Why should I go through all

Mementoes of Syria belonging to Halah al Shami.

these tests? People my age should relax. But I really want to work without all these tests.

I was exempted from the IELTS and I only need to go through the OET which is not an easy thing at all. Even though our current instructor is a native speaker, he sometimes seems unsure of answers to some of the questions. And I always wonder why on earth do we have to be at such a high level of English? I heard that we are paying the price for a mistake committed by a foreign medical doctor in diagnosing a disease. Since then, the average score mark was raised from 7.0 to 7.5. This 7.5 is

so hard to achieve. This will be followed by two PLABs (Professional and Linguistic Assessments Board) PLAB 1 and PLAB 2. According to the UK system, my long experience in Syria doesn't count as long as I am failing these tests. This is the most difficult part of my journey to settle in the UK. The other side of it is the financial aspect. I am not used to living on benefits, and I feel it is a humiliating process which is very painful indeed. I have been managing my finances to a certain extent so far. But not sure for how long I will survive.

The OET course is run by the DPIA (Displaced People in Action) charity which helps refugees in Wales. One of their objectives is to help displaced medical refugee doctors to go back to work by supporting them through these classes. There were some Syrian refugees who graduated from European countries who were exempted from the series of tests. They only had to do the OET. That was a big incentive to them, when they had to do just one type of exam. Moreover, they are all very young graduates who wouldn't hesitate to re-sit as many exams as they can.

Integration was made possible and easier through the English classes and the OET lessons. My instructor thinks that I attend these classes to socialise! To be honest, the initial stages were too hard for me as I couldn't do my homework properly. At one point, I had to take a leave and go to London to help my daughter-in-law with her new baby. And on another occasion, I had to spend time with my daughter who came to visit us from Canada. So, the teacher thought I was attending classes for entertainment. The people I met were nice and supportive. But I can't say that I found a close friend whom I trust and depend on through difficult times. No, I haven't made close friends.

My best friend is my sister who used to live in the same building. She used to come to my place for coffee daily when her husband went to work. She is still in Syria and we constantly connect via social media. My sister is safe so far. Her sons left the country. And at some stage her husband was detained by the Syrian forces who accused him of helping the revolutionaries. But luckily, he was released a short time after that. My brother-in-law is a gynaecologist and is financially sufficient. He refused to leave Syria. He didn't want to leave because he didn't want to put himself in a similar position to myself. He was aware that once he left Syria, he would lose his career and be on benefits. My sister suffered a lot when we all left. When her sons left, she became very ill and had surgery in the USA recently.

I talk to my sister and my daughter in Canada through video calls and FaceTime nearly every day. I love to see my daughter and my grandchildren. These social media apps made it easier for us. My other son moved from London to Aberdeen after his PhD. He has a teaching post in Aberdeen University. I contact him via these apps and talk to his wife and child frequently.

When I started my ESOL classes, I met several people from Syria and other countries who were trying to improve their English and facing similar difficulties to mine. I met some Syrians who were reluctant to speak to me when they knew about my previous senior position back home. I always tried to be friendly. I avoided mentioning that position and any confrontation with anyone as I am very aware of our differences. I think wars created this kind of sensitivity, or it might be an agenda to separate us. I have always worked peacefully with people from different ethnic and sectarian backgrounds and we were all based in the same office and same location. We had never bothered to question each other's background. From the onset of the Syrian crisis, the media described it as 'sectarian'. And we all wondered why it was named as such? And who was behind that? The media played a big role in making people believe that there was a sectarian war.

I feel sorry about this because we have always lived together, celebrating each other's religious events and so on. I was brought up in a city which had always celebrated ethnic diversity. Jews were living in separate neighbourhoods and they had their synagogues and we made friends with them because they don't represent Israel. When I first came to the UK, my daughter-in-law introduced me to a Facebook group where Syrians share their experiences, voice their concerns, difficulties and so on. I noticed that those comments could sometimes instigate sectarian feelings. There were always some posts that would spoil the whole idea of the group.

I have a strong faith in Allah (God) and in His ultimate power to control our destinies. I believe that whatever happens to me, happens for a reason and that God's will is stronger than anything else. I also think that whatever happened to me was in my favour. Despite the difficulties I faced while making the decision to come to the UK, I believe that this is the best choice I've ever made, to be closer to my children who are scattered in Turkey, Canada and the UK. If I had stayed where I was in Syria or Lebanon, I would never be able to dream of reuniting with them. If I get British nationality, I will be able to travel to Canada and to Turkey whenever I like.

Once you have faith in Allah and the plans that Allah put to you, you will face difficulties with an open heart and mind and you become stronger in overcoming them. *Alkhayr ma Ikhtarahu Allah* [Goodness lies in God's choice]. If you believe in this Islamic saying, you will feel relief. This saying offers us spiritual satisfaction and acceptance of hardships which we cannot avoid as they are not in our hands. For instance, when I first came to Cardiff I lived in an awful house and had to wait for six months to be able to move somewhere else. I used to pray God to grant me a house like the one I am in now and I found it. God granted me this nice and quiet flat overlooking the bay and I am so happy here.

Alhamdulillah all of [my children] have continued their studies and have made successful careers for themselves. They are very successful people socially and academically and I am proud of them. I am so proud that they are ambitious, and that they are hard workers. I supported them a lot and it has paid off in the end. My son is going to finish his postgraduate studies soon. Then, eventually, he will get married and I will be left alone, and I wish that I could get a job that keeps me engaged and busy. I tried to make friends with people from the Syrian community in Cardiff, but I couldn't get along with them. They either talk about food and recipes or they gossip, and I couldn't stand

that. I attend some of the events they organise and try to take part but I don't feel comfortable enough to participate in everything on a constant basis. I just can't.

Once I left Syria, I started to look at things from a distance with more freedom. I might go back there for a visit. I have my own house, belongings and my furniture. I don't feel comfortable with any of these pillows here. I designed my house in a beautiful manner. I hired a workman, who decorated the house as I planned. My kitchen back home was the size of this living room. It was a spacious house indeed. Look where I ended up. I am renting a flat. I am aware that I am better off and may be luckier than many other refugees in the west. But still this flat is not like my own house back home.

Back home, we used to buy expensive pieces of kitchenware and keep them for special occasions. Here, I buy cheap stuff and use it immediately as there is not enough storage in this house. Besides, I do not know how long I am staying here or what will happen next. We are always moving, and it doesn't feel like there is a final settling down when you keep renting houses and move between houses. Back home there was more certainty because I was the owner of my house. Anyways, *Alhamdulillah*.

I am going to be selective [about what to tell the grandchildren] as I think the older we are, the more selective we become. I think, we will tend to remember the positive side of the story, the bright side, the nice memory, and I will try my best to describe Syria in the good old days.

In Syria, I used to live in a building surrounded by my

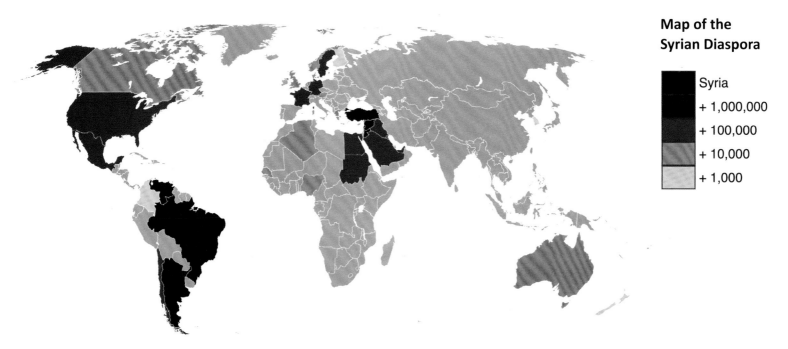

Map of the Syrian Diaspora

	Syria
	+ 1,000,000
	+ 100,000
	+ 10,000
	+ 1,000

Map of the Syrian diaspora. © Allice Hunter, CC BY-SA 4.0, via Wikimedia Commons

siblings. My three sons and daughter, my sister and her children, my brother and his family were all living in the same building. When the crisis began one of my brothers travelled to Jordan where his in-laws lived and then he travelled to Canada. My second brother travelled to the USA because his in-laws are living in the USA and it was easy for him and his family to get there. My third brother, who lives in Lebanon, was moving between Lebanon and Turkey. And my sister remained in Syria. So literally, we were like one family that was spread into five families, each in a different country.

My new grandson is registered British here in the UK and his father is Syrian British and I believe that the third generation will be the same wherever they are. My small family is scattered all over the world as well. My nephews and nieces have also travelled to the USA, Malaysia, Turkey and Germany. The grandchildren speak many languages. Some speak Malaysian, others American English and some use German. So I don't think it will be easy for these children to use Arabic even if their parents use it at home. It will always be easier for the children to speak the language of the host country.

Baher al Abed

I used to live in Lebanon by myself and then once I did work with a charity called Save the Children. It was about the importance of refugees' education in Lebanon. The Head of Save the Children or the CEO of the charity was the former prime minister of Denmark. So, she came to Lebanon to have a look at the campaign, and she liked it. She saw the video on my stories. She liked it. She said she would like to come to my house. She came to my house in 2018 and then she told me her daughter graduated from a school in South Wales. She wanted me to apply, and I applied to a school called the United World College of the Atlantic UWC. I applied and I got it and I came here. I was awarded a full scholarship. Everything. I didn't even pay for the plane ticket. It is IBE International Baccalaureate. Even harder than the A levels. It is more international. More like university preparation. It prepares you for university better than the A levels.

I spent seven years in Lebanon. I went to Lebanon when I was like ten and I never returned to Syria, never came back. I am from the capital city. From Damascus. My family – you know a lot of families had to leave Syria because of the situation. And my family were politically involved. The government started chasing them, so we had to leave. That's after my main family passed away and I had nowhere else to stay there. I had to leave with them and go to study in Lebanon.

I've always liked English and I've always wanted to learn it. I feel it was natural. In Lebanon I used to speak it but not as easily as now. Now I can use it in a better way. I express myself in a better way. But in Lebanon they teach you English from grade seven. But you only study certain subjects in English not all of them. And all the explanations in class happen in Arabic not in English

The Welsh accent? Yes, in the beginning I found it hard to understand because they use a tense accent. So it took me a while to understand it. My school is not Welsh. It is an international school. It had students from all over the world. It is in Saint Donats, it is like an hour and 45 minutes' drive from Cardiff. A boarding school.

It was hard for me in the beginning coming from a really conservative culture and here it is an open-minded culture. There is a lot of sexism back home, a lot of boundaries between girls and boys. You are not allowed to do certain things, while here you can just do anything you want. It was a bit weird for me to accept it. So it took me time to settle in. I didn't settle in during the first term. I hated it in fact. I was like I don't like it here I want to leave. I didn't want to go back to Lebanon, but I wanted to leave there. It was a weird feeling, you know! I don't want to go back to Lebanon, but I don't want to stay in that school either. It was a bit confusing, but I was just figuring things out. But then next term things got easier, and I got used to everything and I started enjoying it and it was nice. Now I am so happy that I went there, and I am so grateful. I made friends from all over the world. We also got the world record of having the largest number of nationalities. Ninety nationalities, I think. When the results came out last week, we were all like checking on one another. A lot of people didn't meet the requirements, sadly.

When I first came it was like I couldn't believe it. These different houses, different streets. The streets are so clean. The grass. I loved how the grass was super green. High buildings, the red buses. All these things we used to see on TV, and I saw them for the first time. It was nice. It was really satisfying. It was the culture shock. I just felt I wasn't fitting in in the beginning, which is normal you know. I had been exposed to something I had never been exposed to before.

When I settled in here, I kind of lost some connection with home. I became a different person. My priorities became different. My ideologies about so many things became different and my preferences of people when I look at people. You know, so many things. For example, I wanted to do engineering when I was in Lebanon and now I want to do politics. See the difference? Think about any real change in this world. What makes it? Politicians, right? Politics is a great source of power that can achieve a lot of change in life which I really want to have access to because I believe that if I use it correctly, I would be able to change millions of lives. Though I am a bit afraid because in Syria they wouldn't agree with everything I agree with, especially now they would call me westernised. Just because I want things to be – it is not about being westernised or something. It is just like – after I've experienced different things, I realised what I think would be good or bad, you know?

I can't wait to have a home country. I just feel that now I don't have any home. I don't have a home. And I am excited for that. Just to feel that I belong somewhere, you know. Just like my home: I can stay here as much as I want. I can do whatever I want to do here. I can come back here

whenever I want. I have a house, I have a place to stay, you know? Can't wait to be at this stage. Like now when I go to Lebanon or Syria, I will feel I am a stranger, you know? Because I am just used to here not there.

I loved Lebanon. I love Lebanon more than Syria even. But Lebanon in general was not welcoming to Syrians or any other foreigners. So, I just wanted to leave because it was obviously not welcoming me. While the UK, here maybe I have a refugee status now. I can work. I can study, I can get a bank account. In Lebanon you can't have a bank account if you are a Syrian. This is like the simplest thing. It is not in the sense that like the UK is my home now. For now, yes,

I belong here. But my heart might go somewhere else in the future. For now, it is yeah. I really wish that I could do a year abroad. Like outside the UK just to experience different things in a different country. But my lawyer said that this would make my status in the UK risky which I think it is a bit unfair, you know?

"I can't wait to have a home country. I just feel that now I don't have any home. I don't have a home. And I am excited for that. Just to feel that I belong somewhere…"

[Syrian identity] is still there. Like whenever I see someone Syrian, I have an amazing connection which I would never have with anyone else. The way they understand my humour maybe, the food. My favourite food is Syrian. I still listen to the music that I used to listen to when I was in Syria, you know? Like so many things. On my social media I put the Syrian flag on all of them. Because I am Syrian. I am not a British. Maybe UK is home for me, but I am not British and I will never be even if a paper would say that. I would never be British.

In the school there was only one Syrian girl. But you know Arabs in general, we had some nice connection, not that much. Because the school looks for a certain type of people and all the Arabs who came here were westernised, didn't really feel that proud of their Arabic identity. They wanted to be more westernised which is their business! But I was willing to embrace my Arabic Syrian identity. Though now I love the UK, you know. But I was thinking of this the other day – once I get my British passport, I will have two countries to fight for – UK and Syria.

Because we use English every day and sometimes when you say things you haven't said for a while, Arabic gets a bit rusty. Like you feel: Oh! how did I use to say this? Oh! How could I say this. You know, you start remembering? Sometimes this happens to me. Some expressions in Arabic don't exist in English because Arabic is a very specific language, it has lots of vocabs, it has a lot of descriptions for like very specific circumstances while English doesn't. However, English has words for things I am dealing with more currently which Arabic hasn't. For example, the word roommate, we don't have the word roommate in Arabic. I had a roommate in school, and I am going to have roommate in university. So, this is how it is.

I talk about politics with people who are into politics. But

Mulukhiyaeh by Osps7, CC BY-SA 4.0, via Wikimedia Commons

most of the Syrian people I've met here were trying to forget what happened in Syria and live a new life. Which I think is a bit wrong. I did one of my school research projects about it, like how refugees come here and they just build a life here and they forget where they came from and then who is going to be building that country if they are going to be living here, you know? But you can't blame them. They have been through so many hard things, and they've had to go on a death journey through the sea to come here. So you can't blame them for trying to forget what happened. But at the same time, if all Syrians go to Germany or come to the UK, who is going to be building Syria after the war?

My favourite Syrian food is Mulukhiyya. I love it. I cooked it a few times. Yeah, but most of the time I don't like cooking just for myself, you know. I like to cook if I have like a group of friends or some people. You know City Road is full of Arabic things, Middle Eastern stuff. Sometimes you have a reason for loving something – it reminds me of home in a nice way. *Shakriyeh*? You know *Shakriyeh*? Yogurt, beef with rice. When was the last time I cooked it? I think I cooked it last year as well. It was so nice! Yes, it reminds me of how we used to eat together. Maybe the gatherings. Yes, you could say that.

In the UK it feels like if you put effort, you get rewarded, you know. While in Lebanon you don't really. Like regardless of how much you work, you try, you don't really get results. But in the UK, you do. People's attitude, the government restrictions – all these things just made people hate their lives in Lebanon. Made things so much harder. It was because Syrian army was in Lebanon in 2006 and they did so many terrible things, so like, Lebanese people kind of hated Syrians a bit because of what the Syrian army did. It's all political, see? Everything. All the issues in the Middle East are political.

I worked, yeah. I worked in different things – in restaurants, construction, and painting. I was never paid. For three years I was not paid at all. It was all for my family. They didn't pay me because they believed that it was their family duty to take care of me. But when I worked a few other jobs, it was never a nice job. Long shifts. Payment was not that good. [I was only] fifteen. But who cares you know?

> *"I just want to become someone who you see on the TV screen, and you believe that this person can do something."*

All these things happening in Lebanon right now, I couldn't imagine myself still living there. Would've been really bad. It is very confusing for me. I just feel like the same things are happening. Repeated. I wouldn't call Syria as still in a war, but it is not in peace. So many things are going on. But repeated things. Nothing is changing. So, it is very complicated in Syria right now. Sometimes when I see tragic stories, I can't watch them. I feel so affected. Especially when I really want to help but I can't. I can't do anything. So, I don't watch them because they just make me feel heartbroken. I just don't follow the story. I don't watch the stories. But I want to know what's going on, you know? Economically, politically, militarily.

I just want to become someone who you see on the TV screen and you believe that this person can do something. You know? I don't know where. But I want to help people. I know it sounds so cliche. A lot of people say I want to help people, but I just want to make a change. In Syria and the UK. I had realised how politics can be destructive. And I just want to use the other face of it which makes it more constructive, you know. Help build Syria again. And help refugees, all over the world, struggling. If they go back to their countries or have better lives at least if they can't go back to their countries. I know these things are easier said than done, but I will be hopeful.

In the beginning I looked so Arabic. But I don't know, something changed in my physique. So now people really get surprised when I speak in Arabic with them. Like when I go to Oasis people were coming to me. They started speaking in English and I realised they were struggling, so

I used Arabic and they were like Oh!! You're Arab? How do you speak? I was like, why? You don't look Arab, you look European, you look Spanish, Italian, you look Turkish, you look Brazilian.

But you don't look Arab. And I am like, this is me, look at me. And then when I am sitting with white people and they hear me speaking in English, they go: Wow! Your English is so good, how did you learn English? So, I just sometimes, most of the time feel like I am too white to be an Arab and I am too Arab to be white, you know? Nobody accepts me. Both see me as an exotic person. Oh! You speak Arabic, how? Oh! your English is so good, how? There are a lot of hows.

For me, what I see is that being an Arab has a lot of good things but at the same time has so many bad things, you know? At the same time, being white has some good things and also bad things. So why not make a combination of the good things of both, you know? Like white people are known for having an interest in being more into themselves, they are interested in something they do. They follow the rules, not all of them – not generalising – but mostly, they follow the rules. They have a certain life pattern. They like to get work done. They are responsible. And Arab people, they are generous, they are nice, they are sympathetic, they like to help each other. So, I'd like to have a combination of these two, you know. I can listen to Arabic music and English music. There shouldn't be only one. I am multicultural and I am bilingual.

So, I just go wherever I feel now, you know! Feel the moment. For example, Arabs get so sensitive about so many things. If someone Arab invited you to their house, you don't have to do the dishes. You can stay and they can serve you everything, while at someone like a British person's house you must kind of try to do the dishes. At a British house, you can't really have more food because they cook exactly enough for you, you know? You always need to put salt to their food. While if you are at an Arab's house, you don't have to clean anything. They don't allow you to stand up. Even if you keep sitting down, because you are the guest. They offer you some nice food, fancier than they offer themselves. They also like offering you tea, fruits, dessert. Anything they have in the house after the food, you know? While white people don't really do that. I don't like British food at all. There is no such thing even. They only have fish and chips and few other things. I hate fish and chips. I used to like fish. Not anymore, just because of this. I eat it because I am respectful. It is rude to reject food, but I wouldn't enjoy it. I love Arabic food. It's kind of my weakness.

I am not ready to go back yet. I need to do certain things. I would save up some money. I have a big to-do list, you know. I know I am a refugee. And if I go to Lebanon, I can't stay for more than two weeks as a tourist. Once in TOK [Theory of Knowledge] we had to do some presentation. We have a topic, and we need to discuss it from two different perspectives. And I was talking about identity and stereotypes. I used examples of how Americans, if they see a brown person, think they are from Pakistan or Afghanistan. They think they are terrorists. But if Americans see a Latino person, a Spanish speaker, a Hispanic person, they assume they are illegal. And I was talking about me – how people when they know I am Syrian assume that I am a refugee or a terrorist. So, I talked about stereotypes. That was one of the presentations I talked about.

The first presentation was on Islamophobia in the UK. I talked about how Muslims struggle from Islamophobia, because at that time I remember there was an incident of how a police officer or a white person attacked a Muslim wife and her children in London. So, I talked about it. My second presentation was about how Russia intervenes in Syria and how they are using it as just a space to practice their skills. And my third was about how the naturalisation of refugees in Lebanon affects the development of Lebanon. There are a lot of people who say that there are four million Syrians in Lebanon, why don't you give them a passport and Lebanese nationality? Well, Lebanon can't handle this because it is too much work. Plus, the definition of a refugee is originally to stay in a country for a certain amount of time and then go back. There are so many things to discuss. And my extended essay, which is like the big research we have to do to pass the IBE, was the question: Who was actually behind escalating the Syrian Civil War? Which was really interesting. I was enjoying it so much. Actually, writing that essay made me realise that I want to do politics. I was really proud.

Khalid al Saeed

It was the first time for me and my family to fly, to be in a plane! Lots of questions came to my mind on board the plane. Am I going to make it? I thought of all the Syrian refugees who were unable to make it, in the final moments as they were approaching their destinations. What was waiting for me? There was a stage between France and Wales when I was so scared. It was the scariest moment when we were over the clouds. There was a severe turbulence. The plane was shaking. I cried out: 'Awlady, Awlady' [My children, my children].

My children's feelings were a mixture of joy and sadness. The eldest ones were sad about leaving their friends in Jordan. The little ones were happier and were so excited. Mohammad, my eldest son, was so excited about going to Cardiff and maybe meeting the Welsh football player Gareth Bale. He is a great fan of Gareth Bale. I had no idea who Gareth Bale was!

When we first arrived, I was so disappointed when I saw the heavy rain. It was raining very heavily in Cardiff. When we left Jordan, the temperature was 43 degrees. During our first days in Cardiff, we were happy for our safe arrival, but the first days were very difficult because of the weather. The constant rain in June, the heavy rain in summer made me think 'If things are so bad and wet in summer, how would they look like in winter then?' I was wondering if we would ever see the sun again! The buildings looked different. I was looking from this window. I was looking at the opposite building and wondering if this was the only building without a *Sateh* [flat roof]. Are all the buildings and houses without *Sateh*? And how come? And what about balconies? No balconies at all?

When the team left, I went for a short walk to explore the area around our house. I walked for about 100 metres

and I was surprised. All the houses, they all look the same! I thought that it was a positive sign. I had a feeling of fairness and of justice once I noticed how similar the houses were. To me, this similarity reflected the fact that people are equal here, at least in the way their houses look. I continued my walk and felt a bit scared. People were looking at me and I felt like a stranger. No words to help me as I couldn't speak English.

We were received by a team of volunteers who work with the resettlement programme and the city council. One of the volunteers spoke Arabic and they helped us in the initial stages. They explained to us all matters to do with the children's school registration, private rent, services like water and energy and the GP registration etc. They helped with the essentials. I also liked the diversity in Cardiff – many nationalities from all over the world. I wasn't sure what would happen next and how we would settle and integrate.

"The constant rain in June, the heavy rain in summer made me think 'If things are so bad and wet in summer, how would they look like in winter then?' I was wondering if we would ever see the sun again!"

Even though I rarely cry, when we first arrived in the airport, when I saw people holding up signs with our names on, I cried. At that moment I shed tears. My wife and children hadn't seen me crying before, but I couldn't help it. I said *Alhamdulillah* that we had all made it safely. If something should happen to me, if I die, I know that my children will be looked after in this country.

Imagine living in that difficult state for eight years. Our hearts were heavy, very heavy with misery. I couldn't sleep for the duration of the flight from Jordan to the UK. I didn't even share my fears with my wife. I was haunted with lots of what ifs. What if the plane crashed and we all ended up in the ocean? What would the media coverage about us look like? I was constantly praying to Allah to make us arrive safely. Once my feet touched the earth, I cried my heart out. I just wanted to let go of that burden. I felt that I had finally succeeded in transferring my plants from water to soil, from sea to land. It was a very difficult moment. The welcoming team at the airport sympathised with me and there was an Arabic-speaking lady who started crying when she saw me crying.

The team escorted me and my family to a van that was waiting for us at the exit gate. While I was heading towards the front right-side car door the driver directed me to the left side and I was confused and embarrassed [laughs]. A couple of days later, when I was waiting to cross the road, I looked to the right side without thinking when cars were coming from the left!

Before coming to the UK, I learned around 20% of the necessary knowledge about some of the rules. I tried to educate myself. I read something about the culture shock. I met some Syrians who arrived in the UK months before me and had no clue about any of this. For instance, 99% of refugees' houses are not provided with TVs. Landlords don't provide a TV because getting a TV requires a TV licence. I knew about this before coming to the UK. So I was not so surprised when I didn't find a TV set in my house. I've heard stories of people who bought their TVs not knowing about the TV licence and they got fined because of their ignorance. No one had explained it to them before. In the Middle East there is no TV licence.

Most refugees were informed about the decision to come to the UK two to three years before the date of their travel. I was informed two years before. The question is why the UNHCR or any other organisation doesn't offer guidance or workshops to refugees before travelling? A pamphlet or a booklet for those who can read and a cassette for others who don't read or write.

Perhaps I was lucky that the volunteer who was responsible for our case had knowledge about some of those issues. The volunteer showed us how to register our children at schools, a GP, a dentist and showed us the way to the nearest supermarket and that was it. I asked the Syrians I met at the mosque or those introduced to me by other friends, and I was lucky that they brought my attention to the Citizens Advice Bureau and other things. But I learned and I can guide others now about the experiences I have been through. They must know their rights and their children's rights. It is a very serious issue when people know nothing. Refugees should learn that things don't happen automatically for them. They should be taught this in advance with clear guidance as where to go and whom to consult.

When we were in Jordan there were twenty-one Syrian families with varying levels of disabilities heading to the UK. We came to Wales and there was an Iraqi family with a 3-year-old severely disabled child. The family was resettled in Newport. In a phone call with the father, I discovered that he didn't have a clue of his rights regarding his son's disability because no one had told him. It is not about the financial aid. If this disabled person is not officially acknowledged as disabled, he will be treated as a healthy person. Disabled children need a special wheelchair, nappies and many other things which are very expensive to buy. Once such children are offered a disabled badge or card, most of these items are available at a very low cost.

When the college offers refugees a place, they have to attend classes for five days a week. As a result, they develop faster than others who can't do the five days. When someone has a disability or is caring for a disabled person, they do part-time study – two lessons a week, that is 8 hours a week which means 13 to 15 hours monthly. Others have around twenty hours weekly whereas people like my wife and I get 13 to 15 hours a month. My wife cares for our son and I have a minor disability. Sometimes these 13 hours are also affected or minimised because those people have appointments with a GP or the hospital. Hospital appointments cannot be easily cancelled, especially when you have been waiting for months to get one.

Online lessons were very difficult to manage. When we were in Jordan, we were struggling to make ends meet and had no time or not enough knowledge about using internet, computer, or laptops. How are we going to deal with remote learning? I spent four months in this country without knowing the meaning of contactless bank cards until I came across someone who explained it to me.

Within one and a half years my English has improved, and I have learned a great deal about places, services and about laws. There are refugees who don't even have an idea about how the visa system works. Five years and then permanent leave to remain and later they can apply for the British Citizenship. Lack of knowledge about this could have a disastrous effect on the whole asylum process. Some have no idea that they are not permitted to spend more than a month or two out of the country. This lack of knowledge has led to some asylum seekers losing their right to stay and apply for the next stage.

I met a friend who was shocked when he had to apply for his British Citizenship. He had no idea that he needed to pay a fortune for it, as he has a big family! He told me 'If I had an idea that it would cost this much, I would have saved for it.' Some think that the Life in the UK test needs to be finalised in the months before the application. They have no idea that they can do the test years before they apply, and that this would allow them plenty of time to revise and prepare rather than squeeze it in before the application date. I wish that the Life in the UK Test could be translated into Arabic and given to refugees before they arrive to the UK for two reasons: firstly, it would give

British Nationality Act 1981

Certificate of naturalisation

as a

BRITISH CITIZEN

The Secretary of State, in exercise of the powers conferred by the British Nationality Act 1981, hereby grants this certificate of naturalisation to the person named below, who shall be a

BRITISH CITIZEN

from the date of this certificate

The goal: a certificate of naturalisation.

refugees a full idea about life in the UK, rules, culture etc and it would also give them a chance to prepare for their test. If they don't already know the language and the rules and if no one is supporting them in the new country, it would be a real disaster. A booklet is necessary.

If I get my citizenship, it would be an acknowledgement. I would be treated as a British Citizen. There is a huge difference between a refugee and a citizen. Now, I can't vote – something which I want to practise freely under a democratic system. I believe all refugees dream of getting that British Passport. I personally feel that the passport will provide me with the freedom to move and to visit my relatives and the people I miss. Despite all the bureaucratic procedures which might exhaust us, I believe that this country treats people fairly. There are laws, and people should abide by the law.

I felt this in the court when my son's application was rejected and then I appealed, and how the judge stood by my side because I was not pretending, and I had evidence etc. I love how the society is open here.

Living in this country has enabled me to meet with people from different backgrounds and educational levels. I sat with the mayor of Cardiff, and he was a nice person. I talk with doctors like you and many others. I gain knowledge and experience and insight from them. During the eight years of that miserable life in Jordan I felt that my life had frozen. My family and I were far behind everything. Here in the UK, I feel like it is time to update our knowledge.

It wasn't an easy path at all. Om Mohammad and I were drained. But it was worth it, wasn't it? We worked hard towards this end, and we are grateful that Allah granted us this opportunity. I realise that in every society and in every country, there are positives and negatives. But I try to look at the positive side of life here. I am happy and satisfied as long as my children are getting their education in a systematic manner. The house we live in is fairly good and is very close to amenities and services. This is an achievement. We have been here for about one and a half years, and we feel like we have learned a lot, because if we don't learn about laws, and how the system works we will be puzzled. The more I learn about the law, the fewer mistakes I make. For instance, let me tell you this funny story about an incident that happened to me. When we first came to live here, I went for a walk and reached the Zebra crossing and was so hesitant to cross. I thought I needed to wait for the traffic lights. I asked someone if it was right to cross and he replied 'yes'. Later, I read about the Zebra crossings and I understood how things work with them. I am so pleased that I learned the meaning of the word 'wait' from the traffic signs! I know what it means to say a 'day ticket' on the bus, 'single' ticket and 'adult' ticket. And because we have children at different levels of education, we learned the different stages of education 'Nursery, reception, primary and high school' plus all the DWP-related expressions like 'council, court and judge'!

We were here over a year and then came Covid-19 and the lockdown. So, no one came. To be honest, we are managing well now. We have learned a lot and we have friends, like you, helping us over the phone for instructions and interpretation. I learned a lot about shopping centres and which ones are better than others. I now know the difference between 'whole milk' with a blue line, and green 'skimmed milk', 'yogurt'.

In the beginning there was an interpreter. Sometimes, the interpreter would be busy or unavailable and it was a hassle to try to ring them each time you needed them. So, I decided to depend on myself, at least for basic conversations. I wrote down all the expressions that I needed to use for – say the GP. I wrote them in Arabic and used Google Translate to listen to the way they are pronounced, and I wrote the pronunciation with Arabic letters. Now I have learned how to tell the receptionist: 'Hi, I have an appointment with Dr X or with the nurse for the injection.' 'I have pain in arm, stomach, shoulder, head.' Om

Mohammad learned expressions related to shopping. She learned them the same way: 'Chicken, drumstick, medium, large, how much and how many... cucumber, garlic...'

ESOL lessons were not very helpful. They focus on grammar. We don't need grammar. When I was using English with a Home Office representative, he was amazed! He asked me: 'How did you learn?' I replied: 'I learned from pressure.' When I get a letter for instance, I scan it and crop it and then I copy it to Google Translate which helps me. Google helps me understand around 75% of the overall meaning. Now, Om Mohammad goes to the pharmacy by herself, and she collects my prescription or Mohammad's prescriptions and she asks about the 'dose' and the instructions. I learned names of places, streets and hospitals because I visited them a lot. My bank account, statement, direct debit and debit card. However, I still prefer paper communications via the post. My wife and I are not very confident with using emails, sending and replying etc. Sometimes, I find it hard to talk to people over the phone. Sometimes they talk too fast when they call for an appointment or inform me about a cancellation. In the beginning I used to ask for an interpreter, then I started asking them to talk more slowly. I started asking essential questions about 'time', 'date' and whether it is 'face-to-face'. If you look over there, I write all our appointments over there. We learned all this during the lockdown. My wife and I are very happy to learn about many places here in Cardiff.

Before lockdown, I used to go to the library building where the city council is based. I met many refugees from

Syrian hospitality: food prepared for Angham, the researcher, by Khalid and his family. © Angham Abdullah

Children don't know what home is. I believe that home for any child is where they feel settled and comfortable. When I was in Jordan, I watched a documentary on a refugee family at one of the camps there. There was a scene of a barefooted girl in the middle of the mud in a camp. I was emotional when I watched it. The presenter asked her father what do you think home means for your daughter? He replied: 'Home for my daughter is a pair of shoes.' So, home means a place where my children feel at home.

Home for my children is definitely here. They are getting their education here, they have made friends and they are learning Welsh and English. My family is back home, and I can't see them or interact with them face-to-face. We must be realistic because we cannot travel unless we have our citizenships, and this needs years to happen. Instead, I am making friends here and I feel that those close friends have become my family. When we first came, we were lonely. Day by day, we met new people and have enlarged our circle of friends and you have become one of them. This is our society now. To be able to go on and be positive, I believe that we shouldn't focus on the past. The past has gone. In English grammar we learned about past, present and future tenses, so the 'past' has gone and won't return. Now we have the 'present' to live in and enjoy and 'the future' is in the hands of Allah. So, let's leave it to Allah to decide the future and let's be positive. As it says in the Arab poem: '*Kun Jamelan Tara al Wojooda Jameela*' [Be beautiful, and you will see beauty].

different parts of the world, and I made friends with some of them. I also met others at the ESOL lessons, and at the park. But the lockdown ruined everything. Hopefully after the lockdown and the vaccine, things will get better. My children made friends with many nationalities. Children make more friends at school.

I have to thank this country for welcoming us here. I feel indebted to this country for taking care of me and my children, especially after our being destitute in Jordan. I wish that the authorities could listen to what we raise and find a reasonable solution to so many issues affecting refugees. I wish that there were no refugees in the world anymore. Life is short and I wish that wars would come to an end. Our children need to be happier. They don't deserve to live as refugees. They shouldn't be involved in any conflict. I want refugees coming to Europe to have an effect and an impact. If the father can't be effective for certain reasons, he should encourage his children to be effective humans in the new society. Refugees are not all bad and we shouldn't generalise and judge refugees as all being here for benefits. Thank you for listening to me.

"In English grammar we learned about past, present and future tenses. The 'past' has gone and won't return. Now we have the 'present' to live in and enjoy and 'the future' is in the hands of Allah. So, let's leave it to Allah to decide the future and let's be positive."

Afterword

Hussam Allaham with Reynette Roberts, Director of Oasis Cardiff, at his UK citizenship ceremony. © Oasis Cardiff

As he escaped from Syria into Jordan, surgeon Hussam Allaham recalled

> When the plane took off, I looked from the window and all I saw was smoke… areas were burning. It was an unforgettable image. I flew when the country was burning… And it is still burning. Since the very beginning no one expected that things would come to this stage… We were hopeful. We used to say this month, the next month, the next year… Two years. Sadly, it was terrible.

After more than ten years of civil war, this image of smoke all around can serve as an evocative metaphor of the common refugee experience of losing sight of all the things that gave their former life its meaning and coherence. The interviews have led us to reflect upon the ways in which fleeing from a violent Syria, from a totally different past life impacts on Syrians' current lives in Wales. It raises the question of how one can experience a sense of belonging in a totally different and previously unknown environment?

The life stories offer several leads here. They show how Syrians in Wales manage to create identities and a sense of community as refugees, as ex-patriot Syrians and as new Welsh citizens. These competing identities are integrated into the host society in different ways and to different degrees. Both remembering and forgetting the past play crucial roles here.

Sometimes remembering is done actively. As Latifa Alnajjar, recalls: 'I sit down at night and contemplate and remember. I feel it, I smell it and feel like my soul is still there.' Here the message is one of nostalgic loss. Yet even where the memories are painful, not all refugees want to forget their traumatic pasts. Some take care to preserve the details of their flight, sometimes by writing them down and sometimes through preserving objects such as the clothing which they had with them when they fled. When they achieve refugee status, such objects take on new meanings. For example, Bashar tells of how 'dear objects of difficult memories' are also a record of his survival. This points to how even traumatic memories can assume a positive role in the present if they are embedded in a narrative of survival. Rather than repressing and forgetting their traumatic experiences, the interviewees use them as evidence of their strength.

The narratives suggest that individuals tailor their identities depending on context, but of course they are not always in control and all sorts of factors can trigger disruptive memories. Both types of memories – traumatic and nostalgic – are involuntarily prompted by external factors including for example, images, media representations, objects, smells and sounds. The interviews show clearly that it is not easy to abandon a past life, however much you might want to put it behind you. They

also show that sharing experiences can have beneficial effects. As Ahmad Al Kadri tells us of his regular meetings with other Syrian refugees, 'We usually discuss our present, plans for the future and perhaps the problems we are facing and memories of the past. It is about sharing of feelings, suffering, happy moments. When I talk to them, I feel I am not alone in whatever suffering I am going through.'

In addition to the psychological and emotional difficulties that many Syrian refugees live with, they face a wide range of other challenges on a day-to-day basis, which include serious problems with English, lack of knowledge of life in Wales, and often not being able to work in the professions for which they were trained. Basic areas of everyday life, such as housing, become problematic even though they may be relatively easy for most people to negotiate if they know the ropes in the host society. While it is apparent that social class and education are very significant determinants on how individuals and families cope, we were very impressed by the refugees' resilience and ways of coping in their new lives in Wales, despite the hardships they face.

Clearly sharing memories is crucial to the process of recalling past events, evoking feelings of both pleasure and pain. How memories can be shared depends on various factors. Primary is the question of who one is trying to share them with. These may range from other Syrians and non-Syrian refugees with similar experiences to empathetic listeners without any similar experiences.

Loss is a crucial impetus to memory. It manifests itself as both absence of material things and in emotions. The interviews suggest that painful memories of violence, fear, loss of belonging, absence of the familiar can lie at the root of overwhelming depression and isolation. The ongoing violence and upheaval in Syria and Lebanon also serve to depress refugees. As Baher Al Abed explains, avoiding the news can reduce exposure to negative feelings.

In telling their life stories, the interviewees suggest a range of strategies that would improve the experience of becoming a refugee. These include focussing on the present not the past. How interviewees view the present varies widely from the very positive to those who only see the bad aspects of life in the UK. For most it is a mixture of good and bad.

Many of the suggestions for doing things differently come from refugees who reached the UK legally with the help of organisations such as the UN. They emphasise the need for greater preparation where possible before travelling. This could also be provided for those travelling without the necessary documentation via independent websites. As Khalid Al Saeed puts it 'Refugees should learn that things won't happen automatically for them. They should be taught this in advance with clear guidance as where to go and whom to consult'.

Some refugees reflect that they 'wish that the authorities could listen to what we raise and find a reasonable solution to so many issues affecting refugees.' Others place a lot of emphasis on self-help. Yet this too could be made easier if more accessible information were more readily available. It would also help refugees be more active in shaping their new lives.

Community support is crucial to making a success of life in Wales: 'I am making friends here and I feel that those close friends have become my family. When we first came, we were lonely. Day by day, we met new people and have enlarged our circle of friends'. As Khalid Al Saeed puts it: 'This is our society now. To be able to go on and be positive I believe that we shouldn't focus on the past.' As Noor relates, social media has made it much easier for the Syrian community to identify and help newcomers.

Ronahi Hassan suggests that refugees are a positive addition to British society. 'Diversity and accepting diversity will benefit society. Refugees are great people. They risk their lives, head to the unknown and do their best to build their lives'. This country should be proud of any refugee who succeeds in 'building a life from scratch'. Some interviewees stress integration must be a two-way process in which the host society must make some 'effort to get to know us better'.

The interviews strongly suggest that traces of the past impact on the present and that challenging pasts are rarely just simply past. This means that the past almost always impinges on and has implications for the present. Both Syrian and other refugees would be helped to participate in the life of Wales if members of the host community were to acquire greater knowledge and empathetic understanding of their former and current lives. This is something that we hope this book has helped to provide.

Glossary

Arabic (using English alphabet)	Meaning	Arabic
A'mtu	His Aunt (father's side)	عمته
Ahla wsahla	You are most welcome	آهلا وسهلا
Ajaneb	Foreigners	أجانب
Al Hamdulillah	Praise be to God: phrase used in many different situations as an expression of relief for completing an action.	ألحمد لله
Al Salamu Alaykum	Peace be upon you	ألسلام عليكم
Al Sham	Sham is the historic Arabic name for "Syria" and "Damascus". In English and French, the old name for that region is the Levant.	ألشام
Alawite	A religious sect of Shia Islam, based in Syria and believed to have been founded during the ninth century.	ألعلوية
Alkhayr ma khtarahu Allah	Goodness lies in God's choice.	ألخير ماا ختاره الله
Allah	God	ألله
Allah Yerhamu	May Allah bless his soul	ألله يرحمه
Argeileh	Hookah	أركيله
Asylum seeker	Someone who has fled their home country and is seeking protection from persecution or conflict in another country as a recognised refugee.	طالب اللجوء
Awlady	My children	أولادي
Ba'ath Party	The political party that has governed Syria since a coup brought the Ba'athists to power in 1963.	حزب البعث

Bab al-Hara	One of the most popular television series in the Arab world. It was reportedly watched by millions of people in the Arab world. The series chronicles the daily happenings and family dramas in a neighbourhood in Damascus.	باب الحارة
Badini/ Bahdini Kurdish	A language spoken by about two million Kurds in Northern Iraq.	اللهجة البادينيه أو البهدينيه
Badr Shakir Al Sayyab	A leading Iraqi poet and one of the most influential Arab poets during the 1950s. He was exiled for his political views. From his exile Al Sayyab wrote poems on home, longing and belonging.	بدر شاكر السياب
Bahra	A fountain in the middle of an open yard in a traditional Syrian house.	بَحرة
Baklava	Sweet pastry made with layers of honey-soaked crispy phyllo pastry and a delicious nut mixture.	بقلاوة
Basboosah	Sweet, syrup-soaked semolina cake	بسبوسة
Beet A'rabi	Arabic house that is a traditional Syrian house with an open courtyard.	بيت عربي
Bismillah	By the name of God	بسم الله
Burgul	Cereal grain made from dried, cracked wheat. Durum wheat is used most often. The flavour is earthy and nutty, much like quinoa.	برغل
Burka	A one-piece veil that covers the face and the whole body	برقع
Dougar	Traffic jam where trucks entering a city or town form a long queue and can sometimes get stuck in that queue for hours.	دوغار
Eid	Religious celebration: Muslims have two Eid celebrations: Eid al Fitr that falls at the end of the fasting month of Ramadan and Eid al Adha which falls on the last day of the Hajj (pilgrimage to Makkah in Saudi Arabia).	عيد
Esh Al-Bulbul	Nightingale's nest – a type of sweet pastry shaped like the nest of the nightingale and stuffed with nuts.	عش البلبل
ESOL	English for Speakers of Other Languages	ايسول

Fadhfadha	To get things off one's chest	فضفضه
Faraket Batatah	Cooked potatoes with beef or eggs	فركة بطاطا
Fattoush	A Mediterranean salad that typically includes lettuce, tomatoes, cucumbers, radishes, and fried pieces of pita.	فتوش
Freekeh	A cereal food made from green durum wheat that is roasted and rubbed to create its flavour.	فريكة
FSA	Free Syrian Army: rebel forces fighting Asad's regime. It is made up of diverse battalions and brigades, including military defectors from the Syrian Army and moderates.	الجيش السوري الحر
Halal	Used to describe food and drink prepared in accordance with Islamic law. In more general terms, any object or action that is permissible according to Islamic law.	حلال
Halawt al Jibn	A Syrian dessert made of a semolina and cheese dough, filled with cream.	حلاوة الجبن
Haram	An act that is sinful and forbidden by Allah. The word has other usages according to the context.	حرام
Haresah	Semolina cake sweetened with rose water syrup.	هريسة
Hijab	A veil covering the head worn by women in the presence of adult males outside the immediate family.	حجاب
IELTS	The International English Language Testing System; a test designed to assess your ability to listen, read, write, and speak in English.	ايلتس
Illegal immigrant	Someone who migrates into a country in violation of the immigration laws of that country, or the continued residence without the legal right to live in that country.	المهاجر الغير شرعي
Indefinite leave to remain	Also called "settlement" or "ILR". It gives the person the right to live, work and study in the UK for as long as they like and apply for benefits if eligible. It can be used to apply for British citizenship.	رخصة أقامة إلى أجل غير مسمى
Inshallah	If God wills	ان شاءالله
Istikhbarat	A secret police organisation, also known as Mukhabarat.	ألأستخبارات

Jallab	A drink made with date molasses, rose water, and topped with pine nuts.	جَلّاب
Khaltu	His aunt on the mother's side	خالته
Kheer	Goodness	خير
Khemar	A head covering or veil typically concealing the head, neck, and shoulders.	خِمار
Kibbeh	A dough made of bulgur (cracked wheat), onions and mint leaves, formed into football shaped croquettes, and filled with meat, pine nuts and Middle Eastern spices. They are then deep fried, so they are crisp on the outside and soft inside.	كبة
Knafeh	A dessert with a shredded filo dough crust, a sweet cheese filling, topped with rose water flavoured sweet syrup.	كنافه
Kun Jamelan Tara al Wojooda Jameela	A line from a poem by the Lebanese poet Elia Abu Madi. It is about inner beauty and the positive outlook to life. The line literally translates as: "Be beautiful, you see the universe beautiful".	كُن جميلاً ترى الوجود جميلاً
Kurds	An ethnic group spanning parts of modern-day Iran, Iraq, Syria, and Turkey	الأكراد
Kurmanji Kurdish	The northern dialect of the Kurdish languages, spoken predominantly in southeast Turkey, northwest and northeast Iran, northern Iraq, northern Syria and the Caucasus and Khorasan regions. It is also called Northern Kurdish.	اللهجة الكرمانجيه الكردية
Labaniyyeh	A classic Middle Eastern dish of kibbeh in a cooked garlic yogurt sauce.	لبنية
Life in the UK test	A computer-based test constituting one of the requirements for anyone seeking Indefinite Leave to Remain in the UK or naturalisation as a British citizen.	أختبار الحياة في المملكة المتحدة
Ma'amoul	A filled butter cookie made with semolina flour. The filling can be made with dried fruits like figs or dates or nuts such as pistachios or walnuts and occasionally almonds.	معمول
Mabrook	Congratulations	مبروك

Mahashi	Stuffed vegetables. The vegetables are filled with rice, green herbs and minced meat and cooked with tomato sauce and lemons.	محاشي
Makdous	A typical dish of Levantine cuisine, consisting of small eggplants, boiled, salted, and stuffed with a mixture of crushed nuts, garlic and chili pepper. The young eggplants are then marinated in olive oil and fermented in a jar.	مكدوس
Manaqeesh	A flatbread typically eaten for breakfast. The crispy homemade dough is topped with a za'atar topping or a blend of cheeses for two different variety of Manaqeesh.	مناقيش
Marhaba	Hello	مرحبا
Mashallah	Literally "what God has willed." It is generally used to express amazement, praise, thankfulness, gratitude, or joy for an event that has already occurred.	ماشاءالله
Mawaleh	Salty nuts and biscuits	موالح
Misk	Musk. The word is used metaphorically to describe extreme kindness.	المِسك
Mooneh	A seasonal food supply that people collect in summer and prepare for the winter's season.	مونة
Mubarak	Blessed	مبارك
Muhalabiyyah	A milk pudding commonly made with rice, sugar, milk and either rice flour, starch, or semolina. It is popular as a dessert in the Middle East.	مهلبية
Mukasarat	Nuts and seeds.	مكسرات
Mulukhiyya	A classic Middle Eastern dish, a delicious soupy vegetable dish made with Jew's Mallow, a distinctive tasting leafy green.	ملوخية
Mushabak	A sweet and crispy dessert made of flour, milk and rose water. It is fried and topped with a sweet syrup.	مُشبّك
Mushallalieh	String cheese. It is often available flavoured with nigella seeds or caraway seeds or some other flavourings.	مشلّله
Nahr al Furat	Euphrates river	نهر الفرات

Niqab	A veil for the face that leaves the area around the eyes clear.	نقاب
Om Mohammad	Mother of Mohammad. Middle Eastern parents are traditionally named after their firstborn son. Parents take great pride in being called for example, Om Mohammad (the mother of Mohammad) and Abu Mohammad (the father of Mohammad). If they don't have a son, then they will be named after their eldest daughter. This practice is a show of respect for the married parent with children.	أم محمد
Qatayef	Filled pancakes that come in the form of cones stuffed with sweet cheese, cream, or nuts. They are served with honey or sweet syrup on the side.	قطايف
Qate'a al-Ahjar	Stone breaking. A ceremony celebrating the appearance of the baby's first steps.	قطع الاحجار
Qura'an	The central religious text of Islam, believed by Muslims to be a revelation from God (Allah).	ألقرآن
Rafiqat al Darb	Road mate	رفيقة الدرب
Ramadan	The ninth month of the Islamic year, during which fasting is observed from sunrise to sunset. This includes abstaining from drinking, eating, immoral acts and anger. Acts of worship such as prayer, reading the Quran and charity are also encouraged during the holy month.	رمضان
Reef Halab	The countryside of Aleppo	ريف حلب
Refugee	A person who, owing to a well-founded fear of persecution, on the grounds of race, religion, nationality, or membership of a social group, find themselves outside their country of origin, and are unable or unwilling to avail themselves of the protection of that country.	اللاجئ
Sahlab	A drink made up of milk, corn flower, sugar, cinnamon, coconut flakes and nuts.	سحلب
Samen	The most common fat used in cooking rice and meat, in the preparation of sweets or simply for seasoning. It is prepared by putting raw sheep milk inside a sheepskin bag and shaking it until the fat separates from the whey.	سمن

Sateh	Flat fenced rooftops, a typical feature of houses in the Middle East. In the summertime, people often sleep on the rooftop to keep cool. The rooftops of village houses, filled with greenery, are spaces where family gatherings take place in summer.	سطح
Shakriyeh	Dish made of yogurt and beef served with rice	شاكرية
Sharab Eriq Alsus	Liquorice juice	شراب عرق السوس
Shawarma	A Levantine dish consisting of meat cut into thin slices, stacked in a cone-like shape, and roasted on a slowly turning vertical rotisserie or spit. Originally made of lamb or mutton, today's shawarma may also be chicken, turkey, beef, or veal.	شاورمة
Shia	The second largest denomination of Islam, who regard Ali, the fourth caliph, as Mohammad's first true successor.	الشيعة
Shish Barak	Little ravioli-like dumplings filled with seasoned lamb, onions, and pine nuts that are cooked in a yogurt stew, baked, or fried and served.	شيش برك
Shukran	Thank you	شكراً
Sorani Kurdish	A North-western Iranian language and the second most widely spoken Kurdish language (after Kurmanji), with at least 9 million speakers in Iran and Iraq. It is also known as Central Kurdish.	اللهجة السورانية الكردية
Subhan Allah	While there is no exact translation in English, the term can mean, among other things, both "God is perfect" and "Glory to God". It is often used when praising God or expressing awe at God's attributes, bounty, or creation.	سبحان الله
Sufra	Dining table	سُفرة
Sunni	The largest denomination of Islam, differing from Shia in its understanding of the Sunnah (the traditional portion of Islamic law based on the Prophet Mohammad's words and acts) and its acceptance of the first three caliphs.	السُنة
Sura	Qura'anic Verse	سورة

Tabarruj	Elegance that attracts men.	تَبَرُّج
Tafadhaly	Come over	تفضّلي
Talae'a Al Ba'ath	The Ba'ath Vanguard Organization, established in Syria in 1974. It was a political educational organization for primary schools based on the ideology of the Ba'ath Party. At high school level, pupils were enrolled into Al Shabiba: Ba'ath Youth Groups. Both organizations have now been replaced by the compulsory National Education course.	طلائع البعث
Umrah or O'mrah	An Islamic pilgrimage to Mecca, in Saudi Arabia, that can be undertaken at any time of the year.	ألعُمرة
Wallah	By God	والله
Waraq al Enab	Vine leaves stuffed with rice and vegetables.	ورق العنب
Ward al Joori	Damask Roses	ورد الجوري
Yarab	My God, a word used in prayers.	يارب
Yasmeen	Damascene Jasmine, a white fragrant flower that has a symbolic value for most Syrians.	الياسمين الدمشقي

Contributors and Credits

EDITORS

Angham Abdullah is originally from Iraq. She moved to the UK in 2009 for her doctoral degree at the University of York. Before that, she was a lecturer in comparative literary studies and a translator of Arabic in the Middle East. Her research focusses on issues related to Iraqi women's narratives of war, displacement and exile. Herself a former refugee, her role as a researcher on the Refugee Wales project has been to record and document the oral histories of Syrian refugees in Wales.

Beth Thomas worked for over forty years for Amgueddfa Cymru-National Museum Wales, based at St Fagans. As Keeper of History and Archaeology, she played a key role in the redevelopment of St Fagans as a National Museum of History. Her work has always involved collecting and archiving oral testimony. She is a long-standing trustee and former chair of the Oral History Society and has trained people from all over Wales to collect and archive oral history.

Chris Weedon is Professor Emerita at Cardiff University where she directed the Centre for Critical and Cultural Theory. She has published widely on feminist theory, cultural politics, culture and identity, women's writing, British Black and Asian writing and multi-ethnic Britain. She was involved in Butetown History & Arts Centre for twenty-six years and has worked on many community-based oral history projects with people from minority communities.

POETRY

Jehan Bseiso, the author of *No Search, No Rescue* is a poet, writer and aid worker. Her poetry has been published on several online platforms. In 2016, her co-authored book *I Remember My Name* won the Palestine Book Awards in the creative category. She is the co-editor of *Making Mirrors: Writing/Righting by and for Refugees* (2019). She has been working with Médecins sans Frontières/Doctors Without Borders since 2008 and has worked in Afghanistan, Pakistan, Iraq, Ethiopia, Jordan and other countries.

PAINTINGS

The artworks reproduced in this book are those of Alison Lochhead, an artist living in mid Wales. Alison is an artist whose work reflects upon the fragmentation of memory and witness of injustices. It explores the impact war and conflict has on the world and the environment; the destruction of livelihoods, identities, securities, homes, the migrations, the inhumanities, the hope of change. She is best known as a sculptor working with materials transformed by fire; cast iron, clay, earth. In 2019 Alison had volunteered in refugee camps: in Calais and in Ioannina in Greece. Stories, images and feelings from these times took time to process and came out in paint rather than three dimensionally.

PHOTOS

The people we interviewed left most of their possessions behind when they left Syria. They had very few photos to illustrate their lives before or during the war. We are therefore grateful to the many photographers who have shared images of Syria via Creative Commons.

Cover image

"All at Sea 2" by Alison Lochhead. Photography: Luke Unsworth.

The War in Syria

Political map of Syria by © pbardocz /Adobe Stock

Syrian Dynasty by Amerune, available under a Creative Commons Attribution Licence 2.0 at https://www.flickr.com/photos/amerune/174613514

Bashar al Asad propaganda, 2007 by Michael Goodine, available under a Creative Commons Attribution Licence 2.0 at https://www.flickr.com/photos/7741046@N06/1457463017

Baniyas Demos – Syria, 2011, by Syria-Frames-Of-Freedom, available under a Creative Commons Attribution Licence 2.0 at https://www.flickr.com/photos/syrian-freedom-captured/5736128537

People search for survivors in the rubble in a damaged area in Al-Suwkkari neighbourhood in Aleppo. © REUTERS / Aref Haj Youssef – stock.adobe.com

Still from animated map by Alexpl, available under CC BY-SA 4.0, via Wikimedia Commons at https://en.wikipedia.org/wiki/Timeline_of_the_Syrian_civil_war#/media/File:SyrianWarAnimation2011-2019.gif

The Human Cost

Infographic by Beth Thomas. Data source: https://commonslibrary.parliament.uk/research-briefings/cbp-9381/; https://gov.wales/new-refugee-and-asylum-seeker-plan-wales-launched

AZEZ, SYRIA – MAY 19: Refugee camp for Syrian people in Burseya hill on May 19, 2019, in Azez, Syria. © hikrcn /Adobe Stock

Map showing the outflow of Syrian refugees to adjacent countries and beyond, Sources: https://data2.unhcr.org/en/situations/syria; https://migrationobservatory.ox.ac.uk/resources/briefings/migration-to-the-uk-asylum/

Syrian refugees resting on the floor of Keleti railway station, Budapest, Hungary, 5 September 2015. By Mstyslav Chernov, available under CC BY-SA 4.0 licence, via Wikimedia Commons at https://commons.wikimedia.org/wiki/File:Syrian_refugees_having_rest_at_the_floor_of_Keleti_railway_station._Refugee_crisis._Budapest,_Hungary,_Central_Europe,_5_September_2015.jpg

The Storytellers

'Looking for Exile' – calligraphy by Abduljaleel Olayyane, inspired by an article written by Ali Zain.

Before the War

Syria – Aleppo © Dario Bajurin/Adobe Stock

Homs – Syria (CC BY 2.0) by Beshr Abdulhadi. Available at https://www.flickr.com/photos/beshro/7684924520

Esh Al-Bulbul, a Syrian sweet. © Syrian Dinner Project.

Raqqa by Beshr Abdulhadi, available under a Creative Commons Attribution Licence 2.0 at https://www.flickr.com/photos/beshro/5965461429

"Azimhof" by captain.orange, available under a Creative Commons Attribution Licence 2.0 at https://www.flickr.com/photos/10527553@N03/1000271762/

The village of Al Hajar Al-Abyadh, photo courtesy of Ali Zain.

Home in Al-Ratoniyyah, photo courtesy of Ali Zain

"Khalid ibn Al-Walid Mosque" (CC BY 2.0) by Beshr Abdulhadi. Available at
https://www.flickr.com/photos/beshro/7685048046

A rose growing in an Aleppo garden

A photo of Aleppo taken by Mohamad Karkoubi

Panoramic view of Ayn al-Bayda in the countryside of Latakia, Syria by Jadd Haidar, available under a CC BY-SA 4.0
licence at https://commons.wikimedia.org/w/index.php?curid=61223485

Jasmine growing on the garden wall, © Mohammed S.

A street view of Manbij city by Jacky Lee available under a Creative Commons Attribution Licence 3.0
at https://commons.wikimedia.org/wiki/File:A_street_view_of_manbij_city_-_panoramio.jpg

Shukri al-Qiwatly street, Qamishli, Syria by Arab Salsa. Public domain, available via Wikimedia Commons
at https://commons.wikimedia.org/wiki/File:Kamishly_view.jpg

"Al Qamishli" by Beshr Abdulhadi, available under a Creative Commons Attribution Licence 2.0
at https://www.flickr.com/photos/beshro/8653882715/

Kurdistan map © lesniewski/Adobe Stock

Newroz at Girê Tertebê, near Qamishli, in 1997 by MikaelF, available under a CC BY-SA 3.0 licence, via Wikimedia
Commons at https://commons.wikimedia.org/wiki/File:Newroz_Girê_Tertebê_1997.jpg

Kurds, Assyrians, and Arabs demonstrate against the government in the city of Qamishli, northeastern Syria.
By KurdWatch.org available under a CC BY 3.0 licence, via Wikimedia Commons
at https://commons.wikimedia.org/wiki/File:Demonstration_in_Qamishli_against_the_Syrian_government.jpg

Houses and farms in Zabadani Valley by Wesamt, available under a CC BY-SA 4.0 licence via Wikimedia Commons
at https://en.wikipedia.org/wiki/Al-Zabadani#/media/File:06242009585_Zabadani_Valley.jpg

The Umayyad Mosque, Damascus. © ali/Adobe Stock.

Syria by Marc Veraart, available under a Creative Commons Attribution Licence 2.0
at https://www.flickr.com/photos/marcveraart/5492439519

City of Damascus pictured from Mt Qasioun by ZCU, available under a CC BY-SA 3.0 licence, via Wikipedia Commons
at https://commons.wikimedia.org/wiki/File:City_of_Damascus_pictured_from_Mt_Qasioun.jpg

Damascus © Dudarev Mikhail/Adobe Stock

Our War

"Above or Below – Never Safe" by Alison Lochhead. Photography: Luke Unsworth

A man with bloodstains on his face carries a boy after what activists said was shelling by forces loyal to Syria's President Bashar al Asad in Aleppo's Bustan al-Qasr district, August 16, 2013. © REUTERS/Aref Haj Youssef – stock.adobe.com

The scar on Noor's wrist. Photo courtesy of Noor.

Muslim women © Grzegorz Japol/Adobe Stock

Destroyed neighbourhood in Raqqa. By Mahmoud Bali (VOA). Public domain, via Wikimedia Commons at https://commons.wikimedia.org/wiki/File:Destroyed_neighborhood_in_Raqqa.png

Old city of Hama, Syria. Syrian women in Islamic veils (niqab) © Vyacheslav Argenberg. Available under CC licence 4.0 International via Wikimedia Commons at https://commons.m.wikimedia.org/wiki/File:Hama,_Stone_alleys_of_the_old_city_of_Hama,_Syrian_women_in_niqab,_Syria.jpg

Anti-riot police in central Damascus, Jan. 16, 2012. Photo: Elizabeth Arrott, Public domain, via Wikimedia Commons at https://commons.wikimedia.org/wiki/File:VOA_Arrott_-_A_View_of_Syria,_Under_Government_Crackdown_07.jpg

'Syria: two years of tragedy' by Basma, available under CC BY-ND 2.0 licence at https://flickr.com/photos/foreignoffice/8642756918

Kobani © Ali/Adobe Stock

Hussam Allaham. Photo © Oasis Cardiff

Surgeons in Deraa, Syria, 2014. Photo: Savesyria, available under CC BY-SA 3.0, via Wikimedia Commons at https://commons.wikimedia.org/wiki/File:Chirurgien_save_syria.jpg

Damascus Checkpoint, 2012. Elizabeth Arrott, Public domain, via Wikimedia Commons at https://commons.wikimedia.org/wiki/File:Damascus_Checkpoint.jpeg

Medical staff treating rebel fighters and civilians at a hospital in Aleppo. Scott Bobb, Public domain, via Wikimedia Commons at https://commons.wikimedia.org/wiki/File:Aleppo_hospital.PNG

Long Way from Home

"Maybe Over the Horizon" by Alison Lochhead. Photography: Luke Unsworth

Photo taken from the Calais Jungle, "2016-01-18 15.44.37" (CC BY 2.0) by malachybrowne

Photo of migrants in rubber boat by Mstyslav Chernov/Unframe, CC BY-SA 4.0 via Wikimedia Commons

Refugees on a capsizing boat in the Mediterranean. Ggia, CC BY-SA 4.0, via Wikimedia Commons 2016

'All at Sea 2' by Alison Lochhead. Photography: Luke Unsworth

Group of refugees from Syria and Afghanistan on their way to EU. Balkan route. Thousands of refugees on border between Croatia and Serbia in autumn 2015. © Ajdin Kamber/Adobe Stock

Migrants stand on roadside in hope of hiding inside trucks in Calais. REUTERS / Pascal Rossignol – stock.adobe.com

'Did People Live Here?' by Alison Lochhead. Photography: Luke Unsworth

Hussam and his brother with other refugees being smuggled through Libya. Photo courtesy of Hussam Allaham.

Hussam with other migrants on the boat from Libya to Italy. Photo courtesy of Hussam Allaham

The Greek coast: a photo taken by Ali on his second attempt to cross by boat from Turkey, on a much calmer sea. © Ali Zain

Migrants in Hungary near the border with Serbia, 2015. Photos: Gémes Sándor/SzomSzed, CC BY-SA 3.0, via Wikimedia Commons available at
https://commons.wikimedia.org/wiki/Category:Images_by_Gémes_Sándor#/media/File:Migrants_in_Hungary_2015_Aug _010.jpg

"2016-01-17 13.02.06" by malachybrowne, available under CC BY 2.0 licence
at https://www.flickr.com/photos/67570481@N04/24665508145/

Migrants enter a truck on the A16 highway that leads to the Channel tunnel crossing in Coquelles. © REUTERS/Pascal Rossignol – stock.adobe.com

Mohammad's plane ticket to London to reunite with his family © Mohammad S

Photograph taken by Mohammad from the window of the plane taking him to the UK, to reunite with his family. © Mohammad S

'The Weight of Waiting' by Alison Lochhead. Photography: Luke Unsworth

'Bristol Airport : Drop Off Point' © Lewis Clarke, available under CC BY 2.0 licence
at https://www. geograph.org.uk/photo/3177520

Life in Wales

Photo of Ronahi Hassan, courtesy of Ronahi.

Swansea City Centre © J WILLIAMS, available under CC BY 2.0 licence at https://www.geograph.org.uk/photo/3304999

The Hassans' Cardiff restaurant. © Ronahi Hassan

The interior of the restaurant © Ronahi Hassan

Ronahi on her graduation day, courtesy of Ronahi Hassan

Dentistry students at Cardiff University. © Cardiff University

Match day at Cardiff – Boycezone by Jeremy Segrott (CC BY 2.0).
Available at https://flickr.com/photos/126337928@N05/16626740929

Bashar at the Cardiff restaurant where he used to work. © Bashar Mousa

Bashar after completing his 365-day run. © Bashar Mousa

Bashar at BBC Wales studios for an interview. © Bashar Mousa

Sulaiman Sulaiman working in his own restaurant in Cardiff, 2020. © Angham Abdullah

Jasmin restaurant © Angham Abdullah

ESOL class at Oasis Cardiff. © Oasis Cardiff

Photo taken by Ali Zain in 2014 of the view from his family home in Syria. © Ali Zain.

Ali's hand-painted calligraphy of the word 'Syria'. Photo: Angham Abdullah

Ali's laptop. Photo: Angham Abdullah

Mohamad Karkoubi and his daughter waving the Welsh flag at a St David's Day event. Courtesy of Mohamad Karkoubi

After a stormy day at Aberystwyth. © Marged Elin Thomas

Notes stuck on the wall in Mohamad's home in Aberystwyth for learning English. Photo: Angham Abdullah

Mohamad's Welsh lessons: learning the future tense © Angham Abdullah

Mohamad's children with their new baby sister. © Mohamad Karkoubi

Mohamad and his family having a picnic on the beach at Aberystwyth. Mohamad is playing an oud.
© Mohamad Karkoubi.

Latifa Alnajjar © Beth Thomas

High St, Aberystwyth. © Bill Boaden Available under CC-BY-SA/2.0 licence at https://www.geograph.org.uk/photo/2286922

Latifa's two daughters, in their school uniform © Latifa Alnajjar

Latifa and her friend Eryl, a volunteer at the Red Cross © Latifa Alnajjar

Latifa's friend Eryl with Latifa's two daughters. © Latifa Alnajjar

Rose, who came up with the idea of the Syrian Dinner Project, with Latifa and her friend Rula. © Latifa Alnajjar

Latifa in the kitchen. Photo courtesy of the Syrian Dinner Project

Latifa's husband and their two daughters in Aberystwyth. © Latifa Alnajjar

Latifa with her mother, her friend Rula and Rula's daughter selling their produce at a farmer's market in Lampeter. © Beth Thomas

Latifa's 'international family'. © Latifa Alnajjar

Najla'a little daughter on the beach at Aberystwyth. ©Najla'a Hadle

Footbridge at Aberystwyth © Najla'a Hadle

Syrian coffee © Angham Abdullah

Syrian foods. Individual photos courtesy of the Syrian Dinner Project

Children with horse © Najla'a Hadle

"Catching the bus" by Jeremy Segrott (Dai Lygad), available under CC BY 2.0 licence at https://commons.wikimedia.org/wiki/File:Catching_the_bus_(15413605136).jpg

ESOL class at Oasis Cardiff © Oasis Cardiff

Life in the UK Study Guide, photo by Angham Abdullah.

Notes taken of her own Life in the UK test by Angham Abdullah © Angham Abdullah

Cardiff terraced housing © Beth Thomas

Notes on English words in Arabic. Anonymous donor.

Mohammad S after being interviewed © Angham Abdullah

Fitzalan High School certificate photo, courtesy of Mohammad S.

Mohammad walking in West Wales. © Mohammad S

The window of Jasmin restaurant © Angham Abdullah

A memento of Syria and the fountain in the courtyard of Halah's home in Syria. © Angham Abdullah

Mementoes of Syria belonging to Halah al Shami. © Angham Abdullah

Map of the Syrian diaspora. © Allice Hunter, CC BY-SA 4.0, via Wikimedia Commons
at https://commons.wikimedia.org/wiki/File:Map_of_the_Syrian_Diaspora_in_the_World.svg

Mulukhiyaeh by Osps7, CC BY-SA 4.0, via Wikimedia Commons

Terraced housing in Splott, Cardiff. © Beth Thomas

Residence permit card. Photo taken by Angham Abdullah

Certificate of Naturalisation. Photo taken by Angham Abdullah

Syrian hospitality: food prepared for Angham, the researcher, by Khalid and his family. © Angham Abdullah

Afterword

Hussam Allaham with Reynette Roberts, Director of Oasis Cardiff, at his UK citizenship ceremony. © Oasis Cardiff

Seventy Years of Struggle and Achievement

Life Stories of Ethnic Minority Women Living in Wales

Edited and selected by
**Kirsten Lavine,
Meena Upadhyaya
and Chris Weedon**

Foreword by
Julie Morgan and Jane Hutt

EMWWAA

"It is pleasing to see so many remarkable Black, Asian and Multi-ethnic women marked and celebrated. Packed with beautiful photographs and fascinating life stories, it makes an enduring tribute to a group of truly inspiring women. It is a book to be cherished." Liz Jones, *Gwales*